MW00583974

ECHOES
from Jerusalem

A new abridgment of the ancient text of
THE BOOK OF MORMON

ECHOES
from Jerusalem

A new abridgment of the ancient text of
THE BOOK OF MORMON

abridged and edited by Kirk Van Leuven

Copyright © 2020 by Kirk Van Leuven

All rights reserved. No part of this book may be reproduced, recorded or transmitted in any form, electronic or mechanical, including photocopying, recording, or by any file storage system without permission in writing from the author.

ISBN
978-1-7350533-0-1

www.belovededitions.com
info@belovededitions.com

"A lone survivor placed the record like a seed in the ground sixteen hundred years ago. Now the words of the book speak out of the ground, just as Isaiah foretold, opening the eyes and ears of millions who read it "

ECHOES from Jerusalem

Table of Contents

The people that walked in darkness have seen
a great light . . .

Isaiah 9: 2

Preface

Echoes From Jerusalem is the epic history of a lost race of people. It abridges the ancient records contained in the Book of Mormon. The original passages are cut and stitched together to make a shorter narrative, helping the reader to complete a cover-to-cover experience and consider the book as a whole, where it came from, and its message for our times. The stated purpose of the ancient writers was kept in mind in selecting the passages.

The main author, Mormon, introduces himself as a witness to the total destruction of his people and informs us of the sources he used to chronicle their history. The story begins when two families leave Jerusalem to cross the ocean around 600 B.C. Their faith in God is at the heart of the story. They practiced the law of Moses and looked forward to the fulfillment of Bible prophesies.

Isaiah and other Hebrew prophets are quoted throughout the book. The group saw themselves as part of Isaiah's tapestry of visions. They connected their own lives to events that the prophet foretold, as a validation of their extreme journeys and experiences. In one of his visions, Isaiah saw the arrival of a day when the deaf would hear the words of a book, like the voice of one crying from the dead, even as one speaking out of the dust. And in that day, Isaiah said, the blind would see, and the poor among men would rejoice in the Holy One of Israel, when the twelve tribes of Israel gather together again. [1]

The story in this book revolves around the devotion of the leaders of this ancient people to write and leave a testament of their experience. Using a form of Egyptian script, they engraved their history on metal plates, to preserve the record for future generations. A lone survivor placed the record like a seed in the ground sixteen hundred years ago. Now the words of the book speak out of the ground, just as Isaiah foretold, opening the eyes and ears of millions who read it.

---

[1] Isaiah 29: 11-24

The ancients engraved the purpose of their writings on the front leaf:

"An account written by the hand of Mormon, upon plates taken from the plates of Nephi, . . . written to the Lamanites, who are a remnant of the house of Israel; and also to the Jew and Gentile, . . . which is to show unto the remnant of the House of Israel what great things the Lord hath done for their fathers, that they may know the covenants of the Lord, that they are not cast off forever, and also to the convincing of the Jew and Gentile that Jesus is the Christ, the Eternal God, manifesting himself unto all nations."

The men who wrote and abridged this history were not concerned with receiving credit for their work. Their concern was for those who would eventually read it. They knew it would have a miraculous effect on later generations. They wrote it for their children. It was also written for us. Parallels to our own times echo through the pages. And in the words of the modern proverb, "Those who cannot remember the past, are condemned to repeat it." [2]

Ironically, the history of this doomed people, outnumbered by sworn enemies and threatened with extinction, is inspirational. The resounding message is one of eternal hope, with perspectives that reassure and provide strength. This strength and reassurance came to me personally thirty years ago, as my wife and I faced the facts of her terminal illness. It was then that I recognized a greater personal value of this story. It became a source of light and direction in difficult times. Now I pass the light forward in a smaller version of Mormon's great book.

---

[2] George Santayana, *The Life of Reason*, 1905

Source and References

The language of *Echoes From Jerusalem* is uniquely old-fashioned, because it comes from an ancient source. The authors explained that they used an Egyptian script to write in their Hebrew language. Their record covers a thousand-year history ending around 400 A.D. The English translation first appeared in 1830, using Shakespearean or King James English. This book preserves the original words with only the following changes:

- Passages selected for this abridgement equal about fifty per-cent of the Book of Mormon and have been slightly reordered to make the narrative more linear, following the chain of ancient writers who faithfully kept the record. This is meant to improve reader comprehension.

- The book is rewritten into paragraph form and makes new divisions on chapters to imitate the original style of the 1830 edition that created so much interest and started a movement. Significant changes are made to the punctuation to help improve sentence and paragraph structure without changing the words or meaning.

- Only a few of the verses have words or phrases omitted as part of the abridgement process. These omissions are noted with an asterisk in the footnotes. In almost all cases, the words or phrases omitted are repetitions, and are dropped for brevity or to improve clarity. The meaning of the passage has not changed.

References by chapter and verse are provided in the footnotes for readers who want to locate any part of these writings in a modern edition of the Book of Mormon. Modern chapter and verse divisions were created in 1879 by Orson Pratt, under the direction of President John Taylor. The 1920 edition was the first to use these chapters and verses, with the text formatted into double columns to encourage study like the Bible. References for *Echoes From Jerusalem* were organized using a 1920 edition of the Book of Mormon. The text is taken from an earlier edition, nearly identical to the 1829 printer's manuscript and the first edition.

Part I

Safe Exodus

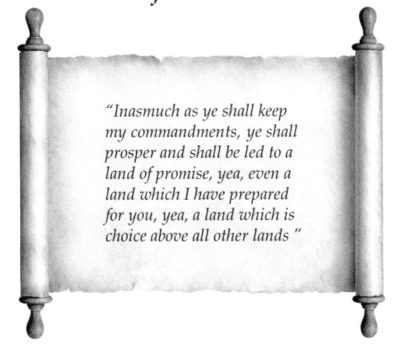

"Inasmuch as ye shall keep my commandments, ye shall prosper and shall be led to a land of promise, yea, even a land which I have prepared for you, yea, a land which is choice above all other lands "

Prologue

Last Words First

About 385 A.D.

And now, I, Mormon, being about to deliver up the record which I have been making into the hands of my son Moroni, behold, I have witnessed almost all the destruction of my people, the Nephites. And it is many hundred years after the coming of Christ that I deliver these records into the hands of my son. And it supposeth me that he will witness the entire destruction of my people. [3]

And it hath become expedient that I, according to the will of God, should make a record of these things which have been done, yea, a small record of that which hath taken place, from the time that Lehi left Jerusalem, even down until the present time. Therefore, I do make my record from the accounts, which have been given by those who were before me, until the commencement of my day, and then do I make a record of the things which I have seen with mine own eyes. [4]

And there had many things transpired which in the eyes of some would be great and marvelous; nevertheless, they cannot all be written in this book. But behold, there are records which do contain all the proceedings of this people. And a more short but a true account was given by Nephi. Therefore, I have made my record of these things according to the record of Nephi, which was engraven on the plates which were called the plates of Nephi. And behold, I do make this record on plates which I have made with mine own hands. [5]

And now, I speak somewhat concerning that which I have written. For, after I had made an abridgment from the plates of Nephi, I searched among the records which had been delivered into my hands, and I found these plates which contained this

---

[3] Words of Mormon 1: 1-2*
[4] 3 Nephi 5: 14*-17
[5] 3 Nephi 5: 8*-11

small account of the prophets from Jacob down to the reign of this King Benjamin, and also many of the words of Nephi. [6] And I cannot write the hundredth part of the things of my people. But behold, I shall take these plates, which contain these prophesyings and revelations, and put them with the remainder of my record, for they are choice unto me. And I know they will be choice unto my brethren. And I do this for a wise purpose, for thus it whispereth me, according to the workings of the Spirit of the Lord which is in me. And now, I do not know all things, but the Lord knoweth all things which are to come, wherefore, he worketh in me to do according to his will. [7]

I am Mormon, and a pure descendant of Lehi. I have reason to bless my God and my Savior Jesus Christ, that he brought our fathers out of the land of Jerusalem, and that he hath given me and my people so much knowledge unto the salvation of our souls. Surely he hath blessed the house of Jacob and hath been merciful unto the seed of Joseph. And insomuch as the children of Lehi have kept his commandments, he hath blessed them and prospered them according to his word. Yea, and surely shall he again bring a remnant of the seed of Joseph to the knowledge of the Lord their God.

And as surely as the Lord liveth will he gather in from the four quarters of the earth all the remnant of the seed of Jacob, who are scattered abroad upon all the face of the earth. And as he hath covenanted with all the house of Jacob, even so shall the covenant be fulfilled, in his own due time, unto the restoring all the house of Jacob unto the knowledge of the covenant that he hath covenanted with them. [8]

Now these things are written unto the remnant of the house of Jacob, and they are written after this manner, because it is known of God that wickedness will not bring them forth unto them. And they are to be hid up unto the Lord that they may come forth in his own due time. And this is the commandment which I

---

[6] Words of Mormon 1: 3*
[7] Words of Mormon 1: 5*-7
[8] 3 Nephi 5: 20*-25*

have received. And behold, they shall come forth according to the commandment of the Lord, when he shall see fit, in his wisdom. [9]

And now I, Mormon, proceed to finish out my record, which I take from the plates of Nephi, and I make it according to the knowledge and the understanding which God has given me. [10]

---

[9] Mormon 5: 12-13
[10] Words of Mormon 1: 9

Chapter 1

Exodus from Jerusalem

About 600 B.C.

I, Nephi, having been born of goodly parents, therefore I was taught somewhat in all the learning of my father; therefore, I make a record of my proceedings in my days. Yea, I make a record in the language of my father, which consists of the learning of the Jews and the language of the Egyptians. And I know that the record which I make is true; and I make it with mine own hand; and I make it according to my knowledge. [1]

For it came to pass in the commencement of the first year of the reign of Zedekiah, king of Judah, there came many prophets, prophesying unto the people that they must repent, or the great city Jerusalem must be destroyed.

Wherefore, it came to pass that my father Lehi, as he went forth, prayed unto the Lord, yea, even with all his heart in behalf of his people. And it came to pass as he prayed unto the Lord, there came a pillar of fire and dwelt upon a rock before him, and he saw and heard much. And because of the things which he saw and heard, he did quake and tremble exceedingly.

And it came to pass that he returned to his own house at Jerusalem, and he cast himself upon his bed, being overcome with the Spirit, and the things which he had seen. And being thus overcome with the Spirit, he was carried away in a vision, even that he saw the heavens open. And he thought he saw God sitting upon his throne, surrounded with numberless concourses of angels in the attitude of singing and praising their God.

And it came to pass that he saw one descending out of the midst of heaven, and he beheld that his luster was above that of the sun at noonday. And he also saw twelve others following him, and their brightness did exceed that of the stars in the firmament. And they came down and went forth upon the face of the earth. And the first came, and stood before my father, and gave unto

---

[1] I Nephi 1: 1*-3

him a book, and bade him that he should read.

And it came to pass that as he read, he was filled with the Spirit of the Lord; and he read, saying, Wo, wo unto Jerusalem! For I have seen thine abominations! Yea, and many things did my father read concerning Jerusalem, that it should be destroyed, and the inhabitants thereof, many should perish by the sword, and many should be carried away captive into Babylon. [2]

Therefore, I would that ye should know that after the Lord had shown so many marvelous things unto my father Lehi, yea, concerning the destruction of Jerusalem, behold, he went forth among the people and began to prophesy and to declare unto them concerning the things which he had both seen and heard. And it came to pass that the Jews did mock him because of the things which he testified of them, for he truly testified of their wickedness and their abominations. And he testified that the things which he saw and heard, and also the things which he read in the book, manifested plainly of the coming of a Messiah and also the redemption of the world.

And when the Jews heard these things, they were angry with him, yea, even as with the prophets of old, whom they had cast out, and stoned, and slain. And they also sought his life, that they might take it away. But behold, I, Nephi, will show unto you that the tender mercies of the Lord are over all those whom he hath chosen, because of their faith, to make them mighty even unto the power of deliverance. [3]

For behold, it came to pass that the Lord spake unto my father, yea, even in a dream, and said unto him, Blessed art thou Lehi, because of the things which thou hast done. And because thou hast been faithful and declared unto this people the things which I commanded thee, behold, they seek to take away thy life.

And it came to pass that the Lord commanded my father, even in a dream, that he should take his family and depart into the wilderness. And it came to pass that he was obedient unto the word of the Lord; wherefore, he did as the Lord commanded him. And it came to pass that he departed into the wilderness. And he

---

[2] 1 Nephi 1: 4*-13
[3] 1 Nephi 1: 18-20

left his house, and the land of his inheritance, and his gold, and his silver, and his precious things, and took nothing with him, save it were his family, and provisions, and tents. And he departed into the wilderness; and he came down by the borders near the shore of the Red Sea. And he did travel in the wilderness with his family, which consisted of my mother Sariah, and my elder brothers, who were Laman, Lemuel, and Sam. [4] And my father dwelt in a tent.

And it came to pass that I, Nephi, being exceeding young, nevertheless, being large in stature, and also having great desires to know of the mysteries of God, wherefore, I did cry unto the Lord. And behold, he did visit me and did soften my heart, that I did believe all the words which had been spoken by my father. Wherefore, I did not rebel against him like unto my brothers. [5]

And it came to pass that the Lord spake unto me, saying, Blessed art thou, Nephi, because of thy faith; for thou hast sought me diligently with lowliness of heart. And inasmuch as ye shall keep my commandments, ye shall prosper and shall be led to a land of promise, yea, even a land which I have prepared for you, yea, a land which is choice above all other lands. And inasmuch as thy brethren shall rebel against thee, they shall be cut off from the presence of the Lord. And inasmuch as thou shalt keep my commandments, thou shalt be made a ruler and a teacher over thy brethren. For behold, in that day that they shall rebel against me, I will curse them even with a sore curse. And they shall have no power over thy seed, except they shall rebel against me also. [6]

And it came to pass that I, Nephi, returned from speaking with the Lord, to the tent of my father. And it came to pass that he spake unto me, saying, Behold, I have dreamed a dream, in the which the Lord hath commanded me that thou and thy brethren shall return to Jerusalem. For behold, Laban hath the record of the Jews, and also a genealogy of thy forefathers. And they are engraven upon plates of brass.

---

[4] 1 Nephi 2: 1-5*
[5] 1 Nephi 2: 15-16
[6] 1 Nephi 2: 19-23

Wherefore, the Lord hath commanded me that thou and thy brothers should go unto the house of Laban, and seek the records, and bring them down hither into the wilderness. And now, behold, thy brothers murmur, saying it is a hard thing which I have required of them; but behold, I have not required it of them, but it is a commandment of the Lord. Therefore, go, my son, and thou shalt be favored of the Lord because thou hast not murmured.

And it came to pass that I, Nephi, said unto my father, I will go and do the things which the Lord hath commanded. For I know that the Lord giveth no commandments unto the children of men save he shall prepare a way for them that they may accomplish the thing which he commandeth them. [7]

And it came to pass that when we had come up to the land of Jerusalem, I and my brethren did consult one with another; and we cast lots, who of us should go in unto the house of Laban. And it came to pass that the lot fell upon Laman. And Laman went in unto the house of Laban, and he talked with him as he sat in his house. And he desired of Laban the records which were engraven upon the plates of brass, which contained the genealogy of my father.

And behold, it came to pass that Laban was angry and thrust him out from his presence; and he would not that he should have the records. Wherefore, he said unto him, Behold, thou art a robber, and I will slay thee. But Laman fled out of his presence and told the things which Laban had done unto us.

And we began to be exceeding sorrowful, and my brethren were about to return unto my father in the wilderness. But behold, I said unto them, that as the Lord liveth, and as we live, we will not go down unto our father in the wilderness until we have accomplished the thing which the Lord hath commanded us. Wherefore, let us be faithful in keeping the commandments of the Lord. Therefore, let us go down to the land of our father's inheritance; for behold, he left gold, and silver, and all manner of riches. And all this he hath done because of the commandments of the Lord. [8] And behold, it is wisdom in God that we should obtain these records, that we may preserve unto our children the language

---

[7] 1 Nephi 3: 1-7
[8] 1 Nephi 3: 10-16

of our fathers, and also that we may preserve unto them the words which have been spoken by the mouth of all the holy prophets, which have been delivered unto them by the Spirit and power of God since the world began, even down unto this present time.

And it came to pass that after this manner of language did I persuade my brethren, that they might be faithful in keeping the commandments of God. And it came to pass that we went down to the land of our inheritance, and we did gather together our gold, and our silver, and our precious things. And after we had gathered these things together, we went up again unto the house of Laban.

And it came to pass that we went in unto Laban and desired him that he would give unto us the records which were engraven upon the plates of brass, for which we would give unto him our gold, and our silver, and all our precious things. And it came to pass that when Laban saw our property, that it was exceeding great, he did lust after it, insomuch that he thrust us out and sent his servants to slay us, that he might obtain our property.

And it came to pass that we did flee before the servants of Laban; and we were obliged to leave behind our property, and it fell into the hands of Laban. And it came to pass that we fled into the wilderness, and the servants of Laban did not overtake us, and we hid ourselves in the cavity of a rock.

And it came to pass that Laman was angry with me and also with my father, and also was Lemuel, for he hearkened unto the words of Laman. Wherefore, Laman and Lemuel did speak many hard words unto us, their younger brothers, and they did smite us even with a rod.

And it came to pass as they smote us with a rod, behold, an angel of the Lord came and stood before them. And he spake unto them saying, Why do ye smite your younger brother with a rod? Know ye not that the Lord hath chosen him to be a ruler over you, and this because of your iniquities? Behold, ye shall go up to Jerusalem again, and the Lord will deliver Laban into your hands.

And after the angel had departed, Laman and Lemuel again began to murmur, saying, How is it possible that the Lord will deliver Laban into our hands? Behold, he is a mighty man, and he can command fifty; yea, even he can slay fifty; then why not us? [9]

And it came to pass that I spake unto my brethren, saying, Let us go up again unto Jerusalem, and let us be faithful in keeping the commandments of the Lord. For behold, he is mightier than all the earth, then why not mightier than Laban and his fifty, yea, or even than his tens of thousands. Therefore, let us go up. Let us be strong like unto Moses; for he truly spake unto the waters of the Red Sea, and they divided hither and thither; and our fathers came through out of captivity on dry ground, and the armies of Pharaoh did follow and were drowned in the waters of the Red Sea.

Now behold, ye know that this is true; and ye also know that an angel hath spoken unto you. Wherefore can ye doubt? Let us go up. The Lord is able to deliver us, even as our fathers, and to destroy Laban, even as the Egyptians.

Now when I had spoken these words, they were yet wroth and did still continue to murmur; nevertheless, they did follow me up until we came without the walls of Jerusalem. And it was by night, and I caused that they should hide themselves without the walls. And after they had hid themselves, I, Nephi, crept into the city and went forth towards the house of Laban.

And I was led by the Spirit, not knowing beforehand the things which I should do. Nevertheless, I went forth and as I came near unto the house of Laban, I beheld a man, and he had fallen to the earth before me, for he was drunken with wine. And when I came to him I found that it was Laban.

And I beheld his sword, and I drew it forth from the sheath thereof; and the hilt thereof was of pure gold, and the workmanship thereof was exceeding fine. And I saw that the blade thereof was of the most precious steel. And it came to pass that I was constrained by the Spirit that I should kill Laban. But I said in my heart, Never at any time have I shed the blood of man; and I shrank and would that I might not slay him.

[9] 1 Nephi 3: 19-29,31

And the Spirit said unto me again, Behold, the Lord hath delivered him into thy hands. [10] Behold, the Lord slayeth the wicked to bring forth his righteous purposes. It is better that one man should perish than that a nation should dwindle and perish in unbelief.

And now, when I, Nephi, had heard these words, I remembered the words of the Lord which he spake unto me in the wilderness, saying that, Inasmuch as thy seed shall keep my commandments, they shall prosper in the land of promise. Yea, and I also thought that they could not keep the commandments of the Lord according to the law of Moses, save they should have the law. And I also knew that the law was engraven upon the plates of brass. And again, I knew that the Lord had delivered Laban into my hands for this cause, that I might obtain the records according to his commandments.

Therefore, I did obey the voice of the Spirit and took Laban by the hair of the head, and I smote off his head with his own sword. And after I had smitten off his head with his own sword, I took the garments of Laban and put them upon mine own body, yea, even every whit. And I did gird on his armor about my loins. And after I had done this, I went forth unto the treasury of Laban.

And as I went forth towards the treasury of Laban, behold, I saw the servant of Laban, who had the keys of the treasury. And I commanded him in the voice of Laban that he should go with me into the treasury. And he supposed me to be his master Laban, for he beheld the garments and also the sword girded about my loins.

And he spake unto me concerning the elders of the Jews, he knowing that his master Laban had been out by night among them. And I spake unto him as if it had been Laban. And I also spake unto him that I should carry the engravings which were upon the plates of brass to my elder brethren, who were without the walls. And I also bade him that he should follow me. And he, supposing that I spake of the brethren of the church and that I was truly that Laban whom I had slain, wherefore, he did follow me. [11]

---

[10] 1 Nephi 4: 1-11*
[11] 1 Nephi 4: 13-26

And it came to pass that when the servant of Laban beheld my brethren, he began to tremble and was about to flee from before me and return to the city of Jerusalem. And now, I, Nephi, being a man large in stature, and also having received much strength of the Lord, therefore, I did seize upon the servant of Laban and held him that he should not flee. [12] And I spake unto him, even with an oath, that he need not fear; that he should be a free man like unto us if he would go down in the wilderness with us. And I also spake unto him, saying, Surely the Lord hath commanded us to do this thing. And shall we not be diligent in keeping the commandments of the Lord? Therefore, if thou wilt go down into the wilderness to my father, thou shalt have place with us.

And it came to pass that Zoram did take courage at the words which I spake. Now Zoram was the name of the servant; and he promised that he would go down into the wilderness unto our father. And he also made an oath unto us that he would tarry with us from that time forth. And it came to pass that we took the plates of brass and the servant of Laban, and departed into the wilderness, and journeyed unto the tent of our father. [13]

And it came to pass that after we had come down into the wilderness unto our father, behold, he was filled with joy; and also my mother Sariah was exceeding glad, for she truly had mourned because of us, for she had supposed that we had perished in the wilderness. And she also had complained against my father, telling him that he was a visionary man, saying, Behold, thou hast led us forth from the land of our inheritance, and my sons are no more, and we perish in the wilderness. And after this manner of language had my mother complained against my father.

And it had come to pass that my father spake unto her, saying, I know that I am a visionary man; for if I had not seen the things of God in a vision, I should not have known the goodness of God, but had tarried at Jerusalem and had perished with my brethren. But behold, I have obtained a land of promise, in the

---

[12] 1 Nephi 4: 30-31
[13] 1 Nephi 4: 33-35,38

which things I do rejoice. Yea, and I know that the Lord will deliver my sons out of the hands of Laban and bring them down again unto us in the wilderness. And after this manner of language did my father Lehi comfort my mother Sariah concerning us, while we journeyed in the wilderness up to the land of Jerusalem to obtain the record of the Jews.

And when we had returned to the tent of my father, behold, their joy was full, and my mother was comforted. And she spake, saying, Now I know of a surety that the Lord hath commanded my husband to flee into the wilderness. Yea, and I also know of a surety that the Lord hath protected my sons, and delivered them out of the hands of Laban, and gave them power whereby they could accomplish the thing which the Lord hath commanded them. And after this manner of language did she speak.

And it came to pass that they did rejoice exceedingly and did offer sacrifice and burnt offerings unto the Lord; and they gave thanks unto the God of Israel. And after they had given thanks unto the God of Israel, my father Lehi took the records which were engraven upon the plates of brass, and he did search them from the beginning.

And he beheld that they did contain the five books of Moses, which gave an account of the creation of the world, and also of Adam and Eve, who were our first parents, and also a record of the Jews from the beginning, even down to the commencement of the reign of Zedekiah, king of Judah, and also the prophecies of the holy prophets, from the beginning, even down to the commencement of the reign of Zedekiah, and also many prophecies which have been spoken by the mouth of Jeremiah.

And it came to pass that my father Lehi also found upon the plates of brass a genealogy of his fathers. Wherefore, he knew that he was a descendant of Joseph, yea, even that Joseph who was the son of Jacob, who was sold into Egypt and who was preserved by the hand of the Lord, that he might preserve his father Jacob and all his household from perishing with famine. And they were also led out of captivity and out of the land of Egypt by that same God who had preserved them.

And thus my father Lehi did discover the genealogy of his fathers. And Laban also was a descendant of Joseph; wherefore, he and his fathers had kept the records. And now, when my father saw all these things, he was filled with the Spirit and began to prophesy concerning his seed, that these plates of brass should go forth unto all nations, kindreds, tongues, and people who were of his seed. Wherefore, he said that these plates of brass should never perish, neither should they be dimmed any more by time. And he prophesied many things concerning his seed.

And it came to pass that, thus far, I and my father had kept the commandments wherewith the Lord had commanded us. And we had obtained the records which the Lord had commanded us, and searched them, and found that they were desirable, yea, even of great worth unto us, insomuch that we could preserve the commandments of the Lord unto our children. Wherefore, it was wisdom in the Lord that we should carry them with us as we journeyed in the wilderness towards the land of promise. [14]

And now, I would that ye might know that after my father Lehi had made an end of prophesying concerning his seed, it came to pass that the Lord spake unto him again, saying that it was not meet for him, Lehi, that he should take his family into the wilderness alone; but that his sons should take daughters to wife, that they might raise up seed unto the Lord in the land of promise. And it came to pass that the Lord commanded him that I, Nephi, and my brethren should again return unto the land of Jerusalem and bring down Ishmael and his family into the wilderness.

And it came to pass that I, Nephi, did again, with my brethren, go forth into the wilderness to go up to Jerusalem. And it came to pass that we went up unto the house of Ishmael, and we did gain favor in the sight of Ishmael, insomuch that we did speak unto him the words of the Lord. And it came to pass that the Lord did soften the heart of Ishmael and also his household, insomuch that they took their journey with us down into the wilderness to the tent of our father.

And it came to pass that as we journeyed in the wilderness, behold, Laman and Lemuel, and two of the daughters of Ishmael, and the two sons of Ishmael, and their families did rebel against us, yea, against me, Nephi, and Sam, and their father Ishmael, and

---

[14] 1 Nephi 5: 1-22

his wife, and his three other daughters. And it came to pass in the which rebellion they were desirous to return unto the land of Jerusalem.

And now, I, Nephi, being grieved for the hardness of their hearts, therefore, I spake unto them, saying, yea, even unto Laman and unto Lemuel, Behold, ye are mine elder brethren, and how is it that ye are so hard in your hearts, and so blind in your minds, that ye have need that I, your younger brother, should speak unto you, yea, and set an example for you?

Yea, and how is it that ye have forgotten that the Lord is able to do all things according to his will for the children of men, if it so be that they exercise faith in him? Wherefore, let us be faithful to him. And if it so be that we are faithful to him, we shall obtain the land of promise. And ye shall know at some future period that the word of the Lord shall be fulfilled concerning the destruction of Jerusalem; for all things which the Lord hath spoken concerning the destruction of Jerusalem must be fulfilled.

For behold, the Spirit of the Lord ceaseth soon to strive with them, for behold, they have rejected the prophets. And Jeremiah have they cast into prison. And they have sought to take away the life of my father, insomuch that they have driven him out of the land. Now behold, I say unto you that if ye will return unto Jerusalem, ye shall also perish with them. And now, if ye have choice, go up to the land and remember the words which I speak unto you, that if ye go, ye will also perish; for thus the Spirit of the Lord constraineth me that I should speak.

And it came to pass that when I, Nephi, had spoken these words unto my brethren, they were angry with me. And it came to pass that they did lay their hands upon me; for behold, they were exceeding wroth. And they did bind me with cords, for they sought to take away my life, that they might leave me in the wilderness to be devoured by wild beasts.

But it came to pass that I prayed unto the Lord, saying, O Lord, according to my faith which is in thee, wilt thou deliver me from the hands of my brethren. Yea, even give me strength that I may burst these bands with which I am bound. And it came to pass that when I had said these words, behold, the bands were

loosed from off my hands and feet, and I stood before my
brethren, and I spake unto them again.

And it came to pass that they were angry with me again and
sought to lay hands upon me. But behold, one of the daughters of
Ishmael, yea, and also her mother, and one of the sons of Ishmael
did plead with my brethren, insomuch that they did soften their
hearts; and they did cease striving to take away my life.

And it came to pass that they were sorrowful because of their
wickedness, insomuch that they did bow down before me and did
plead with me that I would forgive them of the thing that they
had done against me. And it came to pass that I did frankly
forgive them all that they had done, and I did exhort them that
they would pray unto the Lord, their God, for forgiveness. And it
came to pass that they did so. And after they had done praying
unto the Lord, we did again travel on our journey toward the tent
of our father.

And after I, and my brethren, and all the house of Ishmael
had come down unto the tent of my father, they did give thanks
unto the Lord, their God. And they did offer sacrifice and burnt
offerings unto him. [15]

And it came to pass that we had gathered together all manner
of seeds of every kind, both of grain of every kind, and also of the
seeds of fruits of every kind.

And it came to pass that while my father tarried in the
wilderness, he spake unto us, saying, Behold, I have dreamed a
dream; or in other words, I have seen a vision. And behold,
because of the thing which I have seen, I have reason to rejoice in
the Lord because of Nephi and also of Sam, for I have reason to
suppose that they, and also many of their seed will be saved.

But behold, Laman and Lemuel, I fear exceedingly because of
you; for behold, methought I saw in my dream a dark and dreary
wilderness. And it came to pass that I saw a man, and he was
dressed in a white robe; and he came and stood before me. And it
came to pass that he spake unto me and bade me follow him.

And it came to pass that as I followed him, I beheld myself
that I was in a dark and dreary waste. And after I had traveled for

---

[15] I Nephi 7: 1-22*

the space of many hours in darkness, I began to pray unto the Lord that he would have mercy on me according to the multitude of his tender mercies.

And it came to pass after I had prayed unto the Lord, I beheld a large and spacious field. And it came to pass that I beheld a tree, whose fruit was desirable to make one happy. [16] And as I partook of the fruit thereof, it filled my soul with exceeding great joy. Wherefore, I began to be desirous that my family should partake of it also; for I knew that it was desirable above all other fruit.

And as I cast my eyes round about, that perhaps I might discover my family also, I beheld a river of water; and it ran along, and it was near the tree of which I was partaking the fruit. And I looked to behold from whence it came. And I saw the head thereof a little way off, and at the head thereof I beheld your mother Sariah, and Sam, and Nephi; and they stood as if they knew not whither they should go.

And it came to pass that I beckoned unto them; and I also did say unto them with a loud voice that they should come unto me and partake of the fruit, which was desirable above all other fruit. And it came to pass that they did come unto me and partake of the fruit also.

And it came to pass that I was desirous that Laman and Lemuel should come and partake of the fruit also. Wherefore, I cast mine eyes towards the head of the river, that perhaps I might see them. And it came to pass that I saw them, but they would not come unto me and partake of the fruit.

And I beheld a rod of iron, and it extended along the bank of the river and led to the tree by which I stood. And I also beheld a straight and narrow path which came along by the rod of iron, even to the tree by which I stood. And it also led by the head of the fountain unto a large and spacious field, as if it had been a world.

And I saw numberless concourses of people, many of whom were pressing forward, that they might obtain the path which led unto the tree by which I stood. And it came to pass that they did come forth and commence in the path, which led to the tree. And

---

[16] 1 Nephi 8: 1-10

it came to pass that there arose a mist of darkness, yea, even an exceeding great mist of darkness, insomuch that they who had commenced in the path did lose their way, that they wandered off and were lost.

And it came to pass that I beheld others pressing forward, and they came forth and caught hold of the end of the rod of iron. And they did press forward through the mist of darkness, clinging to the rod of iron, even until they did come forth and partake of the fruit of the tree. And after they had partaken of the fruit of the tree, they did cast their eyes about as if they were ashamed.

And I also cast my eyes round about and beheld on the other side of the river of water a great and spacious building. And it stood as it were in the air, high above the earth. And it was filled with people, both old and young, both male and female. And their manner of dress was exceeding fine. And they were in the attitude of mocking and pointing their fingers towards those who had come at and were partaking of the fruit. And after they had tasted of the fruit, they were ashamed because of those that were scoffing at them, and they fell away into forbidden paths and were lost.

And now, I, Nephi, do not speak all the words of my father. But to be short in writing, behold, he saw other multitudes pressing forward; and they came and caught hold of the end of the rod of iron. And they did press their way forward, continually holding fast to the rod of iron until they came forth, and fell down, and partook of the fruit of the tree.

And he also saw other multitudes feeling their way towards that great and spacious building. And it came to pass that many were drowned in the depths of the fountain. And many were lost from his view, wandering in strange roads. And great was the multitude that did enter into that strange building. And after they did enter into that building, they did point the finger of scorn at me and those that were partaking of the fruit also; but we heeded them not. [17]

And Laman and Lemuel partook not of the fruit, said my father. And he did exhort them then, with all the feeling of a tender parent, that they would hearken to his words, that perhaps

[17] 1 Nephi 8: 12-33

the Lord would be merciful to them and not cast them off. Yea, my father did preach unto them. And after he had preached unto them and also prophesied unto them of many things, he bade them to keep the commandments of the Lord. [18]

For behold, it came to pass, after my father had made an end of speaking the words of his dream and also of exhorting them to all diligence, he spake unto them concerning the Jews, that after they should be destroyed, even that great city Jerusalem, and many be carried away captive into Babylon, according to the own due time of the Lord, they should return again, yea, even be brought back out of captivity. And after they should be brought back out of captivity, they should possess again the land of their inheritance.

Yea, even six hundred years from the time that my father left Jerusalem, a prophet would the Lord God raise up among the Jews, even a Messiah, or in other words, a Savior of the world. And he also spake concerning the prophets, how great a number had testified of these things concerning this Messiah of whom he had spoken, or this Redeemer of the world. Wherefore, all mankind were in a lost and in a fallen state and ever would be, save they should rely on this Redeemer. And after this manner of language did my father prophesy and speak unto my brethren. [19]

And it came to pass after I, Nephi, having heard all the words of my father concerning the things which he saw in a vision, and also the things which he spake by the power of the Holy Ghost, which power he received by faith on the Son of God, and the Son of God was the Messiah who should come, I, Nephi, was desirous also that I might see, and hear, and know of these things by the power of the Holy Ghost, which is the gift of God unto all those who diligently seek him, as well in times of old as in the time that he should manifest himself unto the children of men. [20]

For it came to pass after I had desired to know the things that my father had seen, and believing that the Lord was able to make them known unto me, as I sat pondering in mine heart, I was

---

[18] 1 Nephi 8: 35, 37-38*
[19] 1 Nephi 10: 2-6, 15*
[20] 1 Nephi 10: 17

caught away in the Spirit of the Lord, yea, into an exceeding high mountain, which I never had before seen and upon which I never had before set my foot.

And the Spirit said unto me, Behold, what desirest thou?

And I said, I desire to behold the things which my father saw.

And the Spirit said unto me, Believest thou that thy father saw the tree of which he hath spoken?

And I said, Yea, thou knowest that I believe all the words of my father.

And when I had spoken these words, the Spirit cried with a loud voice, saying, Hosanna to the Lord, the most high God, for he is God over all the earth, yea, even above all!

And blessed art thou, Nephi, because thou believest in the Son of the most high God. Therefore, thou shalt behold the things which thou hast desired. And behold, this thing shall be given unto thee for a sign, that after thou hast beheld the tree which bore the fruit which thy father tasted, thou shalt also behold a man descending out of heaven. And him shall ye witness. And after ye have witnessed him, ye shall bear record that it is the Son of God.

And it came to pass that the Spirit said unto me, Look! And I looked and beheld a tree. And it was like unto the tree which my father had seen. And the beauty thereof was far beyond, yea, exceeding of all beauty; and the whiteness thereof did exceed the whiteness of the driven snow.

And it came to pass after I had seen the tree, I said unto the Spirit, I behold thou hast shown unto me the tree which is precious above all.

And he said unto me, What desirest thou?

And I said unto him, To know the interpretation thereof. For I spake unto him as a man speaketh; for I beheld that he was in the form of a man. Yet, nevertheless, I knew that it was the Spirit of the Lord. And he spake unto me as a man speaketh with another.

And it came to pass that he said unto me, Look! And I looked as if to look upon him, and I saw him not; for he had gone from before my presence.

And it came to pass that I looked and beheld the great city of Jerusalem and also other cities. And I beheld the city of Nazareth. And in the city of Nazareth I beheld a virgin, and she was exceedingly fair and white. And it came to pass that I saw the heavens open; and an angel came down and stood before me.

And he said unto me, Nephi, what beholdest thou?

And I said unto him, A virgin, most beautiful and fair above all other virgins.

And he said unto me, Knowest thou the condescension of God?

And I said unto him, I know that he loveth his children; nevertheless, I do not know the meaning of all things.

And he said unto me, Behold, the virgin whom thou seest is the mother of the Son of God, after the manner of the flesh.

And it came to pass that I beheld that she was carried away in the Spirit. And after she had been carried away in the Spirit for the space of a time, the angel spake unto me, saying, Look!

And I looked and beheld the virgin again, bearing a child in her arms.

And the angel said unto me, Behold the Lamb of God, yea, even the Son of the Eternal Father! Knowest thou the meaning of the tree which thy father saw?

And I answered him, saying, Yea, it is the love of God, which sheddeth itself abroad in the hearts of the children of men; wherefore, it is the most desirable above all things.

And he spake unto me, saying, Yea, and the most joyous to the soul.

And after he had said these words, he said unto me, Look! And I looked, and I beheld the Son of God going forth among the children of men. And I saw many fall down at his feet and worship him.

And it came to pass that I beheld that the rod of iron, which my father had seen, was the word of God, which led to the fountain of living waters, or to the tree of life, which waters are a representation of the love of God. And I also beheld that the tree of life was a representation of the love of God. [21]

And it came to pass that the angel spake unto me again, saying, Look! And I looked, and I beheld the heavens open again.

---

[21] 1 Nephi 11: 1-25

And I saw angels descending upon the children of men, and they did minister unto them.

And he spake unto me again, saying, Look! And I looked, and I beheld the Lamb of God going forth among the children of men. And I beheld multitudes of people who were sick and who were afflicted with all manner of diseases, and with devils, and unclean spirits; and the angel spake and showed all these things unto me. And they were healed by the power of the Lamb of God, and the devils and the unclean spirits were cast out.

And it came to pass that the angel spake unto me again, saying, Look! And I looked and beheld the Lamb of God, that he was taken by the people; yea, the Son of the everlasting God was judged of the world; and I saw and bear record. And I, Nephi, saw that he was lifted up upon the cross and slain for the sins of the world.

And after he was slain, I saw the multitudes of the earth, that they were gathered together to fight against the apostles of the Lamb; for thus were the twelve called by the angel of the Lord.

And the multitude of the earth was gathered together; and I beheld that they were in a large and spacious building, like unto the building which my father saw.

And the angel of the Lord spake unto me again, saying, Behold the world and the wisdom thereof. Yea, behold, the house of Israel hath gathered together to fight against the twelve apostles of the Lamb.

And it came to pass that I saw and bear record that the great and spacious building was the pride of the world. And it fell. And the fall thereof was exceeding great. And the angel of the Lord spake unto me again, saying, Thus shall be the destruction of all nations, kindreds, tongues, and people that shall fight against the twelve apostles of the Lamb. [22]

And I bear record that I saw the things which my father saw, and the angel of the Lord did make them known unto me. And now, I make an end of speaking concerning the things which I saw while I was carried away in the Spirit. And if all the things which I

---

[22] 1 Nephi 11:30-36

saw are not written, the things which I have written are true. And thus it is. Amen.[23]

And it came to pass that after I, Nephi, had been carried away in the Spirit and seen all these things, I returned to the tent of my father. And it came to pass that I beheld my brethren, and they were disputing one with another concerning the things which my father had spoken unto them, for he truly spake many great things unto them which were hard to be understood, save a man should inquire of the Lord. And they being hard in their hearts, therefore, they did not look unto the Lord as they ought.

And it came to pass that after I had received strength, I spake unto my brethren, desiring to know of them the cause of their disputations. [24] And it came to pass that they did speak unto me again, saying, What meaneth this thing which our father saw in a dream? What meaneth the tree which he saw?

And I said unto them, It was a representation of the tree of life. And they said unto me, What meaneth the rod of iron which our father saw, that led to the tree?

And I said unto them that it was the word of God; and whoso would hearken unto the word of God and would hold fast unto it, they would never perish; neither could the temptations and the fiery darts of the adversary overpower them unto blindness, to lead them away to destruction.

Wherefore, I, Nephi, did exhort them to give heed unto the word of the Lord. Yea, I did exhort them with all the energies of my soul and with all the faculty which I possessed, that they would give heed to the word of God and remember to keep his commandments always, in all things.

And they said unto me, What meaneth the river of water which our father saw?

And I said unto them that the water which my father saw was filthiness. And so much was his mind swallowed up in other things, that he beheld not the filthiness of the water. And I said unto them that it was an awful gulf, which separateth the wicked from the tree of life and also from the saints of God. And I said

---

[23] 1 Nephi 14:29-30
[24] 1 Nephi 15: 1-3, 6

unto them that it was a representation of that awful hell, which
the angel said unto me was prepared for the wicked.

And I said unto them that our father also saw that the justice
of God did also divide the wicked from the righteous; and the
brightness thereof was like unto the brightness of a flaming fire,
which ascendeth up unto God forever and ever, and hath no end.

And they said unto me, Doth this thing mean the torment of
the body in the days of probation, or doth it mean the final state of
the soul after the death of the temporal body, or doth it speak of
the things which are temporal?

And it came to pass that I said unto them that it was a
representation of things both temporal and spiritual. For the day
should come that they must be judged of their works, yea, even
the works which were done by the temporal body in their days of
probation. Wherefore, if they should die in their wickedness, they
must be cast off also, as to the things which are spiritual, which
are pertaining to righteousness. Wherefore, they must be brought
to stand before God to be judged of their works. And if their
works have been filthiness, they must needs be filthy; and if they
be filthy, it must needs be that they cannot dwell in the kingdom
of God. If so, the kingdom of God must be filthy also.

But behold, I say unto you, The kingdom of God is not filthy,
and there cannot any unclean thing enter into the kingdom of
God. Wherefore, there must needs be a place of filthiness
prepared for that which is filthy. And there is a place prepared,
yea, even that awful hell of which I have spoken; and the devil is
the foundation of it. Wherefore, the final state of the souls of men
is to dwell in the kingdom of God, or to be cast out, because of
that justice of which I have spoken. Wherefore, the wicked are
separated from the righteous and also from that tree of life, whose
fruit is most precious and most desirable above all other fruits.
Yea, and it is the greatest of all the gifts of God. And thus I spake
unto my brethren. Amen.[25]

And now, it came to pass that after I, Nephi, had made an
end of speaking to my brethren, behold, they said unto me, Thou
hast declared unto us hard things, more than we are able to bear.

---

[25] 1 Nephi 15: 21-36

And it came to pass that I said unto them that I knew that I had spoken hard things against the wicked, according to the truth. And the righteous have I justified, and testified that they should be lifted up at the last day. Wherefore, the guilty taketh the truth to be hard, for it cutteth them to the very center. And now, my brethren, if ye were righteous and were willing to hearken to the truth, and give heed unto it, that ye might walk uprightly before God, then ye would not murmur because of the truth, and say, Thou speakest hard things against us.

And it came to pass that I, Nephi, did exhort my brethren, with all diligence, to keep the commandments of the Lord. And it came to pass that they did humble themselves before the Lord, insomuch that I had joy and great hopes of them, that they would walk in the paths of righteousness.

Now all these things were said and done as my father dwelt in a tent in the valley which he called Lemuel.

And it came to pass that I, Nephi, took one of the daughters of Ishmael to wife; and also, my brethren took of the daughters of Ishmael to wife; and also, Zoram took the eldest daughter of Ishmael to wife. And thus my father had fulfilled all the commandments of the Lord which had been given unto him. And also, I, Nephi, had been blessed of the Lord exceedingly.

And it came to pass that the voice of the Lord spake unto my father by night, and commanded him, that on the morrow he should take his journey into the wilderness. [26] And it came to pass that we did again take our journey in the wilderness. And we did travel nearly eastward from that time forth.

And we did travel and wade through much affliction in the wilderness; and our women did bear children in the wilderness. And so great were the blessings of the Lord upon us that, while we did live upon raw meat in the wilderness, our women did give plenty of suck for their children and were strong, yea, even like unto the men; and they began to bear their journeyings without murmurings.

And thus we see that the commandments of God must be fulfilled. And if it so be that the children of men keep the

---

[26] 1 Nephi 16: 1-9

commandments of God, he doth nourish them, and strengthen them, and provide means whereby they can accomplish the thing which he has commanded them. Wherefore, he did provide means for us while we did sojourn in the wilderness.

And we did sojourn for the space of many years, yea, even eight years in the wilderness. And we did come to the land which we called Bountiful because of its much fruit and also wild honey. And all these things were prepared of the Lord that we might not perish.

And we beheld the sea, which we called Irreantum, which, being interpreted, is many waters. And it came to pass that we did pitch our tents by the seashore. And notwithstanding we had suffered many afflictions and much difficulty, yea, even so much that we cannot write them all, we were exceedingly rejoiced when we came to the seashore. And we called the place Bountiful because of its much fruit.

And it came to pass that after I, Nephi, had been in the land of Bountiful for the space of many days, the voice of the Lord came unto me, saying, Arise, and get thee into the mountain. And it came to pass that I arose and went up into the mountain and cried unto the Lord.

And it came to pass that the Lord spake unto me, saying, Thou shalt construct a ship after the manner which I shall show thee, that I may carry thy people across these waters.

And I said, Lord, whither shall I go, that I may find ore to molten, that I may make tools to construct the ship after the manner which thou hast shown unto me?

And it came to pass that the Lord told me whither I should go to find ore, that I might make tools. And it came to pass that I, Nephi, did make bellows, wherewith to blow the fire, of the skins of beasts. And after I had made bellows, that I might have wherewith to blow the fire, I did smite two stones together, that I might make fire.

For the Lord had not hitherto suffered that we should make much fire as we journeyed in the wilderness. For he said, I will make thy food become sweet, that ye cook it not. And I will also be your light in the wilderness. And I will prepare the way before you if it so be that ye shall keep my commandments. Wherefore,

inasmuch as ye shall keep my commandments, ye shall be led
toward the promised land; and ye shall know that it is by me that
ye are led.

Yea, and the Lord said also that, After ye have arrived to the
promised land, ye shall know that I, the Lord, am God, and that I,
the Lord, did deliver you from destruction; yea, that I did bring
you out of the land of Jerusalem.

Wherefore, I, Nephi, did strive to keep the commandments of
the Lord, and I did exhort my brethren to faithfulness and
diligence. And it came to pass that I did make tools of the ore
which I did molten out of the rock.

And when my brethren saw that I was about to build a ship,
they began to murmur against me, saying, Our brother is a fool,
for he thinketh that he can build a ship. Yea, and he also thinketh
that he can cross these great waters. And thus my brethren did
complain against me and were desirous that they might not labor,
for they did not believe that I could build a ship. Neither would
they believe that I was instructed of the Lord.

And now, it came to pass that I, Nephi, was exceeding
sorrowful because of the hardness of their hearts. And now, when
they saw that I began to be sorrowful, they were glad in their
hearts, insomuch that they did rejoice over me, saying, We knew
that ye could not construct a ship, for we knew that ye were
lacking in judgment; wherefore, thou canst not accomplish so
great a work. [27] Behold, these many years we have suffered in the
wilderness, which time we might have enjoyed our possessions
and the land of our inheritance. Yea, and we might have been
happy. And we know that the people who were in the land of
Jerusalem were a righteous people; for they kept the statutes, and
the judgments of the Lord, and all his commandments according
to the law of Moses. Wherefore, we know that they are a righteous
people. And our father hath judged them and hath led us away
because we would hearken unto his word. Yea, and our brother is
like unto him. And after this manner of language did my brethren
murmur and complain against us.

---

[27] 1 Nephi 17: 1-19

And it came to pass that I, Nephi, spake unto them, saying, Do ye believe that our fathers, who were the children of Israel, would have been led away out of the hands of the Egyptians if they had not hearkened unto the words of the Lord? Yea, do ye suppose that they would have been led out of bondage if the Lord had not commanded Moses that he should lead them out of bondage?

Now ye know that the children of Israel were in bondage; and ye know that they were laden with tasks, which were grievous to be borne. Wherefore, ye know that it must needs be a good thing for them, that they should be brought out of bondage.

Now ye know that Moses was commanded of the Lord to do that great work. And ye know that by his word the waters of the Red Sea were divided hither and thither, and they passed through on dry ground. But ye know that the Egyptians were drowned in the Red Sea, who were the armies of Pharaoh.

And ye also know that they were fed with manna in the wilderness. Yea, and ye also know that Moses, by his word, according to the power of God which was in him, smote the rock; and there came forth water, that the children of Israel might quench their thirst.

And notwithstanding they being led, the Lord, their God, their Redeemer, going before them, leading them by day and giving light unto them by night, and doing all things for them which were expedient for man to receive, they hardened their hearts, and blinded their minds, and reviled against Moses and against the true and living God.

And it came to pass that according to his word, he did destroy them; and according to his word, he did lead them; and according to his word, he did do all things for them. And there was not anything done, save it were by his word. [28] And he loveth those who will have him to be their God.

Behold, he loved our fathers; and he covenanted with them, yea, even Abraham, Isaac, and Jacob; and he remembered the covenants which he had made. Wherefore, he did bring them out of the land of Egypt, and he did straiten them in the wilderness

---

[28] 1 Nephi 17: 21-31

with his rod, for they hardened their hearts, even as ye have. And the Lord straitened them because of their iniquity.

He sent fiery flying serpents among them; and after they were bitten, he prepared a way that they might be healed. And the labor which they had to perform was to look. And because of the simpleness of the way, or the easiness of it, there were many who perished.

And they did harden their hearts from time to time, and they did revile against Moses and also against God. Nevertheless, ye know that they were led forth by his matchless power into the land of promise.

And ye also know that by the power of his almighty word he can cause the earth that it shall pass away. Yea, and ye know that by his word he can cause the rough places to be made smooth, and smooth places shall be broken up. Oh, then, why is it that ye can be so hard in your hearts? [29]

And it came to pass that I, Nephi, said unto them that they should murmur no more against their father, neither should they withhold their labor from me, for God had commanded me that I should build a ship.

And I said unto them, If God had commanded me to do all things, I could do them. If he should command me that I should say unto this water, Be thou earth, it should be earth. And if I should say it, it would be done. And now, if the Lord has such great power and has wrought so many miracles among the children of men, how is it that he cannot instruct me that I should build a ship? [30]

And it came to pass that they did worship the Lord and did go forth with me; and we did work timbers of curious workmanship. And the Lord did show me from time to time after what manner I should work the timbers of the ship.

Now I, Nephi, did not work the timbers after the manner which was learned by men, neither did I build the ship after the manner of men. But I did build it after the manner which the Lord had shown unto me; wherefore, it was not after the manner of men.

---

[29] 1 Nephi 17: 40-42, 46
[30] 1 Nephi 17: 49-51

And I, Nephi, did go into the mount oft, and I did pray oft unto the Lord; wherefore, the Lord showed unto me great things. And it came to pass that after I had finished the ship according to the word of the Lord, my brethren beheld that it was good and that the workmanship thereof was exceeding fine; wherefore, they did humble themselves again before the Lord.

And it came to pass that the voice of the Lord came unto my father, that we should arise and go down into the ship. And it came to pass that on the morrow, after we had prepared all things, much fruits and meat from the wilderness, and honey in abundance, and provisions, according to that which the Lord had commanded us, we did go down into the ship with all our loading, and our seeds, and whatsoever thing we had brought with us, everyone according to his age. Wherefore, we did all go down into the ship with our wives and our children.

And now, my father had begotten two sons in the wilderness; the eldest was called Jacob and the younger, Joseph. And it came to pass after we had all gone down into the ship and had taken with us our provisions and things which had been commanded us, we did put forth into the sea and were driven forth before the wind towards the promised land. [31]

---

[31] 1 Nephi 18: 1-8

Chapter 2

Second Exodus — A House Divided

About 590 B.C.

And it came to pass that after we had sailed for the space of many days we did arrive at the promised land. And we went forth upon the land, and did pitch our tents, and we did call it the promised land. And it came to pass that we did begin to till the earth, and we began to plant seeds. Yea, we did put all our seeds into the earth, which we had brought from the land of Jerusalem. And it came to pass that they did grow exceedingly; wherefore, we were blessed in abundance.

And it came to pass that we did find upon the land of promise, as we journeyed in the wilderness, that there were beasts in the forests of every kind, both the cow and the ox, and the ass and the horse, and the goat and the wild goat, and all manner of wild animals, which were for the use of men. And we did find all manner of ore, both of gold and of silver, and of copper. [1]

And it came to pass that the Lord commanded me, wherefore I did make plates of ore that I might engraven upon them the record of my people. And upon the plates which I made, I did engraven the record of my father, and also our journeyings in the wilderness, and the prophecies of my father. And also many of mine own prophecies have I engraven upon them. Nevertheless, I do not write anything upon plates save it be that I think it be sacred. And now, if I do err, even did they err of old. Not that I would excuse myself because of other men, but because of the weakness which is in me according to the flesh, I would excuse myself.

For the things which some men esteem to be of great worth, both to the body and soul, others set at naught and trample under their feet. Yea, even the very God of Israel do men trample under their feet. I say trample under their feet, but I would speak in other words—they set him at naught and hearken not to the voice of his counsels.

---

[1] 1 Nephi 18:23 - 25

And behold he cometh, according to the words of the angel, in six hundred years from the time my father left Jerusalem. And the world, because of their iniquity, shall judge him to be a thing of naught. Wherefore they scourge him, and he suffereth it; and they smite him, and he suffereth it; yea, they spit upon him, and he suffereth it, because of his loving kindness and his long-suffering towards the children of men.

And the God of our fathers who were led out of Egypt, out of bondage, and also were preserved in the wilderness by him, yea, the God of Abraham, and of Isaac, and the God of Jacob, yieldeth himself, according to the words of the angel, as a man, into the hands of wicked men, to be lifted up, according to the words of Zenock, and to be crucified, according to the words of Neum, and to be buried in a sepulchre, according to the words of Zenos, which he spake concerning the three days of darkness, which should be a sign given of his death unto those who should inhabit the isles of the sea, more especially given unto those who are of the house of Israel. [2]

And all these things must surely come, saith the prophet Zenos. And the rocks of the earth must rend. And because of the groanings of the earth, many of the kings of the isles of the sea shall be wrought upon by the Spirit of God to exclaim, The God of nature suffers.

And as for those who are at Jerusalem, saith the prophet, they shall be scourged by all people, because they crucify the God of Israel, and turn their hearts aside, rejecting signs and wonders and the power and glory of the God of Israel. And because they turn their hearts aside, saith the prophet, and have despised the Holy One of Israel, they shall wander in the flesh, and perish, and become a hiss and a byword and be hated among all nations.

Nevertheless, when that day cometh, saith the prophet, that they no more turn aside their hearts against the Holy One of Israel, then will he remember the covenants which he made to their fathers. Yea, then will he remember the isles of the sea. Yea, and all the people who are of the house of Israel, will I gather in, saith the Lord, according to the words of the prophet Zenos, from

---

[2] 1 Nephi 19: 1, 6-10

the four quarters of the earth. Yea, and all the earth shall see the salvation of the Lord, saith the prophet. Every nation, kindred, tongue and people shall be blessed. And I, Nephi, have written these things unto my people, that perhaps I might persuade them that they would remember the Lord their Redeemer. [3]

Now it came to pass that I, Nephi, did teach my brethren these things. And it came to pass that I did read many things to them, which were engraven upon the plates of brass, that they might know concerning the doings of the Lord in other lands, among people of old. And I did read many things unto them which were written in the books of Moses. But that I might more fully persuade them to believe in the Lord their Redeemer I did read unto them that which was written by the prophet Isaiah; for I did liken all scriptures unto us, that it might be for our profit and learning.

Wherefore I spake unto them, saying, Hear ye the words of the prophet, ye who are a remnant of the house of Israel, a branch who have been broken off. Hear ye the words of the prophet, which were written unto all the house of Israel, and liken them unto yourselves, that ye may have hope as well as your brethren from whom ye have been broken off, for after this manner has the prophet written. [4] And again:

Hearken, O ye house of Israel, all ye that are broken off and are driven out because of the wickedness of the pastors of my people; yea, all ye that are broken off, that are scattered abroad, who are of my people, O house of Israel.

Listen, O isles, unto me, and hearken ye people from far; the Lord hath called me from the womb. From the bowels of my mother hath he made mention of my name, and he hath made my mouth like a sharp sword. In the shadow of his hand hath he hid me, and made me a polished shaft. In his quiver hath he hid me, and said unto me, Thou art my servant, O Israel, in whom I will be glorified.

Then I said, I have labored in vain, I have spent my strength for naught and in vain. Surely my judgment is with the Lord, and my work with my God.

And now, saith the Lord, that formed me from the womb that I should be his servant to bring Jacob again to him, Though

---

[3] 1 Nephi 19:12-18
[4] 1 Nephi 19: 22-24

Israel be not gathered, yet shall I be glorious in the eyes of the Lord, and my God shall be my strength. And he said, It is a light thing that thou shouldst be my servant to raise up the tribes of Jacob, and to restore the preserved of Israel. I will also give thee for a light to the Gentiles, that thou mayest be my salvation unto the ends of the earth!

Thus saith the Lord, the Redeemer of Israel, his Holy One, to him whom man despiseth, to him whom the nations abhorreth, to servant of rulers. Kings shall see and arise, princes also shall worship, because of the Lord that is faithful!

Thus saith the Lord, In an acceptable time have I heard thee, O isles of the sea, and in a day of salvation have I helped thee. And I will preserve thee, and give thee my servant for a covenant of the people, to establish the earth, to cause to inherit the desolate heritages, that thou mayest say to the prisoners: Go forth; to them that sit in darkness, Show yourselves!

They shall feed in the ways, and their pastures shall be in all high places. They shall not hunger nor thirst, neither shall the heat nor the sun smite them. For he that hath mercy on them shall lead them, even by the springs of water shall he guide them. And I will make all my mountains a way, and my highways shall be exalted. And then, O house of Israel, behold, these shall come from far; and lo, these from the north and from the west, and these from the land of Sinim.

Sing, O heavens; and be joyful, O earth! For the feet of those who are in the east shall be established and break forth into singing, O mountains! For they shall be smitten no more, for the Lord hath comforted his people, and will have mercy upon his afflicted.

But, behold, Zion hath said, The Lord hath forsaken me, and my Lord hath forgotten me. But he will show that he hath not. For can a woman forget her sucking child, that she should not have compassion on the son of her womb? Yea, they may forget, yet will I not forget thee, O house of Israel!

Behold, I have graven thee upon the palms of my hands; thy walls are continually before me. Thy children shall make haste against thy destroyers; and they that made thee waste shall go forth of thee.

Lift up thine eyes round about and behold: All these gather themselves together, and they shall come to thee. And as I live, saith the Lord, thou shalt surely clothe thee with them all, as with an ornament, and bind them on even as a bride.

For thy waste and thy desolate places, and the land of thy destruction shall even now be too narrow by reason of the inhabitants. And they that swallowed thee up shall be far away. The children whom thou shalt have after thou hast lost the first shall again in thine ears say, The place is too strait for me; give place to me that I may dwell.

Then shalt thou say in thine heart, Who hath begotten me these, seeing I have lost my children, and am desolate, a captive, and removing to and fro? And who hath brought up these? Behold, I was left alone; these, where have they been?

Thus saith the Lord God, Behold, I will lift up mine hand to the Gentiles, and set up my standard to the people; and they shall bring thy sons in their arms, and thy daughters shall be carried upon their shoulders. And kings shall be thy nursing fathers, and their queens thy nursing mothers; they shall bow down to thee with their face towards the earth and lick up the dust of thy feet. And thou shalt know that I am the Lord; for they shall not be ashamed that wait for me.

For shall the prey be taken from the mighty, or the lawful captives delivered? But thus saith the Lord, even the captives of the mighty shall be taken away, and the prey of the terrible shall be delivered; for I will contend with him that contendeth with thee; and I will save thy children. And I will feed them that oppress thee with their own flesh; they shall be drunken with their own blood as with sweet wine. And all flesh shall know that I, the Lord, am thy Savior and thy Redeemer, the Mighty One of Jacob. [5]

And now it came to pass that after I, Nephi, had read these things which were engraven upon the plates of brass, my brethren came unto me and said unto me, What meaneth these things which ye have read? Behold, are they to be understood according to things which are spiritual, which shall come to pass according to the spirit, and not the flesh?

And I, Nephi, said unto them: Behold they were manifest unto the prophet by the voice of the Spirit; for by the Spirit are all things made known unto the prophets which shall come upon the children of men according to the flesh. Wherefore, the things of which I have read are things pertaining to things both temporal and spiritual.

---

[5] 1 Nephi 21:1-26 (Compare Isaiah 49)

For it appears that the house of Israel, sooner or later, will be scattered upon all the face of the earth, and also among all nations. And behold, there are many who are already lost from the knowledge of those who are at Jerusalem. Yea, the more part of all the tribes have been led away, and they are scattered to and fro upon the isles of the sea, and whither they are none of us knoweth, save that we know that they have been led away.

And since they have been led away, these things have been prophesied concerning them, and also concerning all those who shall hereafter be scattered and be confounded, because of the Holy One of Israel. For against him will they harden their hearts. Wherefore, they shall be scattered among all nations and shall be hated of all men.

Nevertheless, after they shall be nursed by the Gentiles, and the Lord has lifted up his hand upon the Gentiles, and set them up for a standard, and their children have been carried in their arms, and their daughters have been carried upon their shoulders— behold these things of which are spoken are temporal, for thus are the covenants of the Lord with our fathers—and it meaneth us in the days to come, and also all our brethren who are of the house of Israel. And it meaneth that the time cometh that after all the house of Israel have been scattered and confounded, that the Lord God will raise up a mighty nation among the Gentiles, yea, even upon the face of this land. And by them shall our seed be scattered. And after our seed is scattered, the Lord God will proceed to do a marvelous work among the Gentiles, which shall be of great worth unto our seed. Wherefore, it is likened unto their being nourished by the Gentiles and being carried in their arms and upon their shoulders.

And it shall also be of worth unto the Gentiles; and not only unto the Gentiles but unto all the house of Israel, unto the making known of the covenants of the Father of heaven unto Abraham, saying: In thy seed shall all the kindreds of the earth be blessed.

And I would, my brethren, that ye should know that all the kindreds of the earth cannot be blessed unless he shall make bare his arm in the eyes of the nations. Wherefore, the Lord God will proceed to make bare his arm in the eyes of all the nations, in bringing about his covenants and his gospel unto those who are of the house of Israel. Wherefore, he will bring them again out of captivity, and they shall be gathered together to the lands of their inheritance. And they shall be brought out of obscurity and out of darkness. And they shall know that the Lord is their Savior and their Redeemer, the Mighty One of Israel. [6]

And every nation which shall war against thee, O house of Israel, shall be turned one against another, and they shall fall into the pit which they digged to ensnare the people of the Lord. And all that fight against Zion shall be destroyed. And that great whore, who hath perverted the right ways of the Lord, yea, that great and abominable church, shall tumble to the dust and great shall be the fall of it.

For behold, saith the prophet, the time cometh speedily that Satan shall have no more power over the hearts of the children of men. For the day soon cometh that all the proud and they who do wickedly shall be as stubble; and the day cometh that they must be burned. For the time soon cometh that the fulness of the wrath of God shall be poured out upon all the children of men, for he will not suffer that the wicked shall destroy the righteous. [7]

Behold, my brethren, I say unto you, that these things must shortly come; yea, even blood, and fire, and vapor of smoke must come. And it must needs be upon the face of this earth. And it cometh unto men according to the flesh, if it so be that they will harden their hearts against the Holy One of Israel. For behold, the righteous shall not perish.

For the time surely must come that all they who fight against Zion shall be cut off. And the Lord will surely prepare a way for his people, unto the fulfilling of the words of Moses, which he spake, saying: A prophet shall the Lord your God raise up unto you, like unto me. Him shall ye hear in all things whatsoever he shall say unto you. And it shall come to pass that all those who will not hear that prophet shall be cut off from among the people. [8]

And now I, Nephi, declare unto you, that this prophet of whom Moses spake was the Holy One of Israel; wherefore, he

---

[6] 1 Nephi 22: 1-12
[7] 1 Nephi 22: 14-16
[8] 1 Nephi 22: 20 (Compare Deuteronomy 18: 18-20)

shall execute judgment in righteousness. [9] And he gathereth his children from the four quarters of the earth; and he numbereth his sheep, and they know him. And there shall be one fold and one shepherd. And he shall feed his sheep; and in him they shall find pasture.

And now behold, I, Nephi, say unto you that all these things must come according to the flesh. But, behold, all nations, kindreds, tongues, and people shall dwell safely in the Holy One of Israel, if it so be that they will repent.

And now I, Nephi, make an end; for I durst not speak further as yet concerning these things. Wherefore, my brethren, I would that ye should consider that the things which have been written upon the plates of brass are true. And they testify that a man must be obedient to the commandments of God. Wherefore, ye need not suppose that I and my father are the only ones that have testified, and also taught them. Wherefore, if ye shall be obedient to the commandments, and endure to the end, ye shall be saved at the last day. And thus it is. Amen.[10]

And now it came to pass that after I, Nephi, had made an end of teaching my brethren, our father, Lehi, also spake many things unto them, and rehearsed unto them, how great things the Lord had done for them in bringing them out of the land of Jerusalem.

For, behold, said he, I have seen a vision, in which I know that Jerusalem is destroyed; and had we remained in Jerusalem we should also have perished. But, said he, Notwithstanding our afflictions, we have obtained a land of promise, a land which is choice above all other lands; a land which the Lord God hath covenanted with me should be a land for the inheritance of my seed.

Yea, the Lord hath covenanted this land unto me, and to my children forever, and also all those who should be led out of other countries by the hand of the Lord. Wherefore, I, Lehi, prophesy according to the workings of the Spirit which is in me, that there shall none come into this land save they shall be brought by the hand of the Lord. Wherefore, this land is consecrated unto him

---

[9] 1 Nephi 22: 18-21
[10] 1 Nephi 22: 25, 27-31

whom he shall bring. And if it so be that they shall serve him according to the commandments which he hath given, it shall be a land of liberty unto them. Wherefore, they shall never be brought down into captivity; if so, it shall be because of iniquity. For if iniquity shall abound, cursed shall be the land for their sakes, but unto the righteous it shall be blessed forever. [11]

And I desire that ye should remember to observe the statutes and the judgments of the Lord. Behold, this hath been the anxiety of my soul from the beginning. Rebel no more against your brother, whose views have been glorious, and who hath kept the commandments from the time that we left Jerusalem, and who hath been an instrument in the hands of God, in bringing us forth into the land of promise. For were it not for him, we must have perished with hunger in the wilderness; nevertheless, ye sought to take away his life. Yea, and he hath suffered much sorrow because of you. [12]

And now my son, Laman, and also Lemuel and Sam, and also my sons who are the sons of Ishmael, behold, if ye will hearken unto the voice of Nephi ye shall not perish. And if ye will hearken unto him I leave unto you a blessing, yea, even my first blessing. But if ye will not hearken unto him I take away my first blessing, yea, even my blessing, and it shall rest upon him. [13]

And now, Jacob, I speak unto you: Thou art my firstborn in the days of my tribulation in the wilderness. And behold, in thy childhood thou hast suffered afflictions and much sorrow, because of the rudeness of thy brethren. Nevertheless, Jacob, my firstborn in the wilderness, thou knowest the greatness of God, and he shall consecrate thine afflictions for thy gain. Wherefore, thy soul shall be blessed, and thou shalt dwell safely with thy brother, Nephi. And thy days shall be spent in the service of thy God.

Wherefore, I know that thou art redeemed, because of the righteousness of thy Redeemer; for thou hast beheld that in the fulness of time he cometh to bring salvation unto men. And thou hast beheld in thy youth his glory; wherefore, thou art blessed even as they unto whom he shall minister in the flesh. For the

---

[11] 2 Nephi 1: 1, 4-7
[12] 2 Nephi 1: 16, 24
[13] 2 Nephi 1: 28 - 29

Spirit is the same, yesterday, today, and forever. And the way is prepared from the fall of man, and salvation is free. [14]

Wherefore, redemption cometh in and through the Holy Messiah, for he is full of grace and truth. Behold, he offereth himself a sacrifice for sin, to answer the ends of the law, unto all those who have a broken heart and a contrite spirit. And unto none else can the ends of the law be answered.

Wherefore, how great the importance to make these things known unto the inhabitants of the earth, that they may know that there is no flesh that can dwell in the presence of God, save it be through the merits, and mercy, and grace of the Holy Messiah, who layeth down his life according to the flesh, and taketh it again by the power of the Spirit, that he may bring to pass the resurrection of the dead, being the first that should rise. Wherefore, he is the firstfruits unto God, inasmuch as he shall make intercession for all the children of men. And they that believe in him shall be saved. And because of the intercession for all, all men come unto God. Wherefore, they stand in the presence of him, to be judged of him, according to the truth and holiness which is in him. [15]

And now, my son, I speak unto you these things for your profit and learning. For there is a God, and he hath created all things, both the heavens, and the earth, and all things that in them are, both things to act, and things to be acted upon. And to bring about his eternal purposes in the end of man, after he had created our first parents, and the beasts of the field and the fowls of the air, and in fine, all things which are created, it must needs be that there was an opposition, even the forbidden fruit in opposition to the tree of life; the one being sweet and the other bitter.

Wherefore, the Lord God gave unto man that he should act for himself. Wherefore, man could not act for himself save it should be that he was enticed by the one or the other. And I, Lehi, according to the things which I have read, must needs suppose that an angel of God, according to that which is written, had fallen from heaven. Wherefore, he became a devil, having sought that which was evil before God. And because he had fallen from

---

[14] 2 Nephi 2: 1-4
[15] 2 Nephi 2: 6-10*

heaven, and had become miserable forever, he sought also the misery of all mankind. Wherefore, he said unto Eve, yea, even that old serpent, who is the devil, who is the father of all lies, wherefore, he said, Partake of the forbidden fruit, and ye shall not die, but ye shall be as God, knowing good and evil.

And after Adam and Eve had partaken of the forbidden fruit they were driven out of the garden of Eden, to till the earth. And they have brought forth children, yea, even the family of all the earth. And the days of the children of men were prolonged according to the will of God, that they might repent while in the flesh. Wherefore, their state became a state of probation, and their time was lengthened, according to the commandments which the Lord God gave unto the children of men. For he gave commandment that all men must repent; for he showed unto all men that they were lost, because of the transgression of their parents. [16]

And men are instructed sufficiently, that they know good from evil, and the law is given unto men. And by the law, no flesh is justified; or, by the law, men are cut off. Yea, by the temporal law they were cut off; and also by the spiritual law they perish from that which is good and become miserable forever. [17]

And now, behold, if Adam had not transgressed he would not have fallen, but he would have remained in the garden of Eden. And all things which were created must have remained in the same state in which they were after they were created; and they must have remained forever and had no end. And they would have had no children. Wherefore they would have remained in a state of innocence, having no joy, for they knew no misery; doing no good, for they knew no sin. [18]

For it must needs be that there is an opposition in all things. If not so, my firstborn in the wilderness, righteousness could not be brought to pass, neither wickedness, neither holiness nor misery, neither good nor bad. Wherefore, if it should be one body, it must needs remain as dead — having no life, neither death, nor

---

[16] 2 Nephi 2: 14-21
[17] 2 Nephi 2: 5
[18] 2 Nephi 2: 22-23

corruption, nor incorruption, happiness nor misery, neither sense nor insensibility. Wherefore, it must needs have been created for a thing of naught. Wherefore, there would have been no purpose in the end of its creation. Wherefore, this thing must needs destroy the wisdom of God and his eternal purposes, and also the power, and the mercy, and the justice of God.

And if ye shall say there is no law, ye shall also say there is no sin. If ye shall say there is no sin, ye shall also say there is no righteousness. And if there be no righteousness there be no happiness. [19] But behold, all things have been done in the wisdom of him who knoweth all things. Adam fell that men might be; and men are, that they might have joy. And the Messiah cometh in the fulness of time, that he may redeem the children of men from the fall. And because that they are redeemed from the fall, they have become free forever, knowing good from evil, to act for themselves and not to be acted upon, save it be by the punishment of the law at the great and last day, according to the commandments which God hath given.

Wherefore, men are free according to the flesh, and all things are given them which are expedient unto man. And they are free to choose liberty and eternal life, through the great Mediator of all men, or to choose captivity and death, according to the captivity and power of the devil; for he seeketh that all men might be miserable like unto himself.

And now, my sons, I would that ye should look to the great Mediator, and hearken unto his great commandments, and be faithful unto his words, and choose eternal life, according to the will of his Holy Spirit. I have spoken these few words unto you all, my sons, in the last days of my probation; and I have chosen the good part, according to the words of the prophet. And I have none other object save it be the everlasting welfare of your souls. Amen. [20]

---

[19] 2 Nephi 2: 11*-13*
[20] 2 Nephi 2: 24-28, 30

About 588 B.C.

And it came to pass after my father, Lehi, had spoken unto all his household, according to the feelings of his heart and the Spirit of the Lord which was in him, he waxed old. And it came to pass that he died and was buried.

And it came to pass that not many days after his death, Laman and Lemuel and the sons of Ishmael were angry with me because of the admonitions of the Lord. [21] Behold, it came to pass that I, Nephi, did cry much unto the Lord my God, because of the anger of my brethren. But behold, their anger did increase against me, insomuch that they did seek to take away my life. Yea, they did murmur against me, saying, Our younger brother thinks to rule over us; and we have had much trial because of him; wherefore, now let us slay him, that we may not be afflicted more because of his words. For behold, we will not have him to be our ruler; for it belongs unto us, who are the elder brethren, to rule over this people.

Now I do not write upon these plates all the words which they murmured against me. But it sufficeth me to say, that they did seek to take away my life. And it came to pass that the Lord did warn me, that I, Nephi, should depart from them and flee into the wilderness, and all those who would go with me. Wherefore, it came to pass that I, Nephi, did take my family, and also Zoram and his family, and Sam, mine elder brother and his family, and Jacob and Joseph, my younger brethren, and also my sisters, and all those who would go with me. And all those who would go with me were those who believed in the warnings and the revelations of God, wherefore, they did hearken unto my words.

And we did take our tents and whatsoever things were possible for us and did journey in the wilderness for the space of many days. And after we had journeyed for the space of many days, we did pitch our tents.

And my people would that we should call the name of the place Nephi, wherefore, we did call it Nephi. And all those who

---

[21] 2 Nephi 4:12-13

were with me did take upon them to call themselves the people of Nephi.

And we did observe to keep the judgments, and the statutes, and the commandments of the Lord in all things, according to the law of Moses. And the Lord was with us. And we did prosper exceedingly; for we did sow seed, and we did reap again in abundance. And we began to raise flocks, and herds, and animals of every kind. [22] And it came to pass that we began to prosper exceedingly, and to multiply in the land.

And I, Nephi, did take the sword of Laban, and after the manner of it did make many swords, lest by any means the people who were now called Lamanites should come upon us and destroy us; for I knew their hatred towards me and my children and those who were called my people.

And I did teach my people to build buildings, and to work in all manner of wood, and of iron, and of copper, and of brass, and of steel, and of gold, and of silver, and of precious ores, which were in great abundance.

And I, Nephi, did build a temple; and I did construct it after the manner of the temple of Solomon save it were not built of so many precious things, for they were not to be found upon the land, wherefore, it could not be built like unto Solomon's temple. But the manner of the construction was like unto the temple of Solomon, and the workmanship thereof was exceedingly fine.

And it came to pass that I, Nephi, did cause my people to be industrious, and to labor with their hands. And it came to pass that they would that I should be their king. But I, Nephi, was desirous that they should have no king; nevertheless, I did for them according to that which was in my power. And behold, the words of the Lord had been fulfilled unto my brethren, which he spake concerning them, that I should be their ruler and their teacher. Wherefore, I had been their ruler and their teacher, according to the commandments of the Lord, until the time they sought to take away my life.

Wherefore, the word of the Lord was fulfilled which he spake unto me, saying that: Inasmuch as they will not hearken unto thy

---

[22] 2 Nephi 5: 1-11

words they shall be cut off from the presence of the Lord. And behold, they were cut off from his presence. And he had caused the cursing to come upon them, yea, even a sore cursing, because of their iniquity. For behold, they had hardened their hearts against him, that they had become like unto a flint. Wherefore, as they were white and exceedingly fair and delightsome, that they might not be enticing unto my people, the Lord God did cause a skin of blackness to come upon them.

And thus saith the Lord God: I will cause that they shall be loathsome unto thy people, save they shall repent of their iniquities. And cursed shall be the seed of him that mixeth with their seed; for they shall be cursed even with the same cursing. And the Lord spake it, and it was done. And because of their cursing which was upon them they did become an idle people, full of mischief and subtlety, and did seek in the wilderness for beasts of prey.

And the Lord God said unto me, They shall be a scourge unto thy seed, to stir them up in remembrance of me. And inasmuch as they will not remember me, and hearken unto my words, they shall scourge them even unto destruction.

About 570 B.C

And it came to pass that I, Nephi, did consecrate Jacob and Joseph, that they should be priests and teachers over the land of my people. And it came to pass that we lived after the manner of happiness. [23] And thirty years had passed away from the time we left Jerusalem. And I, Nephi, had kept the records upon my plates, which I had made, of my people thus far.

And it came to pass that the Lord God said unto me, Make other plates; and thou shalt engraven many things upon them which are good in my sight, for the profit of thy people. Wherefore, I, Nephi, to be obedient to the commandments of the Lord, went and made these plates upon which I have engraven these things. And I engraved that which is pleasing unto God. And if my people are pleased with the things of God, they will be

---

[23] 2 Nephi 5: 13 - 27

pleased with mine engravings which are upon these plates. And if my people desire to know the more particular part of the history of my people, they must search mine other plates. And it sufficeth me to say that forty years had passed away, and we had already had wars and contentions with our brethren. [24]

And now I, Nephi, write more of the words of Isaiah, for my soul delighteth in his words. For I will liken his words unto my people, and I will send them forth unto all my children, for he verily saw my Redeemer, even as I have seen him. And my brother Jacob has seen him as I have seen him. Wherefore, I will send their words forth unto my children to prove unto men that my words are true. Wherefore, by the words of three, God has said, I will establish my word. Nevertheless, God sendeth more witnesses, and proveth all his words.

Behold, my soul delighteth in proving unto my people the truth of the coming of Christ. For, for this end hath the law of Moses been given. And all things which have been given of God, from the beginning of the world, unto man, are the typifying of him. And also my soul delighteth in the covenants of the Lord which he hath made to our fathers. Yea, my soul delighteth in his grace, and in his justice, and power, and mercy in the great and eternal plan of deliverance from death. And my soul delighteth in proving unto my people that save Christ should come all men must perish. For if there be no Christ there be no God; and if there be no God we are not, for there could have been no creation. But there is a God, and he is Christ, and he cometh in the fulness of his own time.

And now I write some of the words of Isaiah, that whoso of my people shall see these words may lift up their hearts and rejoice for all men. Now these are the words, and ye may liken them unto you and unto all men: [25]

The word that Isaiah the son of Amoz saw concerning Judah and Jerusalem: And it shall come to pass in the last days, when the mountain of the Lord's house shall be established in the top of the mountains, and shall be exalted above the hills, and all nations shall flow unto it, and many people shall go and say, Come ye, and let us go up to the mountain of the Lord, to the

---

[24] 2 Nephi 5: 28- 34
[25] 2 Nephi 11: 2 - 8

house of the God of Jacob, and he will teach us of his ways; and we will walk in his paths. For out of Zion shall go forth the law, and the word of the Lord from Jerusalem.

And he shall judge among the nations and shall rebuke many people, and they shall beat their swords into plow-shares, and their spears into pruning-hooks. Nation shall not lift up sword against nation, neither shall they learn war any more.

O house of Jacob, come ye and let us walk in the light of the Lord; yea, come, for ye have all gone astray, every one to his wicked ways. Therefore, O Lord, thou hast forsaken thy people, the house of Jacob, because they be replenished from the east, and hearken unto soothsayers like the Philistines, and they please themselves in the children of strangers.

Their land also is full of silver and gold, neither is there any end of their treasures. Their land is also full of horses, neither is there any end of their chariots. Their land is also full of idols. They worship the work of their own hands, that which their own fingers have made. And the mean man boweth not down, and the great man humbleth himself not; therefore, forgive him not.

O ye wicked ones, enter into the rock, and hide thee in the dust, for the fear of the Lord and the glory of his majesty shall smite thee. And it shall come to pass that the lofty looks of man shall be humbled, and the haughtiness of men shall be bowed down, and the Lord alone shall be exalted in that day. For the day of the Lord of Hosts soon cometh upon all nations, yea, upon every one; yea, upon the proud and lofty, and upon every one who is lifted up, and he shall be brought low. [26]

In that day a man shall cast his idols of silver, and his idols of gold, which he hath made for himself to worship, to the moles and to the bats, to go into the clefts of the rocks, and into the tops of the ragged rocks; for the fear of the Lord shall come upon them and the majesty of his glory shall smite them, when he ariseth to shake terribly the earth. Cease ye from man, whose breath is in his nostrils; for wherein is he to be accounted of? [27]

In that day shall the branch of the Lord be beautiful and glorious, the fruit of the earth excellent and comely, to them that are escaped of Israel. And it shall come to pass, they that are left in Zion and remain in Jerusalem shall be called holy, every one that is written among the living in Jerusalem, when the Lord shall

---

[26] 2 Nephi 12:1 – 12 (Compare Isaiah 2: 1-12)
[27] 2 Nephi 12:20-22 (Compare Isaiah 2: 20-22)

have washed away the filth of the daughters of Zion, and shall have purged the blood of Jerusalem from the midst thereof, by the spirit of judgment and by the spirit of burning.

And the Lord will create upon every dwelling place of mount Zion, and upon her assemblies, a cloud and smoke by day and the shining of a flaming fire by night; for upon all the glory of Zion shall be a defense. And there shall be a tabernacle for a shadow in the daytime from the heat, and for a place of refuge, and a covert from storm and from rain. [28]

The people that walked in darkness have seen a great light; they that dwell in the land of the shadow of death, upon them hath the light shined. Thou hast multiplied the nation and increased the joy. They joy before thee according to the joy in harvest, and as men rejoice when they divide the spoil; for thou hast broken the yoke of his burden, and the staff of his shoulder, the rod of his oppressor. For every battle of the warrior is with confused noise and garments rolled in blood; but this shall be with burning and fuel of fire.

For unto us a child is born; unto us a son is given; and the government shall be upon his shoulder. And his name shall be called Wonderful, Counselor, The Mighty God, The Everlasting Father, The Prince of Peace. Of the increase of government and peace there is no end upon the throne of David, and upon his kingdom, to order it, and to establish it with judgment and with justice, from henceforth even forever. The zeal of the Lord of Hosts will perform this. The Lord sent his word unto Jacob and it hath lighted upon Israel. [29]

And there shall come forth a rod out of the stem of Jesse, and a branch shall grow out of his roots. And the Spirit of the Lord shall rest upon him, the spirit of wisdom and understanding, the spirit of counsel and might, the spirit of knowledge and of the fear of the Lord, and shall make him of quick understanding in the fear of the Lord.

And he shall not judge after the sight of his eyes, neither reprove after the hearing of his ears, but with righteousness shall he judge the poor, and reprove with equity for the meek of the earth. And he shall smite the earth with the rod of his mouth; and with the breath of his lips shall he slay the wicked. And

---

[28] 2 Nephi 14:2-6 (Compare Isaiah 4: 2-6)
[29] 2 Nephi 19:2-8 (Compare Isaiah 9: 2-8)

righteousness shall be the girdle of his loins, and faithfulness the girdle of his reins.

The wolf also shall dwell with the lamb, and the leopard shall lie down with the kid, and the calf, and the young lion, and fatling together; and a little child shall lead them. And the cow and the bear shall feed; their young ones shall lie down together; and the lion shall eat straw like the ox. And the sucking child shall play on the hole of the asp, and the weaned child shall put his hand on the cockatrice's den. They shall not hurt nor destroy in all my holy mountain, for the earth shall be full of the knowledge of the Lord, as the waters cover the sea.

And in that day there shall be a root of Jesse, which shall stand for an ensign of the people. To it shall the Gentiles seek; and his rest shall be glorious. And it shall come to pass in that day that the Lord shall set his hand again the second time to recover the remnant of his people which shall be left, from Assyria, and from Egypt, and from Pathros, and from Cush, and from Elam, and from Shinar, and from Hamath, and from the islands of the sea. And he shall set up an ensign for the nations, and shall assemble the outcasts of Israel, and gather together the dispersed of Judah from the four corners of the earth. And there shall be a highway for the remnant of his people which shall be left from Assyria, like as it was to Israel in the day that he came up out of the land of Egypt. [30]

And in that day thou shalt say, O Lord, I will praise thee! Though thou wast angry with me, thine anger is turned away, and thou comfortedst me. Behold, God is my salvation! I will trust and not be afraid, for the Lord Jehova is my strength and my song! He also is become my salvation. Therefore, with joy shall ye draw water out of the wells of salvation.

And in that day shall ye say, Praise the Lord! Call upon his name; declare his doings among the people; make mention that his name is exalted! Sing unto the Lord, for he hath done excellent things! This is known in all the earth. Cry out and shout, thou inhabitant of Zion, for great is the Holy One of Israel in the midst of thee! [31]

Now I, Nephi, do speak somewhat concerning the words which I have written, which have been spoken by the mouth of Isaiah. For behold, Isaiah spake many things which were hard for

---

[30] 2 Nephi 21:1 – 12, 16 (Compare Isaiah 11: 1-12, 16)
[31] 2 Nephi 22: 1-6 (Compare Isaiah 12: 1-6)

many of my people to understand, for they know not concerning the manner of prophesying among the Jews. Wherefore, I write unto my people, unto all those that shall receive hereafter these things which I write, that they may know the judgments of God, that they come upon all nations, according to the word which he hath spoken.

But behold, I proceed with mine own prophecy, according to my plainness, in the which I know that no man can err. Nevertheless, in the days that the prophecies of Isaiah shall be fulfilled men shall know of a surety, at the times when they shall come to pass. Wherefore, they are of worth unto the children of men. And he that supposeth that they are not, unto them will I speak particularly, and confine the words unto mine own people, for I know that they shall be of great worth unto them in the last days. For in that day shall they understand them. Wherefore, for their good have I written them.

And as one generation hath been destroyed among the Jews because of iniquity, even so have they been destroyed from generation to generation according to their iniquities. And never hath any of them been destroyed save it were foretold them by the prophets of the Lord.

But, behold, they shall have wars, and rumors of wars. And when the day cometh that the Only Begotten of the Father, yea, even the Father of heaven and of earth, shall manifest himself unto them in the flesh, behold, they will reject him, because of their iniquities, and the hardness of their hearts, and the stiffness of their necks.

Behold, they will crucify him. And after he is laid in a sepulchre for the space of three days he shall rise from the dead, with healing in his wings. And all those who shall believe on his name shall be saved in the kingdom of God. Wherefore, my soul delighteth to prophesy concerning him, for I have seen his day, and my heart doth magnify his holy name.

And behold it shall come to pass that after the Messiah hath risen from the dead, and hath manifested himself unto his people, unto as many as will believe on his name, behold, Jerusalem shall be destroyed again, for wo unto them that fight against God and the people of his church. Wherefore, the Jews shall be scattered among all nations; yea, and also Babylon shall be destroyed; wherefore, the Jews shall be scattered by other nations.

And after they have been scattered, and the Lord God hath scourged them by other nations for the space of many generations, yea, even down from generation to generation until they shall be persuaded to believe in Christ, the Son of God, and the atonement, which is infinite for all mankind—and when that day shall come that they shall believe in Christ, and worship the Father in his name, with pure hearts and clean hands, and look not forward any more for another Messiah, then, at that time, the day will come that it must needs be expedient that they should believe these things.

And the Lord will set his hand again the second time to restore his people from their lost and fallen state. Wherefore, he will proceed to do a marvelous work and a wonder among the children of men. Wherefore, he shall bring forth his words unto them, which words shall judge them at the last day, for they shall be given them for the purpose of convincing them of the true Messiah, who was rejected by them, and unto the convincing of them that they need not look forward any more for a Messiah to come. For there should not any come, save it should be a false Messiah which should deceive the people.

For there is save one Messiah spoken of by the prophets, and that Messiah is he who should be rejected of the Jews. For according to the words of the prophets, the Messiah cometh in six hundred years from the time that my father left Jerusalem. And according to the words of the prophets, and also the word of the angel of God, his name shall be Jesus Christ, the Son of God.

And now, my brethren, I have spoken plainly that ye cannot err. And as the Lord God liveth that brought Israel up out of the land of Egypt, and gave unto Moses power that he should heal the nations after they had been bitten by the poisonous serpents, if they would cast their eyes unto the serpent which he did raise up before them, and also gave him power that he should smite the rock and the water should come forth; yea, behold I say unto you, that as these things are true, and as the Lord God liveth, there is none other name given under heaven save it be this Jesus Christ, of which I have spoken, whereby man can be saved.

Wherefore, for this cause hath the Lord God promised unto me that these things which I write shall be kept and preserved and handed down unto my seed, from generation to generation, that the promise may be fulfilled unto Joseph, that his seed should never perish as long as the earth should stand. Wherefore, these things shall go from generation to generation as long as the earth shall stand. And they shall go according to the will and pleasure of God. And the nations who shall possess them shall be judged of them according to the words which are written. For we labor diligently to write, to persuade our children, and also our brethren, to believe in Christ, and to be reconciled to God; for we know that it is by grace that we are saved, after all we can do.

And, notwithstanding we believe in Christ, we keep the law of Moses, and look forward with steadfastness unto Christ, until the law shall be fulfilled. For, for this end was the law given. Wherefore the law hath become dead unto us, and we are made alive in Christ because of our faith; yet we keep the law because of the commandments.

And we talk of Christ, we rejoice in Christ, we preach of Christ, we prophesy of Christ, and we write according to our prophecies, that our children may know to what source they may look for a remission of their sins. [32] He doeth not anything save it be for the benefit of the world; for he loveth the world, even that he layeth down his own life that he may draw all men unto him. Wherefore, he commandeth none that they shall not partake of his salvation.

Behold, doth he cry unto any, saying: Depart from me? Behold, I say unto you, Nay! But he saith, Come unto me all ye ends of the earth, buy milk and honey, without money and without price.

Behold, hath he commanded any that they should depart out of the synagogues or out of the houses of worship? Behold, I say unto you, Nay! [33] But all men are privileged, the one like unto the other, and none are forbidden.

He commandeth that there shall be no priestcrafts; for, behold, priestcrafts are that men preach and set themselves up for a light

[32] 2 Nephi 25:1-26
[33] 2 Nephi 26:24-26

unto the world, that they may get gain and praise of the world; but they seek not the welfare of Zion. But the laborer in Zion shall labor for Zion; for if they labor for money, they shall perish. [34]

And again, the Lord God hath commanded that men should not murder; that they should not lie; that they should not steal; that they should not take the name of the Lord their God in vain; that they should not envy; that they should not have malice; that they should not contend one with another; that they should not commit whoredoms; and that they should do none of these things; for whoso doeth them shall perish. For none of these iniquities come of the Lord.

For he doeth that which is good among the children of men; and he doeth nothing save it be plain unto the children of men. And he inviteth them all to come unto him and partake of his goodness. And he denieth none that come unto him, black and white, bond and free, male and female; and he remembereth the heathen; and all are alike unto God, both Jew and Gentile. [35]

But, behold, in the last days, or in the days of the Gentiles, yea, behold all the nations of the Gentiles and also the Jews, both those who shall come upon this land and those who shall be upon other lands, yea, even upon all the lands of the earth, behold, they will be drunken with iniquity and all manner of abominations:

And when that day shall come, they shall be visited of the Lord of Hosts, with thunder and with earthquake, and with a great noise, and with storm, and with tempest, and with the flame of devouring fire.

And all the nations that fight against Zion, and that distress her, shall be as a dream of a night vision; yea, it shall be unto them, even as unto a hungry man which dreameth. And behold he eateth, but he awaketh and his soul is empty; or like unto a thirsty man which dreameth, and behold he drinketh, but he awaketh and behold he is faint, and his soul hath appetite. Yea, even so shall the multitude of all the nations be that fight against Mount Zion.

For behold, all ye that doeth iniquity, stay yourselves and wonder; for ye shall cry out, and cry. Yea, ye shall be drunken but not with wine, ye shall stagger but not with strong drink. For behold, the Lord hath poured out upon you the spirit of deep

[34] 2 Nephi 26: 28*-29, 31
[35] 2 Nephi 26:32 -33

sleep. For behold, ye have closed your eyes, and ye have rejected the prophets; and your rulers, and the seers hath he covered because of your iniquity.

And it shall come to pass that the Lord God shall bring forth unto you the words of a book, and they shall be the words of them which have slumbered. And behold, the book shall be sealed; and in the book shall be a revelation from God, from the beginning of the world to the ending thereof. Wherefore, because of the things which are sealed up, the things which are sealed shall not be delivered in the day of the wickedness and abominations of the people. Wherefore the book shall be kept from them. [36]

And the day cometh that the words of the book, which were sealed, shall be read upon the house tops; and they shall be read by the power of Christ. And all things shall be revealed unto the children of men which ever have been among the children of men, and which ever will be, even unto the end of the earth. Wherefore, the Lord God will proceed to bring forth the words of the book. And in the mouth of as many witnesses as seemeth him good will he establish his word. And wo be unto him that rejecteth the word of God! [37]

Wherefore it shall come to pass, that the Lord God will deliver again the book, and the words thereof, to him that is not learned. And the man that is not learned shall say: I am not learned.

Then shall the Lord God say unto him: The learned shall not read them, for they have rejected them, and I am able to do mine own work; wherefore thou shalt read the words which I shall give unto thee. Touch not the things which are sealed, for I will bring them forth in mine own due time; for I will show unto the children of men that I am able to do mine own work. [38]

For behold, I am God; and I am a God of miracles. And I will show unto the world that I am the same yesterday, today, and forever; and I work not among the children of men save it be according to their faith.

And again it shall come to pass that the Lord shall say unto him that shall read the words that shall be delivered him,

---

[36] 2 Nephi 27:1-8 (Compare Isaiah 29: 6-10)
[37] 2 Nephi 27: 11, 14
[38] 2 Nephi 27: 19-21 (Compare Isaiah 29:12)

Forasmuch as this people draw near unto me with their mouth, and with their lips do honor me, but have removed their hearts far from me, and their fear towards me is taught by the precepts of men, therefore, I will proceed to do a marvelous work among this people, yea, a marvelous work and a wonder. For the wisdom of their wise and learned shall perish, and the understanding of their prudent shall be hid.

And wo unto them that seek deep to hide their counsel from the Lord, and their works are in the dark; and they say, Who seeth us, and who knoweth us? And they also say, Surely, your turning of things upside down shall be esteemed as the potter's clay. But behold, I will show unto them, saith the Lord of Hosts, that I know all their works. For shall the work say of him that made it, he made me not? Or shall the thing framed say of him that framed it, he had no understanding?

But behold, saith the Lord of Hosts: I will show unto the children of men that it is yet a very little while and Lebanon shall be turned into a fruitful field, and the fruitful field shall be esteemed as a forest.

And in that day shall the deaf hear the words of the book, and the eyes of the blind shall see out of obscurity and out of darkness. And the meek also shall increase, and their joy shall be in the Lord, and the poor among men shall rejoice in the Holy One of Israel.

For assuredly as the Lord liveth, they shall see that the terrible one is brought to naught; and the scorner is consumed; and all that watch for iniquity are cut off, and they that make a man an offender for a word, and lay a snare for him that reproveth in the gate, and turn aside the just for a thing of naught.

Therefore, thus saith the Lord, who redeemed Abraham, concerning the house of Jacob: Jacob shall not now be ashamed, neither shall his face now wax pale. But when he seeth his children, the work of my hands in the midst of him, they shall sanctify my name, and sanctify the Holy One of Jacob, and shall fear the God of Israel. They also that erred in spirit shall come to understanding, and they that murmured shall learn doctrine. [39]

Wherefore murmur ye, because that ye shall receive more of my word? Know ye not that the testimony of two nations is a witness unto you that I am God, that I remember one nation like unto another? Wherefore, I speak the same words unto one nation

---

[39] 2 Nephi 27: 23 -35 (Compare Isaiah 29: 13-24)

like unto another. And when the two nations shall run together, the testimony of the two nations shall run together also. And I do this that I may prove unto many that I am the same yesterday, today, and forever, and that I speak forth my words according to mine own pleasure. And because that I have spoken one word, ye need not suppose that I cannot speak another; for my work is not yet finished, neither shall it be until the end of man, neither from that time henceforth and forever.

For I command all men, both in the east and in the west, and in the north, and in the south, and in the islands of the sea, that they shall write the words which I speak unto them. For out of the books which shall be written I will judge the world, every man according to their works, according to that which is written.

For behold, I shall speak unto the Jews and they shall write it; and I shall also speak unto the Nephites and they shall write it; and I shall also speak unto the other tribes of the house of Israel, which I have led away, and they shall write it; and I shall also speak unto all nations of the earth and they shall write it.

And it shall come to pass that the Jews shall have the words of the Nephites, and the Nephites shall have the words of the Jews; and the Nephites and the Jews shall have the words of the lost tribes of Israel; and the lost tribes of Israel shall have the words of the Nephites and the Jews.

And it shall come to pass that my people, which are of the house of Israel, shall be gathered home unto the lands of their possessions. And my word also shall be gathered in one. And I will show unto them that fight against my word, and against my people, who are of the house of Israel, that I am God, and that I covenanted with Abraham that I would remember his seed forever. [40]

And now, I would prophesy somewhat more concerning the Jews and the Gentiles. For after the book of which I have spoken shall come forth, and be written unto the Gentiles, and sealed up again unto the Lord, there shall be many which shall believe the words which are written. And they shall carry them forth unto the remnant of our seed. And then shall the remnant of our seed know concerning us, how that we came out from Jerusalem, and

---

[40] 2 Nephi 29: 8-9, 11-14

that they are descendants of the Jews. And the gospel of Jesus Christ shall be declared among them. Wherefore, they shall be restored unto the knowledge of their fathers, and also to the knowledge of Jesus Christ, which was had among their fathers.

And then shall they rejoice; for they shall know that it is a blessing unto them from the hand of God. And their scales of darkness shall begin to fall from their eyes. And many generations shall not pass away among them, save they shall be a pure and a delightsome people.

And it shall come to pass that the Jews which are scattered also shall begin to believe in Christ; and they shall begin to gather in upon the face of the land. And as many as shall believe in Christ shall also become a delightsome people.

And it shall come to pass that the Lord God shall commence his work among all nations, kindreds, tongues, and people, to bring about the restoration of his people upon the earth. And with righteousness shall the Lord God judge the poor, and reprove with equity for the meek of the earth. And he shall smite the earth with the rod of his mouth, and with the breath of his lips shall he slay the wicked.

For the time speedily cometh that the Lord God shall cause a great division among the people, and the wicked will he destroy. And he will spare his people, yea, even if it so be that he must destroy the wicked by fire. And righteousness shall be the girdle of his loins, and faithfulness the girdle of his reins.

And then shall the wolf dwell with the lamb; and the leopard shall lie down with the kid, and the calf, and the young lion, and the fatling, together; and a little child shall lead them. And the cow and the bear shall feed; their young ones shall lie down together; and the lion shall eat straw like the ox. And the sucking child shall play on the hole of the asp, and the weaned child shall put his hand on the cockatrice's den. They shall not hurt nor destroy in all my holy mountain, for the earth shall be full of the knowledge of the Lord, as the waters cover the sea.

Wherefore, the things of all nations shall be made known; yea, all things shall be made known unto the children of men. There is nothing which is secret save it shall be revealed. There is no work of darkness save it shall be made manifest in the light; and there is nothing which is sealed upon the earth, save it shall be loosed.

Wherefore, all things which have been revealed unto the children of men, shall at that day be revealed. And Satan shall have power over the hearts of the children of men no more, for a long time. [41]

And now, I, Nephi, cannot write all the things which were taught among my people; neither am I mighty in writing, like unto speaking. For when a man speaketh by the power of the Holy Ghost, the power of the Holy Ghost carrieth it unto the hearts of the children of men.

But behold, there are many that harden their hearts against the Holy Spirit, that it hath no place in them. Wherefore, they cast many things away which are written and esteem them as things of naught. But I, Nephi, have written what I have written; and I esteem it as of great worth, and especially unto my people.

For I pray continually for them by day, and mine eyes water my pillow by night because of them; and I cry unto my God in faith. And I know that he will hear my cry; and I know that the Lord God will consecrate my prayers for the gain of my people. And the words which I have written in weakness will he make strong unto them, for it persuadeth them to do good. It maketh known unto them of their fathers, and it speaketh of Jesus, and persuadeth them to believe in him and to endure to the end, which is life eternal.

And now, my beloved brethren, all those who are of the house of Israel and all ye ends of the earth, I speak unto you, as the voice of one crying from the dust: Farewell until that great day shall come.[42]

---

[41] 2 Nephi 30: 3-18* (Compare Isaiah 11:4-9)
[42] 2 Nephi 33: 1-4, 13

Chapter 3

Third Exodus — The Servant Kings

About 550 B.C.

The word of Jacob, the brother of Nephi, which he spake unto the people of Nephi: Behold, my beloved brethren, I, Jacob, having been called of God, and ordained after the manner of his holy order, and having been consecrated by my brother, Nephi, unto whom ye look as a king or a protector, and on whom ye depend for safety, behold, ye know that I have spoken unto you exceeding many things. Nevertheless, I speak unto you again, for I am desirous for the welfare of your souls. Yea, mine anxiety is great for you; and ye yourselves know that it ever has been. For I have exhorted you with all diligence; and I have taught you the words of my father, and I have spoken unto you concerning all things which are written from the creation of the world.

And now, behold, I would speak unto you concerning things which are, and which are to come; wherefore, I will read you the words of Isaiah. And they are the words which my brother has desired that I should speak unto you. And I speak them unto you for your sakes, that ye may learn and glorify the name of your God. And now, the words which I shall read are they which Isaiah spake concerning all the house of Israel. Wherefore, they may be likened unto you, for ye are of the house of Israel. [1] And now, these are the words:

Thus saith the Lord God, Behold, I will lift up mine hand to the Gentiles and set up my standard to the people; and they shall bring thy sons in their arms, and thy daughters shall be carried upon their shoulders. And kings shall be thy nursing fathers, and their queens thy nursing mothers. They shall bow down to thee with their faces toward the earth and lick up the dust of thy feet. And thou shalt know that I am the Lord; for they shall not be ashamed that wait for me. [2]

---

[1] 2 Nephi 6: 1-5*
[2] 2 Nephi 6: 6-7 (Compare Isaiah 49: 22-23)

And now, I, Jacob, would speak somewhat concerning these words. For behold, the Lord has shown me that those who were at Jerusalem, from whence we came, have been slain and carried away captive. Nevertheless, the Lord has shown unto me that they should return again. And he also has shown unto me that the Lord God, the Holy One of Israel, should manifest himself unto them in the flesh. And after he should manifest himself, they should scourge him and crucify him, according to the words of the angel who spake it unto me.

And after they have hardened their hearts and stiffened their necks against the Holy One of Israel, behold, the judgments of the Holy One of Israel shall come upon them. And the day cometh that they shall be smitten and afflicted. Wherefore, after they are driven to and fro, for thus saith the angel, many shall be afflicted in the flesh and shall not be suffered to perish because of the prayers of the faithful. They shall be scattered, and smitten, and hated. Nevertheless, the Lord will be merciful unto them, that when they shall come to the knowledge of their Redeemer, they shall be gathered together again to the lands of their inheritance.

And blessed are the Gentiles, they of whom the prophet has written. For behold, if it so be that they shall repent, and fight not against Zion, and do not unite themselves to that great and abominable church, they shall be saved. For the Lord God will fulfill his covenants which he has made unto his children. And for this cause the prophet has written these things.

Wherefore, they that fight against Zion and the covenant people of the Lord shall lick up the dust of their feet; and the people of the Lord shall not be ashamed. For the people of the Lord are they who wait for him; for they still wait for the coming of the Messiah.

And behold, according to the words of the prophet, the Messiah will set himself again the second time to recover them. Wherefore, he will manifest himself unto them in power and great glory, unto the destruction of their enemies, when that day cometh when they shall believe in him. And none will he destroy that believe in him. And they that believe not in him shall be destroyed, both by fire, and by tempest, and by earthquakes, and by bloodsheds, and by pestilence, and by famine. And they shall know that the Lord is God, the Holy One of Israel. [3]

Hearken unto me, ye that follow after righteousness. Look unto the rock from whence ye are hewn and to the hole of the pit from whence ye are digged. Look unto Abraham, your father, and unto Sarah, she that bare you. For I called him alone and blessed him. For the Lord shall comfort Zion. He will comfort all her waste places; and he will make her wilderness like Eden and her desert like the garden of the Lord. Joy and gladness shall be found therein, thanksgiving and the voice of melody.

Hearken unto me, my people, and give ear unto me, O my nation: For a law shall proceed from me, and I will make my judgment to rest for a light for the people. My righteousness is near; my salvation is gone forth; and mine arm shall judge the people. The isles shall wait upon me, and on mine arm shall they trust. Lift up your eyes to the heavens and look upon the earth beneath. For the heavens shall vanish away like smoke, and the earth shall wax old like a garment; and they that dwell therein shall die in like manner. But my salvation shall be forever; and my righteousness shall not be abolished.

Hearken unto me, ye that know righteousness, the people in whose heart I have written my law. Fear ye not the reproach of men; neither be ye afraid of their revilings. For the moth shall eat them up like a garment, and the worm shall eat them like wool. But my righteousness shall be forever, and my salvation from generation to generation.

Awake, awake! Put on strength, O arm of the Lord! Awake as in the ancient days. Art thou not it that hath cut Rahab and wounded the dragon? Art thou not it which hath dried the sea, the waters of the great deep, that hath made the depths of the sea a way for the ransomed to pass over? Therefore, the redeemed of the Lord shall return and come with singing unto Zion, and everlasting joy and holiness shall be upon their heads. And they shall obtain gladness and joy. Sorrow and mourning shall flee away. [4]

And now, my beloved brethren, I have read these things that ye might know concerning the covenants of the Lord that he has covenanted with all the house of Israel, that he has spoken unto

---

[3] 2 Nephi: 6: 8-15
[4] 2 Nephi 8: 1-11 (Compare Isaiah 51:1-11)

the Jews by the mouth of his holy prophets, even from the beginning down, from generation to generation, until the time comes that they shall be restored to the true church and fold of God, when they shall be gathered home to the lands of their inheritance, and shall be established in all their lands of promise.

Behold, my beloved brethren, I speak unto you these things that ye may rejoice and lift up your heads forever because of the blessings which the Lord God shall bestow upon your children. For I know that ye have searched much, many of you, to know of things to come. Wherefore, I know that ye know that our flesh must waste away and die; nevertheless, in our bodies we shall see God.

Yea, I know that ye know that in the body he shall show himself unto those at Jerusalem, from whence we came. For it is expedient that it should be among them. For it behooveth the great Creator that he suffereth himself to become subject unto man in the flesh, and die for all men, that all men might become subject unto him. For as death hath passed upon all men, to fulfill the merciful plan of the great Creator, there must needs be a power of resurrection. [5]

Oh, how great the goodness of our God, who prepareth a way for our escape from the grasp of this awful monster, yea, that monster, death and hell, which I call the death of the body, and also the death of the spirit. And because of the way of deliverance of our God, the Holy One of Israel, this death of which I have spoken, which is the temporal, shall deliver up its dead, which death is the grave. And this death of which I have spoken, which is the spiritual death, shall deliver up its dead, which spiritual death is hell. Wherefore, death and hell must deliver up their dead, and the bodies and the spirits of men will be restored, one to the other. And it is by the power of the resurrection of the Holy One of Israel. [6]

And it shall come to pass that when all men shall have passed from this first death unto life, insomuch as they have become immortal, they must appear before the judgment seat of the Holy One of Israel. And then cometh the judgment; and then must they

---

[5] 2 Nephi 9: 1-6*
[6] 2 Nephi 9: 10-12*

be judged according to the holy judgment of God. And assuredly, as the Lord liveth, for the Lord God hath spoken it, and it is his eternal word, which cannot pass away, that they who are righteous shall be righteous still, and they who are filthy shall be filthy still.

Wherefore, they who are filthy are the devil and his angels. And they shall go away into everlasting fire prepared for them. And their torment is as a lake of fire and brimstone, whose flames ascendeth up forever and ever and has no end. But behold, the righteous, the saints of the Holy One of Israel, they who have believed in the Holy One of Israel, they who have endured the crosses of the world and despised the shame of it, they shall inherit the kingdom of God which was prepared for them from the foundation of the world. And their joy shall be full forever. [7]

O my beloved brethren, remember the awfulness in transgressing against that Holy God, and also the awfulness of yielding to the enticings of that cunning one. Remember, to be carnally minded is death, and to be spiritually minded is life eternal.

O, then, my beloved brethren, come unto the Lord, the Holy One. Remember that his paths are righteousness. Behold, the way for man is narrow, but it lieth in a straight course before him; and the keeper of the gate is the Holy One of Israel. And he employeth no servant there. And there is none other way, save it be by the gate, for he cannot be deceived, for the Lord God is his name. [8]

O my beloved brethren, turn away from your sins; shake off the chains of him that would bind you fast. Come unto that God who is the rock of your salvation. Prepare your souls for that glorious day, when justice shall be administered unto the righteous, even the day of judgment, that ye may not shrink with awful fear, that ye may not remember your awful guilt in perfectness and be constrained to exclaim, Holy, holy are thy judgments, O Lord God Almighty! But I know my guilt; I

---

[7] 2 Nephi 9: 15-16,18
[8] 2 Nephi 9: 39,41

transgressed thy law, and my transgressions are mine; and the devil hath obtained me, that I am a prey to his awful misery.[9]

Come, my brethren, everyone that thirsteth; come ye to the waters. And he that hath no money, come, buy and eat! Yea, come buy wine and milk without money and without price! Wherefore, do not spend money for that which is of no worth, nor your labor for that which cannot satisfy. Hearken diligently unto me, and remember the words which I have spoken, and come unto the Holy One of Israel, and feast upon that which perisheth not, neither can be corrupted, and let your soul delight in fatness.

Behold, my beloved brethren, remember the words of your God. Pray unto him continually by day, and give thanks unto his holy name by night. Let your hearts rejoice and behold how great the covenants of the Lord, and how great his condescensions unto the children of men. And because of his greatness and his grace and mercy, he has promised unto us that our seed shall not utterly be destroyed according to the flesh, but that he would preserve them. And in future generations they shall become a righteous branch unto the house of Israel. [10]

For behold, the promises which we have obtained are promises unto us according to the flesh. Wherefore, as it has been shown unto me that many of our children shall perish in the flesh because of unbelief; nevertheless, God will be merciful unto many. And our children shall be restored, that they may come to that which will give them the true knowledge of their Redeemer.

Wherefore, as I said unto you, it must needs be expedient that Christ (for in the last night the angel spake unto me that this should be his name) should come among the Jews, among those who are the more wicked part of the world. And they shall crucify him; for thus it behooveth our God. And there is none other nation on earth that would crucify their God. For should the mighty miracles be wrought among other nations, they would repent and know that he be their God. But because of priestcrafts and iniquities, they at Jerusalem will stiffen their necks against him, that he be crucified.

---

[9] 2 Nephi 9: 45-46
[10] 2 Nephi 9: 50-53

Wherefore, because of their iniquities, destructions, famines, pestilence, and bloodsheds shall come upon them. And they who shall not be destroyed shall be scattered among all nations. But behold, thus saith the Lord God, when the day cometh that they shall believe in me, that I am Christ, then have I covenanted with their fathers that they shall be restored in the flesh upon the earth, unto the lands of their inheritance.

And it shall come to pass that they shall be gathered in from their long dispersion from the isles of the sea and from the four parts of the earth. And the nations of the Gentiles shall be great in the eyes of me, saith God, in carrying them forth to the lands of their inheritance. Yea, the kings of the Gentiles shall be nursing fathers unto them, and their queens shall become nursing mothers. Wherefore, the promises of the Lord are great unto the Gentiles, for he hath spoken it. And who can dispute?

But behold, this land, saith God, shall be a land of thine inheritance; and the Gentiles shall be blessed upon the land. And this land shall be a land of liberty unto the Gentiles; and there shall be no kings upon the land who shall rise up unto the Gentiles. And I will fortify this land against all other nations. And he that fighteth against Zion shall perish, saith God. [11]

For I will fulfill my promises which I have made unto the children of men, that I will do unto them while they are in the flesh. Wherefore, my beloved brethren, thus saith our God, I will afflict thy seed by the hand of the Gentiles; nevertheless, I will soften the hearts of the Gentiles, that they shall be like unto a father to them. Wherefore, the Gentiles shall be blessed and numbered among the house of Israel.

Wherefore, I will consecrate this land unto thy seed, and they who shall be numbered among thy seed, forever, for the land of their inheritance. For it is a choice land, saith God, unto me, above all other lands. Wherefore, I will have all men that dwell thereon, that they shall worship me, saith God.

And now, my beloved brethren, seeing that our merciful God has given us so great knowledge concerning these things, let us remember him, and lay aside our sins, and not hang down our

[11] 2 Nephi 10: 2-13

heads. For we are not cast off. Nevertheless, we have been driven out of the land of our inheritance; but we have been led to a better land. For the Lord has made the sea our path, and we are upon an isle of the sea.

But great are the promises of the Lord unto those who are upon the isles of the sea. Wherefore, as it says isles, there must needs be more than this. And they are inhabited also by our brethren. For behold, the Lord God has led away from time to time from the house of Israel according to his will and pleasure. And now, behold, the Lord remembereth all those who have been broken off; wherefore, he remembereth us also. Therefore, cheer up your hearts and remember that ye are free to act for yourselves, to choose the way of everlasting death or the way of eternal life. [12]

About 545 B.C.

For behold, it came to pass that fifty and five years had passed away from the time that Lehi left Jerusalem; wherefore, Nephi gave me, Jacob, a commandment concerning these small plates upon which these things are engraven. And he gave me, Jacob, a commandment that I should write upon these plates a few of the things which I considered to be most precious, that I should not touch, save it were lightly, concerning the history of this people, which are called the people of Nephi. For he said that the history of his people should be engraven upon his other plates, and that I should preserve these plates and hand them down unto my seed from generation to generation. And if there were preaching which was sacred, or revelation which was great, or prophesying, that I should engrave the heads of them upon these plates, and touch upon them as much as it were possible, for Christ's sake and for the sake of our people.

For because of faith, and great anxiety, it truly had been made manifest unto us concerning our people, what things should happen unto them. And we also had many revelations and the spirit of much prophecy; wherefore, we knew of Christ and his kingdom, which should come. Wherefore, we labored diligently

---

[12] 2 Nephi 10: 17-23

among our people, that we might persuade them to come unto Christ and partake of the goodness of God, that they might enter into his rest; lest by any means he should swear in his wrath they should not enter in, as in the provocation in the days of temptation while the children of Israel were in the wilderness.

Wherefore, we would to God that we could persuade all men not to rebel against God, to provoke him to anger, but that all men would believe in Christ, and view his death, and suffer his cross, and bear the shame of the world. Wherefore, I, Jacob, take it upon me to fulfill the commandment of my brother Nephi, [13] for I, Jacob, and my brother Joseph had been consecrated priests and teachers of this people by the hand of Nephi.

And we did magnify our office unto the Lord, taking upon us the responsibility, answering the sins of the people upon our own heads if we did not teach them the word of God with all diligence; wherefore, by laboring with our mights, their blood might not come upon our garments; otherwise, their blood would come upon our garments, and we would not be found spotless at the last day; [14] wherefore, I, Jacob, gave unto them these words as I taught them in the temple, having firstly obtained mine errand from the Lord. [15]

About 500 B.C.

Now Nephi began to be old, and he saw that he must soon die. Wherefore, he anointed a man to be a king and a ruler over his people, now according to the reigns of the kings, the people, having loved Nephi exceedingly, he having been a great protector for them, having wielded the sword of Laban in their defense, and having labored in all his days for their welfare, wherefore, the people were desirous to retain in remembrance his name. And whoso should reign in his stead were called by the people Second Nephi, Third Nephi, etc., according to the reigns of the kings, and

---

[13] Jacob 1: 1-8
[14] Jacob 1: 18-19
[15] Jacob 1: 17

thus they were called by the people, let them be of whatever name they would. And it came to pass that Nephi died.

Now the people which were not Lamanites were Nephites; nevertheless, they were called Nephites, Jacobites, Josephites, Zoramites, Lamanites, Lemuelites, and Ishmaelites. But I, Jacob, shall not hereafter distinguish them by these names; but I shall call them Lamanites that seek to destroy the people of Nephi; and those who are friendly to Nephi, I shall call Nephites, or the people of Nephi, according to the reigns of the kings.[16] And a hundredth part of the proceedings of this people, which now began to be numerous, cannot be written upon these plates. But many of their proceedings are written upon the larger plates, and their wars, and their contentions, and the reigns of their kings.[17]

Now behold, it came to pass that I, Jacob, having ministered much unto my people in word, and I cannot write but little of my words because of the difficulty of engraving our words upon plates, and we know that the things which we write upon plates must remain, but whatsoever things we write upon anything, save it be upon plates, must perish and vanish away. But we can write a few words upon plates which will give our children, and also our beloved brethren, a small degree of knowledge concerning us or concerning their fathers. [18]

Now in this thing we do rejoice, and we labor diligently to engrave these words upon plates, hoping that our beloved brethren and our children will receive them with thankful hearts, and look upon them that they may learn with joy, and not with sorrow, neither with contempt concerning their first parents. For, for this intent have we written these things, that they may know that we knew of Christ, and we had a hope of his glory many hundred years before his coming. And not only we, ourselves, had a hope of his glory, but also all the holy prophets which were before us.

Behold, they believed in Christ and worshiped the Father in his name, and also we worship the Father in his name. And for this

---

[16] Jacob 1: 9-14
[17] Jacob 3:13
[18] Jacob 4: 1-2

intent we keep the law of Moses, it pointing our souls to him. And for this cause it is sanctified unto us for righteousness, even as it was accounted unto Abraham in the wilderness to be obedient unto the commands of God in offering up his son Isaac, which is a similitude of God and his Only Begotten Son. [19] Wherefore, beloved brethren, be reconciled unto him through the atonement of Christ, his Only Begotten Son, that ye may obtain a resurrection, according to the power of the resurrection which is in Christ.

And now, beloved, marvel not that I tell you these things. For why not speak of the atonement of Christ, and attain to a perfect knowledge of him, as to attain to the knowledge of a resurrection and the world to come? Wherefore, it speaketh of things as they really are, and of things as they really will be. Wherefore, these things are manifested unto us plainly for the salvation of our souls. But behold, we are not witnesses alone in these things, for God also spake them unto prophets of old. [20]

And it came to pass that I, Jacob, began to be old. And the record of this people, being kept on the other plates of Nephi, wherefore, I conclude this record, declaring that I have written according to the best of my knowledge, by saying that the time passed away with us, and also our lives passed away, like as it were unto us a dream. We being a lonesome and a solemn people, wanderers, cast out from Jerusalem, born in tribulation in a wilderness, and hated of our brethren, which caused wars and contentions; wherefore, we did mourn out our days.

And I, Jacob, saw that I must soon go down to my grave; wherefore, I said unto my son Enos, Take these plates, and I told him the things which my brother Nephi had commanded me, and he promised obedience unto the commands. And I make an end of my writing upon these plates, which writing has been small. And to the reader I bid farewell, hoping that many of my brethren may read my words. [21]

---

[19] Jacob 4: 3-5
[20] Jacob 4: 11*-13*
[21] Jacob 7: 26-27*

About 460 B.C.

Behold, it came to pass that I, Enos, knowing my father, that he was a just man, for he taught me in his language and also in the nurture and admonition of the Lord, I will tell you of the wrestle which I had before God, before I received a remission of my sins.

Behold, I went to hunt beasts in the forest, and the words which I had often heard my father speak concerning eternal life and the joy of the saints sank deep into my heart. And my soul hungered, and I kneeled down before my Maker, and I cried unto him in mighty prayer and supplication for mine own soul. And all the day long did I cry unto him; yea, and when the night came, I did still raise my voice high, that it reached the heavens.

And there came a voice unto me saying, Enos, thy sins are forgiven thee, and thou shalt be blessed. And I, Enos, knew that God could not lie; wherefore, my guilt was swept away.

And I said, Lord, how is it done?

And he said unto me, Because of thy faith in Christ, whom thou hast never before heard nor seen. And many years pass away before he shall manifest himself in the flesh. Wherefore, go to. Thy faith hath made thee whole.

Now it came to pass that when I had heard these words, I began to feel a desire for the welfare of my brethren, the Nephites. Wherefore, I did pour out my whole soul unto God for them. And while I was thus struggling in the spirit, behold, the voice of the Lord came into my mind again, saying, I will visit thy brethren according to their diligence in keeping my commandments. I have given unto them this land, and it is a holy land. And I curse it not, save it be for the cause of iniquity. Wherefore, I will visit thy brethren, according as I have said; and their transgressions will I bring down with sorrow upon their own heads.

And after I, Enos, had heard these words, my faith began to be unshaken in the Lord, and I prayed unto him with many long strugglings for my brethren, the Lamanites. [22] For at the present, our strugglings were vain in restoring them to the true faith. And they swore in their wrath that, if it were possible, they would

---

[22] Enos 1: 1*, 2*-11

destroy our records, and us, and also all the traditions of our fathers. Wherefore, I, knowing that the Lord God was able to preserve our records, I cried unto him continually. For he had said unto me, Whatsoever thing ye shall ask in faith, believing that ye shall receive in the name of Christ, ye shall receive it. [23]

And now, it came to pass that I, Enos, went about among the people of Nephi, prophesying of things to come and testifying of the things which I had heard and seen. And I bear record that the people of Nephi did seek diligently to restore the Lamanites unto the true faith in God. But our labors were vain, their hatred was fixed, and they were led by their evil nature, that they became wild, and ferocious, and a bloodthirsty people, full of idolatry and filthiness, feeding upon beasts of prey, dwelling in tents, and wandering about in the wilderness, with a short skin girt about their loins, and their heads shaven. And their skill was in the bow, and the cimeter, and the ax. And many of them did eat nothing save it was raw meat. And they were continually seeking to destroy us. [24]

And I saw wars between the Nephites and the Lamanites in the course of my days, and it came to pass that I began to be old. And a hundred and seventy and nine years had passed away from the time that our father Lehi left Jerusalem. And as I saw that I must soon go down to my grave, having been wrought upon by the power of God, that I must preach and prophesy unto this people, and declare the word, according to the truth which is in Christ. And I have declared it in all my days and have rejoiced in it above that of the world.

And I soon go to the place of my rest, which is with my Redeemer; for I know that in him I shall rest. And I rejoice in the day when my mortal shall put on immortality and shall stand before him. Then shall I see his face with pleasure, and he will say unto me, Come unto me ye blessed, there is a place prepared for you in the mansions of my Father. Amen. [25]

---

[23] Enos 1: 14-15
[24] Enos 1: 19-20
[25] Enos 1: 24-27

About 420 B.C.

Now behold, I, Jarom, write a few words according to the commandment of my father Enos, that our genealogy may be kept. And as these plates are small, and as these things are written for the intent of the benefit of our brethren, the Lamanites, wherefore, it must needs be that I write a little. But I shall not write the things of my prophesying nor of my revelations; for what could I write more than my fathers have written? For have not they revealed the plan of salvation? I say unto you, Yea; and this sufficeth me.

Behold, it is expedient that much should be done among this people because of the hardness of their hearts, and the deafness of their ears, and the blindness of their minds, and the stiffness of their necks. Nevertheless, God is exceeding merciful unto them, and has not as yet swept them off from the face of the land.

And there are many among us who have many revelations, for they are not all stiff-necked. And as many as are not stiffnecked, and have faith, have communion with the Holy Spirit, which maketh manifest unto the children of men according to their faith.

And now, behold, two hundred years had passed away, and the people of Nephi had waxed strong in the land. They observed to keep the law of Moses and the Sabbath day holy unto the Lord. And they profaned not; neither did they blaspheme. And the laws of the land were exceeding strict. And they were scattered upon much of the face of the land, and the Lamanites also. And they were exceeding more numerous than were they of the Nephites. And they loved murder and would drink the blood of beasts.

And it came to pass that they came many times against us, the Nephites, to battle. But our kings and our leaders were mighty men in the faith of the Lord; and they taught the people the ways of the Lord. Wherefore, we withstood the Lamanites, and swept them away out of our lands, and began to fortify our cities, or whatsoever place of our inheritance.

And we multiplied exceedingly, and spread upon the face of the land, and became exceeding rich in gold, and in silver, and in precious things, and in fine workmanship of wood, in buildings, and in machinery, and also in iron, and copper, and brass, and steel, making all manner of tools of every kind to till the ground, and weapons of war, yea, the sharp pointed arrow, and the quiver, and the dart, and the javelin, and all preparations for war. And thus being prepared to meet the Lamanites, they did not prosper against us. But the word of the Lord was verified, which he spake unto our fathers, saying that, inasmuch as ye will keep my commandments, ye shall prosper in the land.

And it came to pass that the prophets of the Lord did threaten the people of Nephi, according to the word of God, that if they did not keep the commandments, but should fall into transgression, they should be destroyed from off the face of the land. Wherefore, the prophets, and the priests, and the teachers did labor diligently, exhorting with all long-suffering the people to diligence, teaching the law of Moses, and the intent for which it was given, persuading them to look forward unto the Messiah, and believe in him to come, as though he already was. And after this manner did they teach them. And it came to pass that, by so doing, they kept them from being destroyed upon the face of the land; for they did prick their hearts with the word, continually stirring them up unto repentance.

And it came to pass that two hundred and thirty and eight years had passed away after the manner of wars, and contentions, and dissensions, for the space of much of the time. And I, Jarom, do not write more, for the plates are small. But behold, my brethren, ye can go to the other plates of Nephi; for behold, upon them the record of our wars are engraven, according to the writings of the kings, or those which they caused to be written. And I deliver these plates into the hands of my son Omni, that they may be kept according to the commandments of my fathers. [26]

About 350 B.C.

Behold, it came to pass that I, Omni, being commanded by my father Jarom that I should write somewhat upon these plates to preserve our genealogy, wherefore, in my days, I would that ye should know that I fought much with the sword to preserve my people, the Nephites, from falling into the hands of their enemies,

---

[26] Jarom 1-15

the Lamanites. But behold, I, of myself, am a wicked man, and I have not kept the statutes and the commandments of the Lord as I ought to have done.

And it came to pass that two hundred and seventy and six years had passed away, and we had many seasons of peace; and we had many seasons of serious war and bloodshed. Yea, and in fine, two hundred and eighty and two years had passed away, and I had kept these plates according to the commandments of my fathers. And I conferred them upon my son Amaron. And I make an end.

About 280 B.C.

And now, I, Amaron, write the things whatsoever I write, which are few, in the book of my father. Behold, it came to pass that three hundred and twenty years had passed away, and the more wicked part of the Nephites were destroyed. [27] Wherefore, the Lord did visit them in great judgment; nevertheless, he did spare the righteous, that they should not perish, but did deliver them out of the hands of their enemies. And it came to pass that I did deliver the plates unto my brother Chemish.

About 250 B.C.

Now I, Chemish, write what few things I write in the same book with my brother; for behold, I saw the last which he wrote, that he wrote it with his own hand; and he wrote it in the day that he delivered them unto me. And after this manner we keep the records, for it is according to the commandments of our fathers. And I make an end.

About 210 B.C.

Behold, I, Abinadom, am the son of Chemish. Behold, it came to pass that I saw much war and contention between my people, the Nephites, and the Lamanites. And I, with mine own

---

[27] Omni 1: 1-5

sword, have taken the lives of many of the Lamanites in the defense of my brethren.

And behold, the record of this people is engraven upon plates, which are had by the kings, according to the generations. And I know of no revelation, save that which has been written, neither prophecy. Wherefore, that which is sufficient is written. And I make an end.

About 170 B.C.

Behold, I am Amaleki, the son of Abinadom. Behold, I will speak unto you somewhat concerning Mosiah, who was made king over the land of Zarahemla.

For behold, he being warned of the Lord, that he should flee out of the land of Nephi, and as many as would hearken unto the voice of the Lord, should also depart out of the land with him into the wilderness. And it came to pass that he did according as the Lord had commanded him. And they departed out of the land into the wilderness, as many as would hearken unto the voice of the Lord. And they were led by many preachings and prophesyings, and they were admonished continually by the word of God. And they were led by the power of his arm through the wilderness, until they came down into the land which is called the land of Zarahemla.

And they discovered a people who were called the people of Zarahemla. Now there was great rejoicing among the people of Zarahemla; and also Zarahemla did rejoice exceedingly because the Lord had sent the people of Mosiah with the plates of brass, which contained the record of the Jews.

Behold, it came to pass that Mosiah discovered that the people of Zarahemla came out from Jerusalem at the time that Zedekiah, king of Judah, was carried away captive into Babylon. And they journeyed in the wilderness and were brought by the hand of the Lord across the great waters into the land where Mosiah discovered them. And they had dwelt there from that time forth. And at the time that Mosiah discovered them, they had become exceeding numerous. Nevertheless, they had had many wars and serious contentions, and had fallen by the sword from time to time. And their language had become corrupted. And they had brought no records with them. And they denied the being of their Creator. And Mosiah, nor the people of Mosiah, could understand them.

But it came to pass that Mosiah caused that they should be taught in his language. And it came to pass that after they were taught in the language of Mosiah, Zarahemla gave a genealogy of his fathers, according to his memory. And they are written, but not in these plates. And it came to pass that the people of Zarahemla and of Mosiah did unite together, and Mosiah was appointed to be their king.

And it came to pass in the days of Mosiah, there was a large stone brought unto him with engravings on it, and he did interpret the engravings by the gift and power of God. And they gave an account of one Coriantumr and the slain of his people. And Coriantumr was discovered by the people of Zarahemla, and he dwelt with them for the space of nine moons. It also spake a few words concerning his fathers. And his first parents came out from the tower at the time the Lord confounded the language of the people. And the severity of the Lord fell upon them, according to his judgments, which are just. And their bones lay scattered in the land northward. [28]

And now, I would speak somewhat concerning a certain number who went up into the wilderness to return to the land of Nephi. For there was a large number who were desirous to possess the land of their inheritance; wherefore, they went up into the wilderness. And their leader, being a strong and a mighty man and a stiff-necked man, wherefore, he caused a contention among them. And they were all slain, save fifty, in the wilderness; and they returned again to the land of Zarahemla. And it came to pass that they also took others, to a considerable number, and took their journey again into the wilderness. And I, Amaleki, had a brother who also went with them. And I have not since known concerning them. And I am about to lie down in my grave, and these plates are full. [29]

---

[28] Omni 7-22
[29] Omni 27-30*

Behold, I, Amaleki, was born in the days of Mosiah and I have lived to see his death. And Benjamin, his son, reigneth in his stead. And it came to pass that I began to be old, and having no seed, and knowing King Benjamin to be a just man before the Lord, wherefore, I shall deliver up these plates unto him, exhorting all men to come unto God, the Holy One of Israel, and believe in prophesying, and in revelations, and in the ministering of angels, and in the gift of speaking with tongues, and in the gift of interpreting languages, and in all things which are good. For there is nothing which is good, save it comes from the Lord; and that which is evil cometh from the devil.

And now, my beloved brethren, I would that ye should come unto Christ, who is the Holy One of Israel, and partake of his salvation and the power of his redemption. Yea, come unto him, and offer your whole souls as an offering unto him, and continue in fasting and praying, and endure to the end. And as the Lord liveth, ye will be saved. [30]

And now concerning this King Benjamin, he had somewhat contentions among his own people. And it came to pass also that the armies of the Lamanites came down out of the land of Nephi to battle against his people. But behold, King Benjamin gathered together his armies, and he did stand against them, and he did fight with the strength of his own arm with the sword of Laban. And in the strength of the Lord they did contend against their enemies until they had slain many thousands of the Lamanites.

And it came to pass that they did contend against the Lamanites until they had driven them out of all the lands of their inheritance. [31] For behold, King Benjamin was a holy man, and he did reign over his people in righteousness. And there were many holy men in the land, and they did speak the word of God with power and with authority. And they did use much sharpness because of the stiff-neckedness of the people. Wherefore, with the help of these, King Benjamin, by laboring with all the might of his body, and the faculty of his whole soul, and also the prophets, did

---

[30] Omni 23-26
[31] Words of Mormon 12-14

once more establish peace in the land. [32]

About 130 B.C.

And now, there was no more contention in all the land of
Zarahemla among all the people who belonged to King Benjamin,
so that King Benjamin had continual peace all the remainder of his
days. And it came to pass that he had three sons; and he called
their names Mosiah, and Helorum, and Helaman. And he caused
that they should be taught in all the language of his fathers, that
thereby they might become men of understanding and that they
might know concerning the prophecies which had been spoken by
the mouths of their fathers, which were delivered them by the
hand of the Lord.

And he also taught them concerning the records which were
engraven on the plates of brass, saying:

My sons, I would that ye should remember that were it not
for these plates, which contain these records and these commandments, we must have suffered in ignorance, even at this present
time, not knowing the mysteries of God. For it were not possible
that our father Lehi could have remembered all these things, to
have taught them to his children, except it were for the help of
these plates. For he, having been taught in the language of the
Egyptians, therefore, he could read these engravings and teach
them to his children, that thereby they could teach them to their
children, and so fulfilling the commandments of God, even down
to this present time.

I say unto you, my sons, were it not for these things, which
have been kept and preserved by the hand of God, that we might
read and understand of his mysteries, and have his commandments always before our eyes, that even our fathers would have
dwindled in unbelief. And we should have been like unto our
brethren, the Lamanites, who know nothing concerning these
things, or even do not believe them when they are taught them,
because of the traditions of their fathers which are not correct.

---

[32] Words of Mormon 17-18

O my sons, I would that ye should remember that these sayings are true, and also that these records are true, and behold, also the plates of Nephi, which contain the records and the sayings of our fathers from the time they left Jerusalem until now. And they are true, and we can know of their surety because we have them before our eyes. And now, my sons, I would that ye should remember to search them diligently, that ye may profit thereby. And I would that ye should keep the commandments of God, that ye may prosper in the land according to the promises which the Lord made unto our fathers.

And many more things did King Benjamin teach his sons, which are not written in this book. And it came to pass that after King Benjamin had made an end of teaching his sons, that he waxed old. And he saw that he must very soon go the way of all the earth; therefore, he thought it expedient that he should confer the kingdom upon one of his sons. Therefore, he had Mosiah brought before him; and these are the words which he spake unto him, saying:

My son, I would that ye should make a proclamation throughout all this land, among all this people, or the people of Zarahemla and the people of Mosiah, who dwell in this land, that thereby they may be gathered together. For on the morrow, I shall proclaim unto this my people, out of mine own mouth, that thou art a king and a ruler over this people whom the Lord, our God, hath given us.

And moreover, I shall give this people a name, that thereby they may be distinguished above all the people which the Lord God hath brought out of the land of Jerusalem. And this I do because they have been a diligent people in keeping the commandments of the Lord. [33]

And now, it came to pass that Mosiah went and did as his father had commanded him and proclaimed unto all the people who were in the land of Zarahemla, that thereby they might gather themselves together, to go up to the temple to hear the words which his father should speak unto them. [34] And there were

---

[33] Mosiah 1: 1-11
[34] Mosiah 1: 18

a great number, even so many that they did not number them, for they had multiplied exceedingly and waxed great in the land.

And they also took of the firstlings of their flocks, that they might offer sacrifice and burnt offerings according to the law of Moses, and also that they might give thanks to the Lord, their God, who had brought them out of the land of Jerusalem, and who had delivered them out of the hands of their enemies, and had appointed just men to be their teachers, and also a just man to be their king, who had established peace in the land of Zarahemla, and who had taught them to keep the commandments of God, that thereby they might rejoice and be filled with love towards God and all men.

And it came to pass that when they came up to the temple, they pitched their tents round about, every man according to his family, consisting of his wife, and his sons, and his daughters, and their sons, and their daughters, from the eldest down to the youngest, every family being separate, one from another. And they pitched their tents round about the temple, every man having his tent with the door thereof towards the temple, that thereby they might remain in their tents and hear the words which King Benjamin should speak unto them. For the multitude being so great that King Benjamin could not teach them all within the walls of the temple; therefore, he caused a tower to be erected, that thereby his people might hear the words which he should speak unto them.

And it came to pass that he began to speak to his people from the tower. And they could not all hear his words because of the greatness of the multitude. Therefore, he caused that the words which he spake should be written and sent forth among those that were not under the sound of his voice, that they might also receive his words.

And these are the words which he spake and caused to be written, saying:

My brethren, all ye that have assembled yourselves together, you that can hear my words which I shall speak unto you this day, for I have not commanded you to come up hither to trifle with the words which I shall speak, but that you should hearken unto me, and open your ears that ye may hear, and your hearts that ye may understand, and your minds, that the mysteries of God may be unfolded to your view.

I have not commanded you to come up hither that ye should fear me, or that ye should think that I, of myself, am more than a mortal man; but I am like as yourselves, subject to all manner of infirmities in body and mind.

Yet, as I have been chosen by this people, and was consecrated by my father, and was suffered by the hand of the Lord, that I should be a ruler and a king over this people, and have been kept and preserved by his matchless power, to serve thee with all the might, mind, and strength which the Lord hath granted unto me— I say unto you, that as I have been suffered to spend my days in your service, even up to this time, and have not sought gold, nor silver, nor any manner of riches of you, neither have I suffered that ye should be confined in dungeons, nor that ye should make slaves one of another, or that ye should murder, or plunder, or steal, or commit adultery, or even I have not suffered that ye should commit any manner of wickedness; and have taught you that ye should keep the commandments of the Lord in all things which he hath commanded you.

And even I, myself, have labored with mine own hands, that I might serve you, and that ye should not be laden with taxes, and that there should nothing come upon you which was grievous to be borne. And of all these things which I have spoken, ye yourselves are witnesses this day. Yet, my brethren, I have not done these things that I might boast; neither do I tell these things that thereby I might accuse you; but I tell you these things that ye may know that I can answer a clear conscience before God this day.

Behold, I say unto you, that because I said unto you that I had spent my days in your service, I do not desire to boast, for I have only been in the service of God. And behold, I tell you these things that ye may learn wisdom— that ye may learn that when ye are in the service of your fellow beings, ye are only in the service of your God.

Behold, ye have called me your king. And if I, whom ye call your king, do labor to serve you, then had not ye ought to labor to serve one another? And behold, also, if I whom ye call your king, who has spent his days in your service, and yet has been in the service of God, doth merit any thanks from you, oh how had you ought to thank your heavenly King! [35]

I say unto you, that if ye should serve him who has created you from the beginning, and is preserving you from day to day, by lending you breath, that ye may live, and move, and do according to your own will, and even supporting you from one moment to another— I say, if ye should serve him with all your whole soul, yet ye would be unprofitable servants.

And behold, all that he requires of you is to keep his commandments. And he has promised you that if ye would keep his commandments ye should prosper in the land. And he never doth vary from that which he hath said. Therefore, if ye do keep his commandments, he doth bless you and prosper you.

And now, in the first place, he hath created you and granted unto you your lives, for which ye are indebted unto him. And secondly, he doth require that ye should do as he hath commanded you, for which, if ye do, he doth immediately bless you. And therefore, he hath paid you. And ye are still indebted unto him, and are, and will be, forever and ever. Therefore, of what have ye to boast? [36]

Ye cannot say that ye are even as much as the dust of the earth. Yet ye were created of the dust of the earth. But behold, it belongeth to him who created you. And I, even I, whom ye call your king, am no better than ye yourselves are; for I am also of the dust. And ye behold that I am old and am about to yield up this mortal frame to its mother earth. [37]

And moreover, I say unto you that I have caused that ye should assemble yourselves together, that I might declare unto you that I can no longer be your teacher nor your king. For even at this time my whole frame doth tremble exceedingly while attempting to speak unto you. But the Lord God doth support me, and hath suffered me that I should speak unto you, and hath commanded me that I should declare unto you this day that my son Mosiah is a king and a ruler over you.

---

[35] Mosiah 2: 2-19
[36] Mosiah 2: 21-24
[37] Mosiah 2: 25*-26

And now, my brethren, I would that ye should do as ye have hitherto done; as ye have kept my commandments, and also the commandments of my father, and have prospered and have been kept from falling into the hands of your enemies; even so, if ye shall keep the commandments of my son, or the commandments of God, which shall be delivered unto you by him, ye shall prosper in the land. And your enemies shall have no power over you. [38]

And now, I say unto you, my brethren, that after ye have known and have been taught all these things, if ye should transgress and go contrary to that which has been spoken, that ye do withdraw yourselves from the Spirit of the Lord, that it may have no place in you, to guide you in wisdom's path, that ye may be blessed, prospered, and preserved. I say unto you that the man that doeth this, the same cometh out in open rebellion against God. Therefore, he listeth to obey the evil spirit and becometh an enemy to all righteousness; therefore, the Lord has no place in him, for he dwelleth not in unholy temples. [39]

And moreover, I would desire that ye should consider on the blessed and happy state of those that keep the commandments of God. For behold, they are blessed in all things, both temporal and spiritual. And if they hold out faithful to the end, they are received into heaven, that thereby they may dwell with God in a state of never-ending happiness.

Oh, remember, remember that these things are true; for the Lord God hath spoken it. [40]

And again, my brethren, I would call your attention, for I have somewhat more to speak unto you. For behold, I have things to tell you concerning that which is to come. And the things which I shall tell you are made known unto me by an angel from God.

And he said unto me, Awake! And I awoke. And behold, he stood before me. And he said unto me, Awake, and hear the words which I shall tell thee; for behold, I am come to declare unto thee glad tidings of great joy. For the Lord hath heard thy prayers, and hath judged of thy righteousness, and hath sent me

---

[38] Mosiah 2: 29-31
[39] Mosiah 2: 36-37
[40] Mosiah 2: 41

to declare unto thee that thou mayest rejoice, and that thou mayest declare unto thy people, that they may also be filled with joy.

For behold, the time cometh, and is not far distant, that with power, the Lord Omnipotent, who reigneth, who was, and is, from all eternity to all eternity, shall come down from heaven among the children of men, and shall dwell in a tabernacle of clay, and shall go forth amongst men, working mighty miracles, such as healing the sick, raising the dead, causing the lame to walk, the blind to receive their sight, and the deaf to hear, and curing all manner of diseases. And he shall cast out devils, or the evil spirits which dwell in the hearts of the children of men.

And lo, he shall suffer temptations, and pain of body, hunger, thirst, and fatigue, even more than man can suffer, except it be unto death. For behold, blood cometh from every pore, so great shall be his anguish for the wickedness and the abominations of his people.

And he shall be called Jesus Christ, the Son of God, the Father of heaven and earth, the Creator of all things from the beginning. And his mother shall be called Mary.

And lo, he cometh unto his own, that salvation might come unto the children of men, even through faith on his name. And even after all this, they shall consider him a man, and say that he hath a devil, and shall scourge him, and shall crucify him. And he shall rise the third day from the dead. And behold, he standeth to judge the world.

And behold, all these things are done, that a righteous judgment might come upon the children of men. For behold, and also, his blood atoneth for the sins of those who have fallen by the transgression of Adam, who have died not knowing the will of God concerning them, or who have ignorantly sinned. But wo, wo unto him who knoweth that he rebelleth against God; for salvation cometh to none such, except it be through repentance and faith on the Lord Jesus Christ. [41]

And the infant perisheth not, that dieth in his infancy; but men drink damnation to their own souls, except they humble themselves, and become as little children, and believe that

---

[41] Mosiah 3: 1-12

salvation is in, and through, the atoning blood of Christ, the Lord Omnipotent. For the natural man is an enemy to God, and has been from the fall of Adam, and will be forever and ever, but if he yields to the enticings of the Holy Spirit, and putteth off the natural man, and becometh a saint through the atonement of Christ the Lord, and becometh as a child —submissive, meek, humble, patient, full of love, willing to submit to all things which the Lord seeth fit to inflict upon him, even as a child doth submit to his father.

And moreover, I say unto you that the time shall come when the knowledge of a Savior shall spread throughout every nation, kindred, tongue, and people. And behold, when that time cometh, none shall be found blameless before God except it be little children— only through repentance and faith on the name of the Lord God Omnipotent.

And now, I have spoken the words which the Lord God hath commanded me. [42]

And now, it came to pass that when King Benjamin had made an end of speaking the words which had been delivered unto him by the angel of the Lord, that he cast his eyes round about on the multitude. And behold, they had fallen to the earth, for the fear of the Lord had come upon them. And they had viewed themselves in their own carnal state, even less than the dust of the earth.

And they all cried aloud with one voice, saying, Oh, have mercy, and apply the atoning blood of Christ, that we may receive forgiveness of our sins, and our hearts may be purified. For we believe in Jesus Christ, the Son of God, who created heaven and earth, and all things, who shall come down among the children of men.

And it came to pass that after they had spoken these words, the Spirit of the Lord came upon them, and they were filled with joy, having received a remission of their sins, and having peace of conscience, because of the exceeding faith which they had in Jesus Christ who should come, according to the words which King Benjamin had spoken unto them.

---

[42] Mosiah 3: 18*-21, 23

And King Benjamin again opened his mouth and began to
speak unto them, saying, My friends and my brethren, my kindred,
and my people, I would again call your attention, that ye may hear
and understand the remainder of my words which I shall speak
unto you: [43]

And again, I say unto you, as I have said before, that as ye
have come to the knowledge of the glory of God, or if ye have
known of his goodness, and have tasted of his love, and have
received a remission of your sins, which causeth such exceeding
great joy in your souls— even so, I would that ye should
remember and always retain in remembrance, the greatness of
God, and your own nothingness, and his goodness and long-
suffering towards you unworthy creatures— and humble
yourselves, even in the depths of humility, calling on the name of
the Lord daily, and standing steadfastly in the faith of that which
is to come, which was spoken by the mouth of the angel.

And behold, I say unto you that if ye do this, ye shall always
rejoice, and be filled with the love of God, and always retain a
remission of your sins. And ye shall grow in the knowledge of the
glory of him that created you, or in the knowledge of that which is
just and true. And ye will not have a mind to injure one another,
but to live peaceably and to render to every man according to that
which is his due.

And ye will not suffer your children, that they go hungry or
naked. Neither will ye suffer that they transgress the laws of God,
and fight and quarrel one with another, and serve the devil, who
is the master of sin, or who is the evil spirit which hath been
spoken of by our fathers; he being an enemy to all righteousness.
But ye will teach them to walk in the ways of truth and soberness.
Ye will teach them to love one another and to serve one another.

And also, ye yourselves will succor those that stand in need
of your succor. Ye will administer of your substance unto him that
standeth in need, and ye will not suffer that the beggar putteth up
his petition to you in vain and turn him out to perish. Perhaps
thou shalt say, The man has brought upon himself his misery;
therefore, I will stay my hand, and will not give unto him of my

---

[43] Mosiah 4: 1-4

food, nor impart unto him of my substance that he may not suffer, for his punishments are just.

But I say unto you, O man, whosoever doeth this, the same hath great cause to repent; and except he repenteth of that which he hath done, he perisheth forever and hath no interest in the kingdom of God.

For behold, are we not all beggars? Do we not all depend upon the same being, even God, for all the substance which we have, for both food, and raiment, and for gold, and for silver, and for all the riches which we have of every kind?

And behold, even at this time, ye have been calling on his name and begging for a remission of your sins. And has he suffered that ye have begged in vain? Nay! He has poured out his Spirit upon you and has caused that your hearts should be filled with joy, and has caused that your mouths should be stopped, that ye could not find utterance, so exceeding great was your joy.

And now, if God who has created you, on whom you are dependent for your lives, and for all that ye have and are, doth grant unto you whatsoever ye ask that is right, in faith, believing that ye shall receive, oh, then, how had ye ought to impart of the substance that ye have, one to another. [44]

And again, I say unto the poor, ye who have not, and yet have sufficient that ye remain from day to day. I mean all you who deny the beggar because ye have not. I would that ye say in your hearts that I give not because I have not; but if I had, I would give. And now, if ye say this in your hearts, ye remain guiltless. Otherwise, ye are condemned, and your condemnation is just; for ye covet that which ye have not received.

And now, for the sake of these things which I have spoken unto you, that is, for the sake of retaining a remission of your sins from day to day, that ye may walk guiltless before God, I would that ye should impart of your substance to the poor, every man according to that which he hath, such as feeding the hungry, clothing the naked, visiting the sick, and administering to their relief, both spiritually and temporally, according to their wants.

---

[44] Mosiah 4: 11-21

And see that all these things are done in wisdom and order; for it is not requisite that a man should run faster than he has strength. And again, it is expedient that he should be diligent, that thereby he might win the prize. Therefore, all things must be done in order.

And I would that ye should remember that whosoever among you that borroweth of his neighbor should return the thing that he borroweth, according as he doth agree, or else thou shalt commit sin. And perhaps thou shalt cause thy neighbor to commit sin also.

And finally, I cannot tell you all the things whereby ye may commit sin, for there are diverse ways and means, even so many that I cannot number them. But this much I can tell you, that if ye do not watch yourselves, and your thoughts, and your words, and your deeds, and observe to keep the commandments of God, and continue in the faith of what ye have heard concerning the coming of our Lord, even unto the end of your lives, ye must perish. And now, O man, remember, and perish not. [45]

And now it came to pass that when King Benjamin had thus spoken to his people, he sent among them, desiring to know of his people if they believed the words which he had spoken unto them. And they all cried with one voice, saying:

Yea, we believe all the words which thou hast spoken unto us; and also we know of their surety and truth because of the Spirit of the Lord Omnipotent, which has wrought a mighty change in us, or in our hearts, that we have no more disposition to do evil, but to do good continually. And we, ourselves, also, through the infinite goodness of God, and the manifestations of his Spirit, have great views of that which is to come. And were it expedient, we could prophesy of all things.

And it is the faith which we have had on the things which our king has spoken unto us, and has brought us to this great knowledge, whereby we do rejoice with such exceeding great joy. And we are willing to enter into a covenant with our God, to do his will and to be obedient to his commandments in all things that he shall command us, all the remainder of our days, that we may not bring upon ourselves a never-ending torment, as has been

---

[45] Mosiah 4: 24-30

spoken by the angel, that we may not drink out of the cup of the wrath of God.

And now, these are the words which King Benjamin desired of them. And therefore he said unto them, Ye have spoken the words that I desired. And the covenant which ye have made is a righteous covenant.

And now, because of the covenant which ye have made, ye shall be called the children of Christ, his sons and his daughters. For behold, this day he hath spiritually begotten you; for ye say that your hearts are changed through faith on his name. Therefore, ye are born of him and have become his sons and his daughters.

And under this head ye are made free; and there is no other head whereby ye can be made free. There is no other name given whereby salvation cometh. Therefore, I would that ye should take upon you the name of Christ, all you that have entered into the covenant with God, that ye should be obedient unto the end of your lives. [46]

Therefore, I would that ye should be steadfast and immovable, always abounding in good works, that Christ, the Lord God Omnipotent, may seal you his, that you may be brought to heaven, that ye may have everlasting salvation and eternal life through the wisdom, and power, and justice, and mercy of him, who created all things in heaven and in earth, who is God above all. Amen. [47]

And now, King Benjamin thought it was expedient, after having finished speaking to the people, that he should take the names of all those who had entered into a covenant with God to keep his commandments. And it came to pass that there was not one soul, except it were little children, but what had entered into the covenant and had taken upon them the name of Christ.

And again, it came to pass that when King Benjamin had made an end of all these things, and had consecrated his son Mosiah to be a ruler and a king over his people, and had given him all the charges concerning the kingdom, and also had appointed priests to teach the people, that thereby they might hear

---

[46] Mosiah 5: 1-8
[47] Mosiah 5: 15

and know the commandments of God, and to stir them up in
remembrance of the oath which they had made, he dismissed the
multitude. And they returned, everyone according to their
families, to their own houses.

And Mosiah began to reign in his father's stead. And he
began to reign in the thirtieth year of his age, making in the whole
about four hundred and seventy-six years from the time that Lehi
left Jerusalem. And King Benjamin lived three years, and he died.

And it came to pass that King Mosiah did walk in the ways of
the Lord, and did observe his judgments and his statutes, and did
keep his commandments in all things whatsoever he commanded
him.

And King Mosiah did cause his people that they should till
the earth. And he also, himself, did till the earth, that thereby he
might not become burdensome to his people, that he might do
according to that which his father had done in all things. [48]

---

[48] Mosiah 6: 1-7*

Chapter 4

Fourth Exodus — The Prophet Martyr

About 124 B.C.

And now, it came to pass that after King Mosiah had had continual peace for the space of three years, he was desirous to know concerning the people who went up to dwell in the land of Nephi, or in the city of Lehi-Nephi, for his people had heard nothing from them from the time they left the land of Zarahemla. Therefore, they wearied him with their teasings.

And it came to pass that King Mosiah granted that sixteen of their strong men might go up to the land of Lehi-Nephi to inquire concerning their brethren. And it came to pass that on the morrow they started to go up, having with them one Ammon, he being a strong and mighty man and a descendant of Zarahemla; and he was also their leader.

And now, they knew not the course they should travel in the wilderness to go up to the land of Lehi-Nephi; therefore, they wandered many days in the wilderness, even forty days did they wander. And when they had wandered forty days, they came to a hill, which is north of the land of Shilom, and there they pitched their tents. And Ammon took three of his brethren, and their names were Amaleki, Helem, and Hem; and they went down into the land of Nephi.

And behold they met the king of the people who were in the land of Nephi, [1] the king having been without the gates of the city with his guard. [2] And they were surrounded by the king's guard, and were taken and were bound, and were committed to prison. And it came to pass that when they had been in prison two days they were again brought before the king, and their bands were loosed, and they stood before the king, and were permitted, or rather commanded that they should answer the questions that the king should ask them.

---

[1] Mosiah 7: 1*-7*
[2] Mosiah 21: 23*

And he said unto them, Behold, I am Limhi, the son of Noah, who was the son of Zeniff, who came up out of the land of Zarahemla to inherit this land which was the land of their fathers, who was made a king by the voice of the people. And now I desire to know the cause whereby ye were so bold as to come near the walls of the city, when I myself was with my guards without the gate? [3]

And now, when Ammon saw that he was permitted to speak, he went forth and bowed himself before the king; and, rising again, he said, O King, I am very thankful before God this day that I am yet alive and am permitted to speak. And I will endeavor to speak with boldness, for I am assured that if ye had known me, ye would not have suffered that I should have worn these bands. For I am Ammon, and am a descendant of Zarahemla, and have come up out of the land of Zarahemla to inquire concerning our brethren, whom Zeniff brought up out of that land.

And now, it came to pass that after Limhi had heard the words of Ammon, he was exceeding glad and said, Now I know of a surety that my brethren who were in the land of Zarahemla are yet alive. And now, I will rejoice; and on the morrow I will cause that my people shall rejoice also. For behold, we are in bondage to the Lamanites and are taxed with a tax which is grievous to be borne. And now, behold, our brethren will deliver us out of our bondage, or out of the hands of the Lamanites, and we will be their slaves. For it is better that we be slaves to the Nephites than to pay tribute to the king of the Lamanites.

And now, King Limhi commanded his guards that they should no more bind Ammon nor his brethren, but caused that they should go to the hill which was north of Shilom and bring their brethren into the city, that thereby they might eat, and drink, and rest themselves from the labors of their journey, for they had suffered many things; they had suffered hunger, thirst, and fatigue.

And now, it came to pass on the morrow that King Limhi sent a proclamation among all his people, that thereby they might gather themselves together to the temple to hear the words which he should speak unto them.

---

[3] Mosiah 7: 7*-10

And it came to pass that when they had gathered themselves together, that he spake unto them on this wise, saying, O ye my people, lift up your heads and be comforted. For behold, the time is at hand, or is not far distant, when we shall no longer be in subjection to our enemies, notwithstanding our many strugglings which have been in vain. Yet I trust there remaineth an effectual struggle to be made. Therefore, lift up your heads, and rejoice, and put your trust in God, in that God who was the God of Abraham, and Isaac, and Jacob, and also that God who brought the children of Israel out of the land of Egypt, and caused that they should walk through the Red Sea on dry ground, and fed them with manna, that they might not perish in the wilderness. And many more things did he do for them.

And again, that same God has brought our fathers out of the land of Jerusalem and has kept and preserved his people, even until now. And behold, it is because of our iniquities and abominations that have brought us into bondage; and ye all are witnesses this day, that Zeniff, who was made king over this people, he being overzealous to inherit the land of his fathers, therefore being deceived by the cunning and craftiness of King Laman, who having entered into a treaty with King Zeniff, and having yielded up into his hands the possessions of a part of the land, or even the city of Lehi-Nephi, and the city of Shilom, and the land round about— and all this he did for the sole purpose of bringing this people into subjection, or into bondage.

And behold, we at this time do pay tribute to the king of the Lamanites, to the amount of one-half of our corn, and our barley, and even all our grain of every kind, and one-half of the increase of our flocks and our herds. And even one-half of all we have or possess the king of the Lamanites doth exact of us, or our lives. And now, is not this grievous to be borne? And is not this our affliction great? Now behold, how great reason have we to mourn. [4]

And it came to pass that after King Limhi had made an end of speaking to his people, he caused that Ammon should stand up before the multitude and rehearse unto them all that had happened unto their brethren, from the time that Zeniff went up out of the

---

[4] Mosiah 7: 12-23

land, even until the time that he himself came up out of the land. And he also rehearsed unto them the last words which King Benjamin had taught them, and explained them to the people of King Limhi, so that they might understand all the words which he spake.

And it came to pass that after he had done all this, that King Limhi dismissed the multitude and caused that they should return, everyone unto his own house. And it came to pass that he caused that the plates which contained the record of his people, from the time that they left the land of Zarahemla, should be brought before Ammon, that he might read them.

Now, as soon as Ammon had read the record, the king inquired of him to know if he could interpret languages. And Ammon told him that he could not.

And the king said unto him, Being grieved for the afflictions of my people, I caused that forty and three of my people should take a journey into the wilderness, that thereby they might find the land of Zarahemla, that we might appeal unto our brethren to deliver us out of bondage. And they were lost in the wilderness for the space of many days. Yet they were diligent, and found not the land of Zarahemla, but returned to this land, having traveled in a land among many waters, having discovered a land which was covered with bones of men and of beasts, etc., and was also covered with ruins of buildings of every kind, having discovered a land which had been peopled with a people who were as numerous as the hosts of Israel.

And for a testimony that the things that they have said are true, they have brought twenty-four plates, which are filled with engravings. And they are of pure gold. And behold, also, they have brought breastplates, which are large. And they are of brass and of copper and are perfectly sound. And again, they have brought swords; the hilts thereof have perished, and the blades thereof were cankered with rust. And there is no one in the land that is able to interpret the language or the engravings that are on the plates. [5]

---

[5] Mosiah 8: 1*, 2*-11*

And I say unto thee again, Knowest thou of anyone that can translate? For I am desirous that these records should be translated into our language. For, perhaps they will give us a knowledge of a remnant of the people who have been destroyed, from whence these records came. And I am desirous to know the cause of their destruction.

Now Ammon said unto him, I can assuredly tell thee, O King, of a man that can translate the records. For he has wherewith that he can look and translate all records that are of ancient date; and it is a gift from God. And the things are called interpreters. And no man can look in them, except he be commanded. And whosoever is commanded to look in them, the same is called seer. [6] And behold, the king of the people who is in the land of Zarahemla is the man that is commanded to do these things, and who has this high gift from God.

And the king said that a seer is greater than a prophet.

And Ammon said that a seer is a revelator and a prophet also; and a gift which is greater can no man have, except he should possess the power of God, which no man can; yet a man may have great power given him from God. But a seer can know of things which have passed, and also of things which are to come. And by them shall all things be revealed, or rather, shall secret things be made manifest, and hidden things shall come to light, and things which are not known shall be made known by them. And also, things shall be made known by them which otherwise could not be known. Thus God has provided a means that man, through faith, might work mighty miracles; therefore, he becometh a great benefit to his fellow beings.

And now, when Ammon had made an end of speaking these words, the king rejoiced exceedingly and gave thanks to God, saying, Doubtless, a great mystery is contained within these plates; and these interpreters were doubtless prepared for the purpose of unfolding all such mysteries to the children of men. [7]

And now, it came to pass that Ammon and King Limhi began to consult with the people how they should deliver themselves out

---

[6] Mosiah 8: 12*-13*
[7] Mosiah 8: 14-19

of bondage. And even they did cause that all the people should gather themselves together. And this they did that they might have the voice of the people concerning the matter.

And it came to pass that they could find no way to deliver themselves out of bondage, except it were to take their women and children, and their flocks and their herds, and their tents and depart into the wilderness. For the Lamanites being so numerous that it was impossible for the people of Limhi to contend with them, thinking to deliver themselves out of bondage by the sword.

Now it came to pass that Gideon went forth, and stood before the king, and said unto him, Now, O King, thou hast hitherto hearkened unto my words many times when we have been contending with our brethren, the Lamanites. And now, O King, if thou hast not found me to be an unprofitable servant, or if thou hast hitherto listened to my words in any degree, and they have been of service to thee, even so, I desire that thou wouldest listen to my words at this time, and I will be thy servant and deliver this people out of bondage.

And the king granted unto him that he might speak. And Gideon said unto him, Behold the back pass through the back wall, on the back side of the city. The Lamanites, or the guards of the Lamanites, by night are drunken; therefore, let us send a proclamation among all this people that they gather together their flocks and herds, that they may drive them into the wilderness by night. And I will go according to thy command and pay the last tribute of wine to the Lamanites, and they will be drunken. And we will pass through the secret pass on the left of their camp when they are drunken and asleep. Thus we will depart with our women and our children, our flocks and our herds, into the wilderness, and we will travel around the land of Shilom.

And it came to pass that the king hearkened unto the words of Gideon. And King Limhi caused that his people should gather their flocks together; and he sent the tribute of wine to the Lamanites; and he also sent more wine as a present unto them. And they did drink freely of the wine which King Limhi did send unto them.

And it came to pass that the people of King Limhi did depart by night into the wilderness with their flocks and their herds. And they went round about the land of Shilom in the wilderness and bent their course towards the land of Zarahemla, being led by Ammon and his brethren. And they had taken all their gold, and silver, and their precious things which they could carry, and also their provisions with them into the wilderness, and they pursued their journey. [8]

And after being many days in the wilderness, they arrived in the land of Zarahemla. And it came to pass that Mosiah received them with joy. And he also received their records and also the records which had been found by the people of Limhi. [9]

And it came to pass that Mosiah did read, and caused to be read, the records of Zeniff to his people. Yea, he read the records of the people of Zeniff, from the time they left the land of Zarahemla until they returned again: [10]

The Record of Zeniff

I, Zeniff, having been taught in all the language of the Nephites, and having had a knowledge of the land of Nephi, or of the land of our fathers' first inheritance, and having been sent as a spy among the Lamanites, that I might spy out their forces, that our army might come upon them and destroy them— but when I saw that which was good among them, I was desirous that they should not be destroyed, therefore, I contended with my brethren in the wilderness, for I would that our ruler should make a treaty with them.

But he, being an austere and a bloodthirsty man, commanded that I should be slain. But I was rescued by the shedding of much blood; for father fought against father, and brother against brother, until the greatest number of our army was destroyed in the wilderness. And we returned, those of us that were spared, to the land of Zarahemla, to relate that tale to their wives and their children.

---

[8] Mosiah 22: 1-12
[9] Mosiah 22: 13*-14
[10] Mosiah 25: 5

And yet, I, being overzealous to inherit the land of our fathers, collected as many as were desirous to go up to possess the land and started again on our journey into the wilderness to go up to the land. But we were smitten with famine and sore afflictions; for we were slow to remember the Lord, our God. Nevertheless, after many days' wandering in the wilderness, we pitched our tents in the place where our brethren were slain, which was near to the land of our fathers.

And it came to pass that I went again with four of my men into the city, in unto the king, that I might know of the disposition of the king and that I might know if I might go in with my people and possess the land in peace. And I went in unto the king, and he covenanted with me that I might possess the land of Lehi-Nephi and the land of Shilom. And he also commanded that his people should depart out of that land. And I and my people went into the land, that we might possess it. And we began to build buildings and to repair the walls of the city, yea, even the walls of the city of Lehi-Nephi and the city of Shilom. [11]

Now, it was the cunning and the craftiness of King Laman to bring my people into bondage that he yielded up the land, that we might possess it. Therefore, it came to pass that after we had dwelt in the land for the space of twelve years, that King Laman began to grow uneasy, lest by any means my people should wax strong in the land; and that they could not overpower them and bring them into bondage, that they might glut themselves with the labors of our hands, yea, that they might feast themselves upon the flocks of our fields. [12]

Therefore, it came to pass that King Laman began to stir up his people, that they should contend with my people. Therefore, there began to be wars and contentions in the land. For in the thirteenth year of my reign in the land of Nephi, away on the south of the land of Shilom, when my people were watering and feeding their flocks and tilling their lands, a numerous host of Lamanites came upon them, and began to slay them, and to take of their flocks and the corn of their fields. Yea, and it came to pass

---

[11] Mosiah 9: 1-8
[12] Mosiah 9: 10-12*

that they fled, all that were not overtaken, even into the city of Nephi, and did call upon me for protection.

And it came to pass that I did arm them with bows, and with arrows, with swords, and with cimeters, and with clubs, and with slings, and with all manner of weapons which we could invent. And I and my people did go forth against the Lamanites to battle. Yea, in the strength of the Lord did we go forth to battle against the Lamanites, for I and my people did cry mightily to the Lord, that he would deliver us out of the hands of our enemies; for we were awakened to a remembrance of the deliverance of our fathers. And God did hear our cries and did answer our prayers and we did go forth in his might.

Yea, we did go forth against the Lamanites; and in one day and a night we did slay three thousand and forty-three. We did slay them, even until we had driven them out of our land. And I, myself, with mine own hands did help bury their dead. And behold, to our great sorrow and lamentation, two hundred and seventy-nine of our brethren were slain. [13]

And it came to pass that we again began to establish the kingdom, and we again began to possess the land in peace. And I caused that there should be weapons of war made of every kind, that thereby I might have weapons for my people against the time the Lamanites should come up again to war against my people. And I set guards round about the land, that the Lamanites might not come upon us again unawares and destroy us. And thus I did guard my people and my flocks and keep them from falling into the hands of our enemies.

And it came to pass that we did inherit the land of our fathers for many years, yea, for the space of twenty and two years. And I did cause that the men should till the ground and raise all manner of grain and all manner of fruit of every kind. And I did cause that the women should spin, and toil, and work all manner of fine linen, yea, and cloth of every kind, that we might clothe our nakedness. And thus we did prosper in the land; thus we did have continual peace in the land for the space of twenty and two years.

---

[13] Mosiah 9: 13-19

And it came to pass that King Laman died, and his son began to reign in his stead. And he began to stir his people up in rebellion against my people; therefore, they began to prepare for war and to come up to battle against my people. But I had sent my spies out round about the land of Shemlon, that I might discover their preparations, that I might guard against them, that they might not come upon my people and destroy them.

And it came to pass that they came up upon the north of the land of Shilom with their numerous hosts, men armed with bows, and with arrows, and with swords, and with cimeters, and with stones, and with slings. And they had their heads shaved, that they were naked; and they were girded with a leathern girdle about their loins.

And it came to pass that I caused that the women and children of my people should be hid in the wilderness. And I also caused that all my old men that could bear arms, and also all my young men that were able to bear arms, should gather themselves together to go to battle against the Lamanites. And I did place them in their ranks, every man according to his age. And it came to pass that we did go up to battle against the Lamanites. And I, even I, in my old age, did go up to battle against the Lamanites.

And it came to pass that we did go up in the strength of the Lord to battle. Now, the Lamanites knew nothing concerning the Lord, nor the strength of the Lord; therefore, they depended upon their own strength. [14] And now, I, Zeniff, after having told all these things unto my people concerning the Lamanites, I did stimulate them to go to battle with their might, putting their trust in the Lord. Therefore, we did contend with them, face to face.

And it came to pass that we did drive them again out of our land; and we slew them with a great slaughter, even so many that we did not number them. And it came to pass that we returned again to our own land, and my people again began to tend their flocks and to till their ground. And now, I, being old, did confer the kingdom upon one of my sons; therefore, I say no more. And may the Lord bless my people. Amen. [15]

---

[14] Mosiah 10: 1-11*
[15] Mosiah 10: 19-22

And now, it came to pass that Zeniff conferred the kingdom upon Noah, one of his sons; therefore, Noah began to reign in his stead. And he did not walk in the ways of his father; for behold he did not keep the commandments of God, but he did walk after the desires of his own heart. And he had many wives and concubines, and did cause his people to commit sin, and do that which was abominable in the sight of the Lord. [16]

And he laid a tax of one-fifth part of all they possessed: a fifth part of their gold and of their silver, and a fifth part of their ziff, and of their copper, and of their brass and their iron, and a fifth part of their fatlings, and also a fifth part of all their grain. And all this did he take to support himself, and his wives, and his concubines, and also his priests, and their wives, and their concubines.

Thus he had changed the affairs of the kingdom. For he put down all the priests that had been consecrated by his father, and consecrated new ones in their stead, such as were lifted up in the pride of their hearts.

And it came to pass that King Noah built many elegant and spacious buildings, and he ornamented them with fine work of wood and of all manner of precious things: of gold, and of silver, and of iron, and of brass, and of ziff, and of copper. [17]

And it came to pass that he built a tower near the temple, yea, a very high tower, even so high that he could stand upon the top thereof and overlook the land of Shilom and also the land of Shemlon, which was possessed by the Lamanites. And he could even look over all the land round about. And he caused a great tower to be built on the hill north of the land Shilom, which had been a resort for the children of Nephi at the time they fled out of the land. And thus he did do with the riches which he obtained by the taxation of his people. [18]

And it came to pass that he placed his heart upon his riches, and he spent his time in riotous living with his wives and his concubines. And so did also his priests spend their time with harlots. And it came to pass that he planted vineyards round about

---

[16] Mosiah 11: 1-2*
[17] Mosiah 11: 3-5, 8
[18] Mosiah 11: 12-13*

in the land. And he built winepresses and made wine in abundance. And therefore, he became a winebibber, and also his people. [19]

And it came to pass that there was a man among them, whose name was Abinadi. And he went forth among them and began to prophesy, saying, Behold, thus saith the Lord, and thus hath he commanded me, saying, Wo be unto this people, for I have seen their abominations, and their wickedness, and their whoredoms. And except they repent, I will visit them in mine anger. And except they repent and turn to the Lord, their God, behold, I will deliver them into the hands of their enemies. Yea, and they shall be brought into bondage, and they shall be afflicted by the hand of their enemies. And it shall come to pass that they shall know that I am the Lord, their God, and am a jealous God, visiting the iniquities of my people. [20] And except they repent in sackcloth and ashes and cry mightily to the Lord, their God, I will not hear their prayers; neither will I deliver them out of their afflictions. And thus saith the Lord, and thus hath he commanded me.

Now it came to pass that when Abinadi had spoken these words unto them, they were wroth with him and sought to take away his life; but the Lord delivered him out of their hands.

Now when King Noah had heard of the words which Abinadi had spoken unto the people, he was also wroth, and he said, Who is Abinadi, that I and my people should be judged of him? Or who is the Lord, that shall bring upon my people such great afflictions? I command you to bring Abinadi hither, that I may slay him. For he has said these things that he might stir up my people to anger, one with another, and to raise contentions among my people. Therefore, I will slay him. [21]

And it came to pass that after the space of two years, that Abinadi came among them in disguise, that they knew him not, and began again to prophesy among them, saying, Thus hath the Lord commanded me, saying, Abinadi, go and prophesy unto this my people, for they have hardened their hearts against my words. They have repented not of their evil doings.

---

[19] Mosiah 11: 14-15
[20] Mosiah 11: 20*-22
[21] Mosiah 11: 25-28

And the Lord said unto me, Stretch forth thy hand and prophesy, saying, Thus saith the Lord: It shall come to pass that this generation, because of their iniquities, shall be brought into bondage, and shall be smitten on the cheek, yea, and shall be driven by men, and shall be slain. And the vultures of the air, and the dogs, yea, and the wild beasts shall devour their flesh.

And it shall come to pass that the life of King Noah shall be valued even as a garment in a hot furnace, for he shall know that I am the Lord. And it shall come to pass that I will smite this my people with sore afflictions, yea, with famine and with pestilence; and I will cause that they shall howl all the day long. Yea, and I will cause that they shall have burdens lashed upon their backs, and they shall be driven before, like a dumb ass. [22] And it shall come to pass that, except they repent, I will utterly destroy them from off the face of the earth. Yet they shall leave a record behind them, and I will preserve them for other nations which shall possess the land. Yea, even this will I do, that I may discover the abominations of this people to other nations.

And many things did Abinadi prophesy against this people. And it came to pass that they were angry with him; and they took him, and carried him bound before the king, and said unto the king, Behold, we have brought a man before thee who has prophesied evil concerning thy people, and saith that God will destroy them. And he also prophesieth evil concerning thy life and saith that thy life shall be as a garment in a furnace of fire. [23] And again, he saith thou shalt be as the blossoms of a thistle, which when it is fully ripe, if the wind bloweth, it is driven forth upon the face of the land. And he pretendeth the Lord hath spoken it. And he saith all this shall come upon thee except thou repent; and this because of thine iniquities.

And now, O King, what great evil hast thou done, or what great sins have thy people committed, that we should be condemned of God or judged of this man? [24] Behold, here is the man; we deliver him into thy hands. Thou mayest do with him as

---

[22] Mosiah 12: 1*, 2*-5
[23] Mosiah 12: 8-10
[24] Mosiah 12: 12-13

seemeth thee good.

And it came to pass that King Noah caused that Abinadi should be cast into prison. And he commanded that the priests should gather themselves together, that he might hold a council with them what he should do with him. And it came to pass that they said unto the king, Bring him hither, that we may question him. And the king commanded that he should be brought before them.

And they began to question him, that they might cross him, that thereby they might have wherewith to accuse him. But he answered them boldly and withstood all their questions, yea, to their astonishment. For he did withstand them in all their questions, and did confound them in all their words.

And it came to pass that one of them said unto him, What meaneth the words which are written and which have been taught by our fathers, saying, How beautiful upon the mountains are the feet of him that bringeth good tidings, that publisheth peace, that bringeth good tidings of good, that publisheth salvation, that saith unto Zion, thy God reigneth. Thy watchmen shall lift up the voice; with the voice together shall they sing, for they shall see eye to eye, when the Lord shall bring again Zion. Break forth into joy; sing together, ye waste places of Jerusalem; for the Lord hath comforted his people; he hath redeemed Jerusalem. The Lord hath made bare his holy arm in the eyes of all the nations; and all the ends of the earth shall see the salvation of our God. [25]

And now, Abinadi said unto them, Are you priests and pretend to teach this people, and to understand the spirit of prophesying, and yet desire to know of me what these things mean?

I say unto you, Wo be unto you for perverting the ways of the Lord. For if ye understand these things, ye have not taught them. Therefore, ye have perverted the ways of the Lord. Ye have not applied your hearts to understanding; therefore, ye have not been wise. Therefore, what teach ye this people?

And they said, We teach the law of Moses.

And again, he said unto them, If ye teach the law of Moses, why do ye not keep it? Why do ye set your hearts upon riches? Why do ye commit whoredoms, and spend your strength with

---

[25] Mosiah 12: 21-24 (Compare Isaiah 52: 8-10)

harlots, yea, and cause this people to commit sin, that the Lord has cause to send me to prophesy against this people, yea, even a great evil against this people?

Know ye not that I speak the truth? Yea, ye know that I speak the truth; and you ought to tremble before God. And it shall come to pass that ye shall be smitten for your iniquities; for ye have said that ye teach the law of Moses.

And what know ye concerning the law of Moses? Doth salvation come by the law of Moses? What say ye?

And they answered and said that salvation did come by the law of Moses.

But now Abinadi said unto them, I know if ye keep the commandments of God, ye shall be saved; yea, if ye keep the commandments which the Lord delivered unto Moses, in the mount of Sinai, saying, I am the Lord, thy God, who has brought thee out of the land of Egypt, out of the house of bondage.

Thou shalt have no other god before me. Thou shalt not make unto thee any graven image, or any likeness of anything in heaven above, or things which are in the earth beneath.

Now Abinadi said unto them, Have ye done all this? I say unto you, Nay, ye have not. And have ye taught this people that they should do all these things? I say unto you, Nay, ye have not. [26]

And now, when the king had heard these words, he said unto his priests, Away with this fellow, and slay him; for what have we to do with him, for he is mad.

And they stood forth and attempted to lay their hands on him; but he withstood them and said unto them, Touch me not; for God shall smite you if ye lay your hands upon me; for I have not delivered the message which the Lord sent me to deliver. Neither have I told you that which ye requested that I should tell; therefore, God will not suffer that I shall be destroyed at this time. But I must fulfill the commandments wherewith God has commanded me. And because I have told you the truth, ye are angry with me. And again, because I have spoken the word of God, ye have judged me that I am mad.

---

[26] Mosiah 12: 16-37 (Compare Exodus 20: 2-4)

Now it came to pass after Abinadi had spoken these words, that the people of King Noah durst not lay their hands on him, for the Spirit of the Lord was upon him. And his face shone with exceeding luster, even as Moses' did while in the mount of Sinai while speaking with the Lord.

And he spake with power and authority from God. And he continued his words, saying, Ye see that ye have not power to slay me; therefore, I finish my message. Yea, and I perceive that it cuts you to your hearts because I tell you the truth concerning your iniquities. Yea, and my words fill you with wonder, and amazement, and with anger. But I finish my message; and then it matters not whither I go, if it be so that I am saved. But this much I tell you: What you do with me after this shall be as a type and a shadow of things which are to come.

And now, I read unto you the remainder of the commandments of God, for I perceive that they are not written in your hearts. I perceive that ye have studied and taught iniquity the most part of your lives.

And now, ye remember that I said unto you, Thou shalt not make unto thee any graven image, or any likeness of things which are in heaven above, or which are in the earth beneath, or which are in the water under the earth.

And again, Thou shalt not bow down thyself unto them, nor serve them; for I, the Lord, thy God, am a jealous God, visiting the iniquities of the fathers upon the children unto the third and fourth generations of them that hate me, and showing mercy unto thousands of them that love me and keep my commandments.

Thou shalt not take the name of the Lord, thy God, in vain; for the Lord will not hold him guiltless that taketh his name in vain.

Remember the Sabbath day, to keep it holy. Six days shalt thou labor and do all thy work; but the seventh day, the Sabbath of the Lord thy God, thou shalt not do any work, thou, nor thy son, nor thy daughter, thy manservant, nor thy maidservant, nor thy cattle, nor thy stranger that is within thy gates. For in six days the Lord made heaven, and earth, and the sea, and all that in them is; wherefore, the Lord blessed the Sabbath day and hallowed it.

Honor thy father and thy mother, that thy days may be long upon the land which the Lord, thy God, giveth thee.

Thou shalt not kill.

Thou shalt not commit adultery.

Thou shalt not steal.

Thou shalt not bear false witness against thy neighbor.

Thou shalt not covet thy neighbor's house; thou shalt not covet thy neighbor's wife, nor his manservant, nor his maidservant, nor his ox, nor his ass, nor anything that is thy neighbor's.[27]

And it came to pass that after Abinadi had made an end of these sayings, that he said unto them, Have ye taught this people that they should observe to do all these things, for to keep these commandments? I say unto you, Nay; for if you had, the Lord would not have caused me to come forth and to prophesy evil concerning this people.

And now, ye have said that salvation cometh by the law of Moses. But I say unto you that the time shall come when it shall no more be expedient to keep the law of Moses. [28] And moreover, I say unto you that salvation doth not come by the law alone. And were it not for the atonement which God himself shall make for the sins and iniquities of his people, that they must unavoidably perish, notwithstanding the law of Moses.

Therefore, there was a law given them, yea, a law of performances and of ordinances, a law which they were to observe strictly from day to day, to keep them in remembrance of God and their duty towards him. But behold, I say unto you that all these things were types of things to come.

And now, did they understand the law? I say unto you, Nay, they did not all understand the law, and this because of the hardness of their hearts. For they understood not that there could not any man be saved, except it were through the redemption of God.

For behold, did not Moses prophesy unto them concerning the coming of the Messiah, and that God should redeem his people, yea, and even all the prophets who have prophesied ever since the world began? [29]

Yea, even doth not Isaiah say, Who hath believed our report, and to whom is the arm of the Lord revealed? For he shall grow

[27] Compare Exodus 20: 3-17

[28] Mosiah 13: 1-27*

[29] Mosiah 13: 28, 30-33*

up before him as a tender plant, and as a root out of dry ground. He hath no form nor comeliness; and when we shall see him, there is no beauty that we should desire him.

He is despised and rejected of men, a man of sorrows and acquainted with grief. And we hid, as it were, our faces from him. He was despised, and we esteemed him not. Surely he has borne our griefs and carried our sorrows; yet we did esteem him stricken, smitten of God, and afflicted.

But he was wounded for our transgressions; he was bruised for our iniquities; the chastisement of our peace was upon him; and with his stripes we are healed.

All we like sheep have gone astray. We have turned everyone to his own way; and the Lord hath laid on him the iniquities of us all. He was oppressed, and he was afflicted; yet he opened not his mouth. He is brought as a lamb to the slaughter; and as a sheep before her shearers is dumb, so, he opened not his mouth.

He was taken from prison and from judgment. And who shall declare his generation? For he was cut off out of the land of the living. For the transgressions of my people was he stricken.

And he made his grave with the wicked and with the rich in his death, because he had done no evil; neither was any deceit in his mouth. Yet it pleased the Lord to bruise him. He hath put him to grief.

When thou shalt make his soul an offering for sin, he shall see his seed, he shall prolong his days, and the pleasure of the Lord shall prosper in his hand. He shall see of the travail of his soul and shall be satisfied. By his knowledge shall my righteous servant justify many, for he shall bear their iniquities. Therefore will I divide him a portion with the great, and he shall divide the spoil with the strong, because he hath poured out his soul unto death. And he was numbered with the transgressors; and he bare the sins of many and made intercession for the transgressors. [30]

And now, Abinadi said unto them, I would that ye should understand that God himself shall come down among the children of men and shall redeem his people. And because he dwelleth in flesh, he shall be called the Son of God. And having subjected the flesh to the will of the Father, being the Father and the Son— the Father because he was conceived by the power of God, and the Son because of the flesh, thus becoming the Father and Son, and

---

[30] Mosiah 14: 1-12 (Compare Isaiah 53)

they are one God, yea, the very eternal Father of heaven and of earth.

And thus the flesh, becoming subject to the Spirit, or the Son to the Father, being one God, suffereth temptation and yieldeth not to the temptation, but suffereth himself to be mocked, and scourged, and cast out, and disowned by his people.

And after all this, and after working many mighty miracles among the children of men, he shall be led, yea, even as Isaiah said, as a sheep before the shearer is dumb, so he opened not his mouth. Yea, even so he shall be led, crucified, and slain; the flesh becoming subject even unto death, the will of the Son being swallowed up in the will of the Father.

And thus God breaketh the bands of death, having gained the victory over death, giving the Son power to make intercession for the children of men, having ascended into heaven, having the bowels of mercy, being filled with compassion toward the children of men, standing betwixt them and justice, having broken the bands of death, taken upon himself their iniquity and their transgressions, having redeemed them, and satisfied the demands of justice.

And now, I say unto you, Who shall declare his generation?

Behold, I say unto you that when his soul has been made an offering for sin, he shall see his seed. And who shall be his seed?

Behold I say unto you, that whosoever has heard the words of the prophets, yea, all the holy prophets who have prophesied concerning the coming of the Lord, I say unto you, that all those who have hearkened unto their words, and believed that the Lord would redeem his people, and have looked forward to that day for a remission of their sins, I say unto you that these are his seed, or they are heirs of the kingdom of God. For these are they whose sins he has borne. These are they for whom he has died, to redeem them from their transgressions.

And now, are they not his seed? Yea, and are not the prophets, every one that has opened his mouth to prophesy, that has not fallen into transgression, I mean all the holy prophets ever since the world began? I say unto you, that they are his seed. And these are they who have published peace, who have brought good tidings of good, who have published salvation and said unto Zion, Thy God reigneth!

And oh, how beautiful upon the mountains were their feet! And again, how beautiful upon the mountains are the feet of those that are still publishing peace!

And again, how beautiful upon the mountains are the feet of those who shall hereafter publish peace, yea, from this time henceforth and forever!

And behold, I say unto you, This is not all—For oh, how beautiful upon the mountains are the feet of him that bringeth good tidings, that is the founder of peace, yea, even the Lord, who has redeemed his people, yea, he who has granted salvation unto his people. For were it not for the redemption which he hath made for his people, which was prepared from the foundation of the world, I say unto you, Were it not for this, all mankind must have perished.

But behold, the bands of death shall be broken, and the Son reigneth and hath power over the dead. Therefore, he bringeth to pass the resurrection of the dead. [31]

And now, the resurrection of all the prophets, and all those that have believed in their words, or all those that have kept the commandments of God, shall come forth in the first resurrection. Therefore, they are the first resurrection. They are raised to dwell with God who has redeemed them. Thus they have eternal life through Christ, who has broken the bands of death. [32]

But behold, and fear and tremble before God! For ye ought to tremble! For the Lord redeemeth none such that rebel against him and die in their sins, yea, even all those that have perished in their sins ever since the world began, that have willfully rebelled against God, that have known the commandments of God and would not keep them. These are they that have no part in the first resurrection. Therefore, had ye not ought to tremble? For salvation cometh to none such; for the Lord hath redeemed none such. Yea, neither can the Lord redeem such, for he cannot deny himself, for

---

[31] Mosiah 15: 1-20
[32] Mosiah 15: 22-23

he cannot deny justice when it has its claim.

And now, I say unto you that the time shall come that the salvation of the Lord shall be declared to every nation, kindred, tongue, and people. Yea, Lord, thy watchmen shall lift up their voice. With the voice together shall they sing; for they shall see eye to eye, when the Lord shall bring again Zion.

Break forth into joy, sing together, ye waste places of Jerusalem; for the Lord hath comforted his people; he hath redeemed Jerusalem. The Lord hath made bare his holy arm in the eyes of all the nations; and all the ends of the earth shall see the salvation of our God. [33]

And now, it came to pass that after Abinadi had spoken these words, he stretched forth his hand and said, The time shall come when all shall see the salvation of the Lord. He is the light and the life of the world, yea, a light that is endless, that can never be darkened; yea, and also a life which is endless, that there can be no more death. Even this mortal shall put on immortality; and this corruption shall put on incorruption, and shall be brought to stand before the bar of God to be judged of him, according to their works, whether they be good or whether they be evil— if they be good, to the resurrection of endless life and happiness, and if they be evil, to the resurrection of endless damnation. [34]

And now, had ye not ought to tremble, and repent of your sins, and remember only in and through Christ ye can be saved? Therefore, if ye teach the law of Moses, also teach that it is a shadow of those things which are to come, teach them that redemption cometh through Christ the Lord, who is the very eternal Father. Amen. [35]

And now, it came to pass that when Abinadi had finished these sayings, that the king commanded that the priests should take him and cause that he should be put to death. But there was one among them whose name was Alma, he also being a descendant of Nephi. And he was a young man, and he believed the words which Abinadi had spoken; for he knew concerning the iniquity which Abinadi had testified against them.

---

[33] Mosiah 15: 26-31 (Compare Isaiah 52: 8-10)
[34] Mosiah 16: 1*, 9-11*
[35] Mosiah 16: 13-15

Therefore, he began to plead with the king that he would not be angry with Abinadi, but suffer that he might depart in peace. But the king was more wroth, and caused that Alma should be cast out from among them, and sent his servants after him that they might slay him. But he fled from before them and hid himself, that they found him not. And he being concealed for many days, did write all the words which Abinadi had spoken.

And it came to pass that the king caused that his guards should surround Abinadi and take him. And they bound him and cast him into prison. And after three days, having counseled with his priests, he caused that he should again be brought before him. And he said unto him, Abinadi, we have found an accusation against thee, and thou art worthy of death.

For thou hast said that God himself should come down among the children of men. And now, for this cause thou shalt be put to death, unless thou wilt recall all the words which thou hast spoken evil concerning me and my people.

Now Abinadi said unto him, I say unto you, I will not recall the words which I have spoken unto you concerning this people, for they are true. And that ye may know of their surety, I have suffered myself that I have fallen into your hands. Yea, and I will suffer even until death, and I will not recall my words; and they shall stand as a testimony against you. And if ye slay me, ye will shed innocent blood. And this shall also stand as a testimony against you at the last day.

And now, King Noah was about to release him, for he feared his word; for he feared that the judgments of God would come upon him. But the priests lifted up their voices against him and began to accuse him, saying, He has reviled the king. Therefore, the king was stirred up in anger against him, and he delivered him up that he might be slain. And it came to pass that they took him, and bound him, and scourged his skin with fagots, yea, even unto death.

And now, when the flames began to scorch him, he cried unto them, saying, Behold, even as ye have done unto me, so shall it come to pass that thy seed shall cause that many shall suffer the pains that I do suffer, even the pains of death by fire, and this because they believe in the salvation of the Lord, their God.

And it will come to pass that ye shall be afflicted with all manner of diseases because of your iniquities. Yea, and ye shall be smitten on every hand, and shall be driven and scattered, to and fro, even as a wild flock is driven by wild and ferocious beasts. And in that day ye shall be hunted, and ye shall be taken by the hand of your enemies; and then ye shall suffer, as I suffer, the pains of death by fire. Thus God executeth vengeance upon those that destroy his people. O God, receive my soul!

And now, when Abinadi had said these words, he fell, having suffered death by fire, yea, having been put to death because he would not deny the commandments of God, having sealed the truth of his words by his death. [36]

And now, it came to pass that Alma, who had fled from the servants of King Noah, repented of his sins and iniquities, and went about privately among the people, and began to teach the words of Abinadi. And it came to pass that as many as did believe him did go forth to a place which was called Mormon, having received its name from the king, being in the borders of the land, having been infested by times, or at seasons, by wild beasts.

Now there was in Mormon a fountain of pure water, and Alma resorted thither, there being near the water a thicket of small trees where he did hide himself in the daytime from the searches of the king. [37] And it came to pass after many days, there were a goodly number gathered together to the place of Mormon to hear the words of Alma. And he did teach them and did preach unto them repentance, and redemption, and faith on the Lord.

And it came to pass that he said unto them, Behold, here are the waters of Mormon, for thus were they called. And now, as ye are desirous to come into the fold of God, and to be called his people, and are willing to bear one another's burdens, that they may be light, yea, and are willing to mourn with those that mourn, yea, and comfort those that stand in need of comfort, and to stand as witnesses of God, at all times, and in all things, and in all places that ye may be in, even until death; that ye may be redeemed of God, and be numbered with those of the first

---

[36] Mosiah 17: 1-20
[37] Mosiah 18: 1*, 4-5

resurrection, that ye may have eternal life —now I say unto you, if this be the desire of your hearts, what have you against being baptized in the name of the Lord, as a witness before him that ye have entered into a covenant with him, that ye will serve him and keep his commandments, that he may pour out his Spirit more abundantly upon you?

And now, when the people had heard these words, they clapped their hands for joy and exclaimed, This is the desire of our hearts!

And now, it came to pass that Alma took Helam, he being one of the first, and went and stood forth in the water, and cried, saying, O Lord, pour out thy Spirit upon thy servant, that he may do this work with holiness of heart. And when he had said these words, the Spirit of the Lord was upon him.

And he said, Helam, I baptize thee, having authority from the Almighty God, as a testimony that ye have entered into a covenant to serve him until you are dead, as to the mortal body. And may the Spirit of the Lord be poured out upon you. And may he grant unto you eternal life, through the redemption of Christ, whom he has prepared from the foundation of the world.

And after Alma had said these words, both Alma and Helam were buried in the water; and they arose and came forth out of the water rejoicing, being filled with the Spirit. And again, Alma took another, and went forth a second time into the water, and baptized him according to the first, only he did not bury himself again in the water. And after this manner he did baptize everyone that went forth to the place of Mormon. And they were in number about two hundred and four souls. Yea, and they were baptized in the waters of Mormon and were filled with the grace of God. And they were called the church of God, or the church of Christ, from that time forward. [38]

And it came to pass that Alma, having authority from God, ordained priests; even one priest to every fifty of their number did he ordain to preach unto them and to teach them concerning the things pertaining to the kingdom of God. And he commanded them that they should teach nothing save it were the things which

---

[38] Mosiah 18: 7*-17*

he had taught, and which had been spoken by the mouth of the holy prophets.

Yea, even he commanded them that they should preach nothing save it were repentance and faith on the Lord, who had redeemed his people. And he commanded them that there should be no contention one with another, but that they should look forward with one eye, having one faith and one baptism, having their hearts knit together in unity and in love, one towards another. And thus he commanded them to preach. And thus they became the children of God.

And he commanded them that they should observe the Sabbath day and keep it holy, and also every day they should give thanks to the Lord, their God. [39]

And the priests were not to depend upon the people for their support; but for their labor they were to receive the grace of God, that they might wax strong in the Spirit, having the knowledge of God, that they might teach with power and authority from God.

And again, Alma commanded that the people of the church should impart of their substance, everyone according to that which he had. If he had more abundantly, he should impart more abundantly; and he that had but little, but little should be required. And to him that had not should be given. And thus they should impart of their substance of their own free will and good desires towards God, and to those priests that stood in need, yea, and to every needy, naked soul. And this he said unto them, having been commanded of God. And they did walk uprightly before God, imparting to one another, both temporally and spiritually, according to their needs and their wants.

And now, it came to pass that all this was done in Mormon, yea, by the waters of Mormon, in the forest that was near the waters of Mormon, yea, the place of Mormon, the waters of Mormon, the forest of Mormon. How beautiful are they to the eyes of them who there came to the knowledge of their Redeemer. Yea, and how blessed are they, for they shall sing to his praise forever.

And these things were done in the borders of the land, that they might not come to the knowledge of the king. But behold, it

---

[39] Mosiah 18: 18-23

came to pass that the king, having discovered a movement among the people, sent his servants to watch them. Therefore, on the day that they were assembling themselves together to hear the word of the Lord, they were discovered unto the king. And now, the king said that Alma was stirring up the people to rebellion against him. Therefore, he sent his army to destroy them.

And it came to pass that Alma and the people of the Lord were apprised of the coming of the king's army. Therefore, they took their tents and their families and departed into the wilderness. And they were in number about four hundred and fifty souls. [40] And the Lord did strengthen them, that the people of King Noah could not overtake them to destroy them. [41] And it came to pass that the army of the king returned, having searched in vain for the people of the Lord.

And now, behold, the forces of the king were small, having been reduced. And there began to be a division among the remainder of the people. And the lesser part began to breathe out threatenings against the king, and there began to be a great contention among them.

And now, there was a man among them whose name was Gideon. And he, being a strong man and an enemy to the king, therefore, he drew his sword and swore in his wrath that he would slay the king. And it came to pass that he fought with the king. And when the king saw that he was about to overpower him, he fled and ran and got upon the tower which was near the temple. And the king cast his eyes round about towards the land of Shemlon, and behold, the army of the Lamanites were within the borders of the land. [42]

And now, the king cried out in the anguish of his soul, saying, Gideon, spare me! For the Lamanites are upon us, yea, they will destroy my people. And now, the king was not so much concerned about his people as he was about his own life. Nevertheless, Gideon did spare his life. And the king commanded the people that they should flee before the Lamanites, and he himself did go before

---

[40] Mosiah 18: 26-35
[41] Mosiah 23: 2
[42] Mosiah 19: 1-6*

them. And they did flee into the wilderness with their women and their children.

And it came to pass that the Lamanites did pursue them, and did overtake them, and began to slay them. And it came to pass that the king commanded them that all the men should leave their wives and their children and flee before the Lamanites. Now there were many that would not leave them; but had rather stay and perish with them. And the rest left their wives and their children and fled.

And it came to pass that those who tarried with their wives and their children caused that their fair daughters should stand forth and plead with the Lamanites, that they would not slay them. And it came to pass that the Lamanites had compassion on them, for they were charmed with the beauty of their women. Therefore, the Lamanites did spare their lives, and granted unto them that they might possess the land, under the conditions that they would deliver up King Noah into the hands of the Lamanites, and deliver up their property, even one-half of all they possessed: one-half of their gold, and their silver, and all their precious things.

And thus they should pay tribute to the king of the Lamanites from year to year. And also Limhi, being the son of the king, having the kingdom conferred upon him by the people, made an oath unto the king of the Lamanites, that his people should pay tribute unto him, even one-half of all they possessed. [43]

And it came to pass that Gideon sent men into the wilderness secretly to search for the king and those that were with him. And it came to pass that they met the people in the wilderness, all save the king and his priests.

Now they had sworn in their hearts that they would return to the land of Nephi. And if their wives and their children were slain, that they would seek revenge and also perish with them. And the king commanded them that they should not return. And they were angry with the king, and caused that he should suffer, even unto death by fire. And they were about to take the priests also to put them to death, and they fled before them.

---

[43] Mosiah 19: 7-15, 26

And it came to pass that they were about to return to the land of Nephi and they met the men of Gideon. And the men of Gideon told them of all that had happened to their wives and their children, and that the Lamanites had granted unto them that they might possess the land by paying a tribute to the Lamanites of one-half of all they possessed.

And the people told the men of Gideon that they had slain the king, and his priests had fled from them farther into the wilderness. And it came to pass that after they had ended the ceremony, that they returned to the land of Nephi, rejoicing because their wives and their children were not slain. [44]

And the king of the Lamanites set guards round about the land, that he might keep the people of Limhi in the land, that they might not depart into the wilderness. And he did support his guards out of the tribute which he did receive from the Nephites. And now, King Limhi did have continual peace in his kingdom for the space of two years, that the Lamanites did not molest them nor seek to destroy them.[45]

Now, there was a place in Shemlon where the daughters of the Lamanites did gather themselves together to sing and to dance, and to make themselves merry. And it came to pass that there was one day a small number of them gathered together to sing and to dance.

And now, the priests of King Noah, being ashamed to return to the city of Nephi, yea, and also fearing that the people would slay them, therefore, they durst not return to their wives and their children. And having tarried in the wilderness, and having discovered the daughters of the Lamanites, they laid and watched them. And when there were but few of them gathered together to dance, they came forth out of their secret places, and took them, and carried them into the wilderness; yea, twenty and four of the daughters of the Lamanites they carried into the wilderness.

And it came to pass that when the Lamanites found that their daughters had been missing, they were angry with the people of Limhi; for they thought it was the people of Limhi. Therefore, they

---

[44] Mosiah 19: 18-24*
[45] Mosiah 19: 28-29

sent their armies forth; yea, even the king himself went before his people; and they went up to the land of Nephi to destroy the people of Limhi.

And now, Limhi had discovered them from the tower. Even all their preparations for war did he discover; therefore, he gathered his people together and laid in wait for them in the fields and in the forests. And it came to pass that when the Lamanites had come up, that the people of Limhi began to fall upon them from their waiting places and began to slay them.

And it came to pass that the battle became exceeding sore, for they fought like lions for their prey. And it came to pass that the people of Limhi began to drive the Lamanites before them, yet they were not half so numerous as the Lamanites. But they fought for their lives, and for their wives, and for their children; therefore, they exerted themselves, and like dragons did they fight.

And it came to pass that they found the king of the Lamanites among the number of their dead; yet he was not dead, having been wounded and left upon the ground, so speedy was the flight of his people. And they took him, and bound up his wounds, and brought him before Limhi. [46] And Limhi said unto him, What cause have ye to come up to war against my people? Behold, my people have not broken the oath that I made unto you; therefore, why should ye break the oath which ye made unto my people?

And now, the king said, I have broken the oath because thy people did carry away the daughters of my people; therefore, in my anger I did cause my people to come up to war against thy people.

Now Limhi had heard nothing concerning this matter; therefore, he said, I will search among my people, and whosoever has done this thing shall perish. [47]

Now when Gideon had heard these things, he being the king's captain, he went forth and said unto the king, I pray thee forbear, and do not search this people, and lay not this thing to their charge. For do ye not remember the priests of thy father, whom this people sought to destroy? And are they not in the

---

[46] Mosiah 20: 1-13*
[47] Mosiah 20: 14*-16*

wilderness? And are not they the ones who have stolen the daughters of the Lamanites?

And now, behold, and tell the king of these things, that he may tell his people, that they may be pacified towards us. For behold, they are already preparing to come against us; and behold, also, there are but few of us. [48] And now, let us pacify the king, and we fulfill the oath which we have made unto him; for it is better that we should be in bondage than that we should lose our lives. Therefore, let us put a stop to the shedding of so much blood. And now, Limhi told the king all the things concerning his father and the priests that had fled into the wilderness and attributed the carrying away of their daughters to them.

And it came to pass that the king was pacified towards his people. And he said unto them, Let us go forth to meet my people without arms; and I swear unto you with an oath that my people shall not slay thy people. And it came to pass that they followed the king and went forth without arms to meet the Lamanites.

And it came to pass that they did meet the Lamanites; and the king of the Lamanites did bow himself down before them and did plead in behalf of the people of Limhi. And when the Lamanites saw the people of Limhi, that they were without arms, they had compassion on them, and were pacified towards them, and returned with their king in peace to their own land. [49] And it came to pass that Limhi and his people returned to the city of Nephi and began to dwell in the land again in peace.

And it came to pass that after many days, the Lamanites began again to be stirred up in anger against the Nephites; and they began to come into the borders of the land round about. Now they durst not slay them because of the oath which their king had made unto Limhi; but they would smite them on their cheeks, and exercise authority over them, and began to put heavy burdens upon their backs, and drive them as they would a dumb ass. Yea, all this was done that the word of the Lord might be fulfilled.

And now, the afflictions of the Nephites were great; and there was no way that they could deliver themselves out of their

---

[48] Mosiah 20: 17-19
[49] Mosiah 20: 22-26

hands, for the Lamanites had surrounded them on every side. And it came to pass that the people began to murmur with the king because of their afflictions; and they began to be desirous to go against them to battle. And they did afflict the king sorely with their complaints; therefore, he granted unto them that they should do according to their desires. And they gathered themselves together again, and put on their armor, and went forth against the Lamanites to drive them out of their land.

And it came to pass that the Lamanites did beat them, and drove them back, and slew many of them. And now, there was a great mourning and lamentation among the people of Limhi, the widow mourning for her husband, the son and the daughter mourning for their father, and the brothers for their brethren. [50]

And it came to pass that their continual cries did stir up the remainder of the people of Limhi to anger against the Lamanites. And they went again to battle; but they were driven back again, suffering much loss. And those that were not slain returned again to the city of Nephi. [51]

And they did humble themselves even to the dust, subjecting themselves to the yoke of bondage, submitting themselves to be smitten, and to be driven to and fro, and burdened, according to the desires of their enemies. And they did humble themselves, even in the depths of humility. And they did cry mightily to God; yea, even all the day long did they cry unto their God, that he would deliver them out of their afflictions.

And now, the Lord was slow to hear their cry because of their iniquities; nevertheless, the Lord did hear their cries and began to soften the hearts of the Lamanites, that they began to ease their burdens. Yet the Lord did not see fit to deliver them out of their bondage.

And it came to pass that they began to prosper by degrees in the land and began to raise grain more abundantly, and flocks, and herds, that they did not suffer with hunger. Now there was a great number of women more than there was of men; therefore, King Limhi commanded that every man should impart to the

---

[50] Mosiah 21: 1-9
[51] Mosiah 21: 11-12*

support of the widows and their children, that they might not perish with hunger, and this they did because of the greatness of their number that had been slain.

Now the people of Limhi kept together in a body, as much as it was possible. [52] And the king himself did not trust his person without the walls of the city unless he took his guards with him, fearing that he might by some means fall into the hands of the Lamanites. And he caused that his people should watch the land round about, that by some means they might take those priests that fled into the wilderness, who had stolen the daughters of the Lamanites and that had caused such a great destruction to come upon them. For they were desirous to take them that they might punish them; for they had come into the land of Nephi by night and carried off their grain and many of their precious things. Therefore, they laid wait for them.

And it came to pass that there was no more disturbance between the Lamanites and the people of Limhi, even until the time that Ammon and his brethren came into the land. [53] And now since the coming of Ammon, king Limhi had also entered into a covenant with God, and also many of his people, to serve him and keep his commandments. [54]

And it came to pass that the people of King Limhi did depart by night into the wilderness with their flocks and their herds; and they went round about the land of Shilom in the wilderness and bent their course towards the land of Zarahemla, being led by Ammon and his brethren. And after being many days in the wilderness, they arrived in the land of Zarahemla and joined King Mosiah's people, and became his subjects. [55]

---

[52] Mosiah 21: 13-18*
[53] Mosiah 21: 19-22
[54] Mosiah 21: 32
[55] Mosiah 22: 11, 13

Part II

The Price of Peace

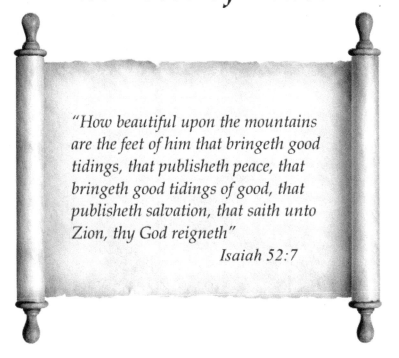

"How beautiful upon the mountains
are the feet of him that bringeth good
tidings, that publisheth peace, that
bringeth good tidings of good, that
publisheth salvation, that saith unto
Zion, thy God reigneth"

Isaiah 52:7

Chapter 5

Fifth Exodus — Foundation of Freedom

The Record of Alma

Now Alma, having been warned of the Lord that the armies of King Noah would come upon them, and had made it known to his people, therefore, they gathered together their flocks, and took of their grain, and departed into the wilderness before the armies of king Noah. And the Lord did strengthen them, that the people of King Noah could not overtake them to destroy them. And they fled eight days' journey into the wilderness.

And they came to a land, yea, even a very beautiful and pleasant land, a land of pure water. And they pitched their tents, and began to till the ground, and began to build buildings, etc.; yea, they were industrious and did labor exceedingly.

And the people were desirous that Alma should be their king, for he was beloved by his people. But he said unto them, Behold, it is not expedient that we should have a king. For thus saith the Lord: Ye shall not esteem one flesh above another, or one man shall not think himself above another. Therefore, I say unto you, It is not expedient that ye should have a king.

Nevertheless, if it were possible that ye could always have just men to be your kings, it would be well for you to have a king. But remember the iniquity of King Noah and his priests. And I, myself, was caught in a snare and did many things which were abominable in the sight of the Lord, which caused me sore repentance. [1]

And now, I say unto you, Ye have been oppressed by King Noah, and have been in bondage to him and his priests, and have been brought into iniquity by them. Therefore, ye were bound with the bands of iniquity. And now, as ye have been delivered by the power of God, out of these bonds, yea, even out of the hands of King Noah and his people, and also from the bonds of iniquity, even so I desire that ye should stand fast in this liberty wherewith ye have been made free, and that ye trust no man to be a king over

---

[1] Mosiah 23: 1-9

you, and also trusting no one to be your teacher nor your minister, except he be a man of God, walking in his ways and keeping his commandments.

Thus did Alma teach his people that every man should love his neighbor as himself, that there should be no contention among them. And now Alma was their high priest, he being the founder of their church. [2] And it came to pass that they did multiply and prosper exceedingly in the land of Helam. And they built a city, which they called the city of Helam.

Nevertheless, the Lord seeth fit to chasten his people. Yea, he trieth their patience and their faith. Nevertheless, whoever putteth his trust in him, the same shall be lifted up at the last day. Yea, and thus it was with this people. For behold, I will show unto you that they were brought into bondage. And none could deliver them but the Lord, their God, yea, even the God of Abraham, and of Isaac, and of Jacob. [3]

And now, it came to pass, when the Lamanites had found that the people of Limhi had departed out of the land by night, they sent an army into the wilderness to pursue them. And after they had pursued them two days, they could no longer follow their tracks; therefore, they were lost in the wilderness. [4] And behold, they had found those priests of King Noah in a place which they called Amulon. And they had begun to possess the land and had begun to till the ground. Now the name of the leader of those priests was Amulon.

And it came to pass that Amulon did plead with the Lamanites, and he also sent forth their wives, who were the daughters of the Lamanites, to plead with their brethren, that they should not destroy their husbands. And the Lamanites had compassion on Amulon and his brethren and did not destroy them because of their wives.

And Amulon and his brethren did join the Lamanites, and they were traveling in the wilderness in search of the land of Nephi when they discovered the land of Helam, which was

---

[2] Mosiah 23: 12-16
[3] Mosiah 23: 20-23
[4] Mosiah 22: 15*-16

possessed by Alma and his brethren. [5]

Now it came to pass that the brethren of Alma fled from their fields and gathered themselves together into the city of Helam, and they were much frightened because of the appearance of the Lamanites. But Alma went forth, and stood among them, and exhorted them that they should not be frightened, but that they should remember the Lord, their God, and he would deliver them. Therefore they hushed their fears and began to cry unto the Lord, that he would soften the hearts of the Lamanites, that they would spare them, and their wives, and their children.

And it came to pass that the Lord did soften the hearts of the Lamanites. And Alma and his brethren went forth and delivered themselves up into their hands. [6] And it came to pass that the Lamanites promised unto Alma and his brethren that if they would show them the way which led to the land of Nephi, that they would grant unto them their lives and their liberty.

But after Alma had shown them the way that led to the land of Nephi, the Lamanites would not keep their promise; but they set guards round about the land of Helam over Alma and his brethren. And the remainder of them went to the land of Nephi. [7]

And it came to pass that Amulon did gain favor in the eyes of the king of the Lamanites; therefore, the king of the Lamanites granted unto him and his brethren that they should be appointed teachers over his people, yea, even over the people who were in the land of Shemlon, and in the land of Shilom, and in the land of Amulon.

And now, the name of the king of the Lamanites was Laman, being called after the name of his father, and therefore, he was called King Laman. And he was king over a numerous people. And he appointed teachers of the brethren of Amulon in every land which was possessed by his people.

And thus the language of Nephi began to be taught among all the people of the Lamanites. And they were a people friendly one with another, nevertheless, they knew not God. Neither did

---

[5] Mosiah 23: 31-35
[6] Mosiah 23: 26-29*
[7] Mosiah 23: 36-38*

the brethren of Amulon teach them anything concerning the Lord
their God, neither the law of Moses. Nor did they teach them the
words of Abinadi. But they taught them that they should keep
their record and that they might write one to another.

And thus the Lamanites began to increase in riches, and
began to trade one with another, and wax great, and began to be a
cunning and a wise people, as to the wisdom of the world, yea, a
very cunning people, delighting in all manner of wickedness and
plunder, except it were among their own brethren. [8]

And the king of the Lamanites had granted unto Amulon that
he should be a king and a ruler over his people who were in the
land of Helam; nevertheless, he should have no power to do
anything contrary to the will of the king of the Lamanites. [9] And
now, it came to pass that Amulon began to exercise authority over
Alma and his brethren, and began to persecute him, and cause
that his children should persecute their children. For Amulon
knew Alma, that he had been one of the king's priests, and that it
was he that believed the words of Abinadi, and was driven out
before the king; and therefore, he was wroth with him, and put
tasks upon them, and put taskmasters over them. [10]

And it came to pass that so great were their afflictions that
they began to cry mightily to God. And Amulon commanded
them that they should stop their cries. And he put guards over
them to watch them, that whosoever should be found calling upon
God should be put to death.

And Alma and his people did not raise their voices to the
Lord, their God, but did pour out their hearts to him; and he did
know the thoughts of their hearts.

And it came to pass that the voice of the Lord came to them
in their afflictions, saying, Lift up your heads and be of good
comfort, for I know of the covenant which ye have made unto me.
And I will covenant with this my people and deliver them out of
bondage. And I will also ease the burdens which are put upon
your shoulders, that even you cannot feel them upon your backs,

---

[8] Mosiah 24: 1, 3-6
[9] Mosiah 23: 39
[10] Moisah 24: 8-9*

even while you are in bondage. And this will I do, that ye may stand as witnesses for me hereafter and that ye may know of a surety that I, the Lord God, do visit my people in their afflictions.

And now, it came to pass that the burdens which were laid upon Alma and his brethren were made light. Yea, the Lord did strengthen them that they could bear up their burdens with ease, and they did submit cheerfully and with patience to all the will of the Lord.

And it came to pass that so great was their faith and their patience, that the voice of the Lord came unto them again, saying, Be of good comfort, for on the morrow I will deliver you out of bondage. And he said unto Alma, Thou shalt go before this people, and I will go with thee and deliver this people out of bondage.

Now it came to pass that Alma and his people in the nighttime gathered their flocks together, and also of their grain; yea, even all the nighttime were they gathering their flocks together. And in the morning the Lord caused a deep sleep to come upon the Lamanites, yea, and all their taskmasters were in a profound sleep.

And Alma and his people departed into the wilderness; and when they had traveled all day, they pitched their tents in a valley. And they called the valley Alma because he led their way in the wilderness. Yea, and in the valley of Alma they poured out their thanks to God because he had been merciful unto them, and eased their burdens, and had delivered them out of bondage. For they were in bondage, and none could deliver them, except it were the Lord, their God. And they gave thanks to God, yea, all their men, and all their women, and all their children that could speak, lifted their voices in the praises of their God.

And now, the Lord said unto Alma, Haste thee and get thou and this people out of this land, for the Lamanites have awakened and do pursue thee. Therefore, get thee out of this land and I will stop the Lamanites in this valley, that they come no further in pursuit of this people.

And it came to pass that they departed out of the valley and took their journey into the wilderness. And after they had been in the wilderness twelve days, they arrived to the land of Zarahemla. And King Mosiah did also receive them with joy. [11]

And now, King Mosiah caused that all the people should be gathered together. Now there were not so many of the children of Nephi, or so many of those who were descendants of Nephi, as there were of the people of Zarahemla, who was a descendant of Mulek, and those who came with him into the wilderness. And there were not so many of the people of Nephi and of the people of Zarahemla as there were of the Lamanites. Yea, they were not half so numerous.

And now, all the people of Nephi were assembled together, and also all the people of Zarahemla, and they were gathered together in two bodies. And it came to pass that Mosiah did read, and caused to be read, the records of Zeniff to his people. [12] And he also read the account of Alma, and his brethren, and all their afflictions, from the time they left the land of Zarahemla until the time they returned again.

And now, when Mosiah had made an end of reading the records, his people who tarried in the land were struck with wonder and amazement, for they knew not what to think. For when they beheld those that had been delivered out of bondage, they were filled with exceeding great joy.

And again, when they thought of their brethren who had been slain by the Lamanites, they were filled with sorrow and even shed many tears of sorrow.

And again, when they thought of the immediate goodness of God, and his power in delivering Alma and his brethren out of the hands of the Lamanites and of bondage, they did raise their voices and give thanks to God.

And again, when they thought upon the Lamanites who were their brethren, of their sinful and polluted state, they were filled with pain and anguish for the welfare of their souls. [13]

And now, all the people of Zarahemla were numbered with the Nephites, and this because the kingdom had been conferred

---

[11] Mosiah 24: 10-25
[12] Mosiah 25: 1-5*
[13] Mosiah 25: 6-11

upon none but those who were descendants of Nephi.

And now, it came to pass that when Mosiah had made an end of speaking and reading to the people, he desired that Alma should also speak to the people. And Alma did speak unto them when they were assembled together in large bodies, and he went from one body to another, preaching unto the people repentance and faith on the Lord. And he did exhort the people of Limhi and his brethren, all those that had been delivered out of bondage, that they should remember that it was the Lord that did deliver them.

And it came to pass that after Alma had taught the people many things and had made an end of speaking to them, that King Limhi was desirous that he might be baptized. And all his people were desirous that they might be baptized also. Therefore, Alma did go forth into the water and did baptize them; yea, he did baptize them after the manner he did his brethren in the waters of Mormon. Yea, and as many as he did baptize did belong to the church of God; and this because of their belief on the words of Alma.

And it came to pass that King Mosiah granted unto Alma that he might establish churches throughout all the land of Zarahemla, and gave him power to ordain priests and teachers over every church. Now this was done because there were so many people that they could not all be governed by one teacher; neither could they all hear the word of God in one assembly; therefore, they did assemble themselves together in different bodies, being called churches, every church having their priests and their teachers, and every priest preaching the word according as it was delivered to him by the mouth of Alma. And thus, notwithstanding there being many churches, they were all one church, yea, even the church of God, for there was nothing preached in all the churches except it were repentance and faith in God.

And now, there were seven churches in the land of Zarahemla. And it came to pass that whosoever were desirous to take upon them the name of Christ, or of God, they did join the churches of God. And they were called the people of God. And the Lord did pour out his Spirit upon them, and they were blessed and prospered in the land. [14]

About 100 B.C.

Now it came to pass that there were many of the rising generation that could not understand the words of King Benjamin, being little children at the time he spake unto his people; and they did not believe the tradition of their fathers. They did not believe what had been said concerning the resurrection of the dead; neither did they believe concerning the coming of Christ. And now, because of their unbelief, they could not understand the word of God; and their hearts were hardened. And they would not be baptized, neither would they join the church. And they were a separate people as to their faith and remained so ever after, even in their carnal and sinful state; for they would not call upon the Lord, their God.

And now, in the reign of Mosiah, they were not half so numerous as the people of God, but because of the dissensions among the brethren, they became more numerous. For it came to pass that they did deceive many with their flattering words, who were in the church, and did cause them to commit many sins. Therefore, it became expedient that those who committed sin that were in the church should be admonished by the church. And it came to pass that they were brought before the priests, and delivered up unto the priests by the teachers. And the priests brought them before Alma, who was the high priest.

Now King Mosiah had given Alma the authority over the church. And it came to pass that Alma did not know concerning them, for there were many witnesses against them; yea, the people stood and testified of their iniquity in abundance. Now there had not any such thing happened before in the church. Therefore, Alma was troubled in his spirit, and he caused that they should be brought before the king.

And he said unto the king, Behold, here are many whom we have brought before thee, who are accused of their brethren; yea,

---

[14] Mosiah 25: 13-24

and they have been taken in diverse iniquities. And they do not repent of their iniquities; therefore, we have brought them before thee, that thou mayest judge them according to their crime. But King Mosiah said unto Alma, Behold, I judge them not; therefore, I deliver them into thy hands to be judged.

And now, the spirit of Alma was again troubled. And he went and inquired of the Lord what he should do concerning this matter, for he feared that he should do wrong in the sight of God. And it came to pass that after he had poured out his whole soul to God, the voice of the Lord came to him, saying:

Blessed art thou, Alma, and blessed are they who were baptized in the waters of Mormon. Thou art blessed because of thy exceeding faith in the words alone of my servant Abinadi. And blessed are they because of their exceeding faith in the words which thou hast spoken unto them. And blessed art thou because thou hast established a church among this people. And they shall be established, and they shall be my people. Yea, blessed is this people, who are willing to bear my name. For in my name shall they be called, and they are mine.

And because thou hast inquired of me concerning the transgressor, thou art blessed. Thou art my servant, and I covenant with thee that thou shalt have eternal life. And thou shalt serve me, and go forth in my name, and shalt gather together my sheep. And he that will hear my voice shall be my sheep, and him shall ye receive into the church, and him will I also receive.

For behold, this is my church. Whosoever is baptized shall be baptized unto repentance. And whosoever ye receive shall believe in my name, and him will I freely forgive. For it is I that taketh upon me the sins of the world. For it is I that hath created them; and it is I that granteth unto him that believeth, in the end, a place at my right hand. For behold, in my name are they called. And if they know me, they shall come forth and shall have a place eternally at my right hand.

And it shall come to pass that when the second trump shall sound, then shall they that never knew me come forth and shall stand before me. And then shall they know that I am the Lord, their God, that I am their Redeemer; but they would not be redeemed. [15] Therefore, I say unto you that he that will not hear my voice, the same shall ye not receive into my church, for him I will not receive at the last day.

Therefore, I say unto you, Go; and whosoever transgresseth against me, him shall ye judge according to the sins which he has committed. And if he confess his sins before thee and me, and repenteth in the sincerity of his heart, him shall ye forgive, and I will forgive him also. Yea, and as often as my people repent, will I forgive them their trespasses against me.

And ye shall also forgive one another your trespasses. For verily, I say unto you, He that forgiveth not his neighbor's trespasses, when he says that he repents, the same hath brought himself under condemnation. Now I say unto you, Go, and whosoever will not repent of his sins, the same shall not be numbered among my people. And this shall be observed from this time forward.

And it came to pass when Alma had heard these words, he wrote them down, that he might have them and that he might judge the people of that church according to the commandments of God.

And it came to pass that Alma went and judged those that had been taken in iniquity, according to the word of the Lord. And whosoever repented of their sins and did confess them, them he did number among the people of the church. And those that would not confess their sins and repent of their iniquity, the same were not numbered among the people of the church, and their names were blotted out. [16]

And now, all these things did Alma and his fellow laborers do, who were over the church. And they did admonish their brethren, and they were also admonished, everyone, by the word of God, according to his sins, or to the sins which he had committed, being commanded of God to pray without ceasing and to give thanks in all things. [17]

And now, it came to pass that the persecutions, which were inflicted on the church by the unbelievers became so great that the

---

[15] Mosiah 26: 1-26
[16] Mosiah 26: 28-36
[17] Mosiah 26: 38*-39

church began to murmur and complain to their leaders concerning the matter. And they did complain to Alma. And Alma laid the case before their King Mosiah. And Mosiah consulted with his priests.

And it came to pass that King Mosiah sent a proclamation throughout the land, round about, that there should not any unbeliever persecute any of those who belonged to the church of God. And there was a strict command throughout all the churches that there should be no persecutions among them, that there should be an equality among all men, that they should let no pride nor haughtiness disturb their peace, that every man should esteem his neighbor as himself, laboring with their own hands for their support. Yea, and all their priests and teachers should labor with their own hands for their support in all cases, save it were in sickness or in much want. And, doing these things, they did abound in the grace of God.

And there began to be much peace again in the land. And the people began to be very numerous and began to scatter abroad upon the face of the earth, yea, on the north and on the south, on the east and on the west, building large cities and villages in all quarters of the land. And the Lord did visit them and prosper them, and they became a large and a wealthy people.

Now the sons of Mosiah were numbered among the unbelievers. And also one of the sons of Alma was numbered among them, he being called Alma, after his father; nevertheless, he became a very wicked and an idolatrous man. And he was a man of many words, and did speak much flattery to the people; therefore, he led many of the people to do after the manner of his iniquities. And he became a great hinderment to the prosperity of the church of God, stealing away the hearts of the people, causing much dissension among the people, giving a chance for the enemy of God to exercise his power over them.

And now, it came to pass that while he was going about to destroy the church of God —for he did go about secretly with the sons of Mosiah seeking to destroy the church, and to lead astray the people of the Lord contrary to the commandments of God, or even the king—and, as I said unto you, as they were going about rebelling against God, behold, the angel of the Lord appeared unto them. And he descended as it were in a cloud. And he spake as it were with a voice of thunder, which caused the earth to shake upon which they stood. And so great was their astonishment that they fell to the earth and understood not the words which he spake unto them.

Nevertheless, he cried again, saying, Alma, arise, and stand forth, for why persecuteth thou the church of God? For the Lord hath said, This is my church, and I will establish it, and nothing shall overthrow it, save it is the transgression of my people.

And again, the angel said, Behold, the Lord hath heard the prayers of his people and also the prayers of his servant Alma, who is thy father. For he has prayed with much faith concerning thee, that thou mightest be brought to the knowledge of the truth. Therefore, for this purpose have I come to convince thee of the power and authority of God, that the prayers of his servants might be answered according to their faith.

And now, behold, can ye dispute the power of God? For behold, doth not my voice shake the earth? And can ye not also behold me before you? And I am sent from God. [18] And now, I say unto thee, Alma, Go thy way, and seek to destroy the church no more, that their prayers may be answered; and this, even if thou wilt of thyself be cast off.

And now, it came to pass that these were the last words which the angel spake unto Alma, and he departed. And now, Alma and those that were with him fell again to the earth, for great was their astonishment. For with their own eyes they had beheld an angel of the Lord. And his voice was as thunder, which shook the earth. And they knew that there was nothing, save the power of God, that could shake the earth and cause it to tremble as though it would part asunder.

And now, the astonishment of Alma was so great that he became dumb, that he could not open his mouth. Yea, and he became weak, even that he could not move his hands. Therefore, he was taken by those that were with him and carried helpless, even until he was laid before his father.

And they rehearsed unto his father all that had happened unto them. And his father rejoiced, for he knew that it was the

---

[18] Mosiah 27: 1-15

power of God. And he caused that a multitude should be gathered together, that they might witness what the Lord had done for his son and also for those that were with him. And he caused that the priests should assemble themselves together. And they began to fast and pray to the Lord, their God, that he would open the mouth of Alma, that he might speak, and also that his limbs might receive their strength, that the eyes of the people might be opened to see and know of the goodness and glory of God.

And it came to pass after they had fasted and prayed for the space of two days and two nights, the limbs of Alma received their strength. And he stood up and began to speak unto them, bidding them to be of good comfort.

For, said he, I have repented of my sins and have been redeemed of the Lord. Behold, I am born of the Spirit. And the Lord said unto me, Marvel not that all mankind, yea, men, and women, all nations, kindreds, tongues, and people must be born again, yea, born of God, changed from their carnal and fallen state to a state of righteousness, being redeemed of God, becoming his sons and daughters. And thus they become new creatures. And unless they do this, they can in no wise inherit the kingdom of God. I say unto you, Unless this be the case, they must be cast off.

And this I know because I was like to be cast off. Nevertheless, after wading through much tribulation, repenting nigh unto death, the Lord in mercy hath seen fit to snatch me out of an everlasting burning, and I am born of God. My soul hath been redeemed from the gall of bitterness and bonds of iniquity. I was in the darkest abyss. But now I behold the marvelous light of God.

My soul was racked with eternal torment; but I am snatched, and my soul is pained no more. I rejected my Redeemer and denied that which had been spoken of by our fathers. But now, that they may foresee that he will come, and that he remembereth every creature of his creating, he will make himself manifest unto all. Yea, every knee shall bow, and every tongue confess before him. Yea, even at the last day, when all men shall stand to be judged of him, then shall they confess that he is God. Then shall they confess, who live without God in the world, that the judgment of an everlasting punishment is just upon them. And they shall quake, and tremble, and shrink beneath the glance of his all-searching eye.

And now, it came to pass that Alma began from this time forward to teach the people, and those who were with Alma at the time the angel appeared unto them, traveling round about through all the land, publishing to all the people the things which they had heard and seen, and preaching the word of God in much tribulation, being greatly persecuted by those who were unbelievers, being smitten by many of them. But notwithstanding all this, they did impart much consolation to the church, confirming their faith, and exhorting them with long-suffering and much travail to keep the commandments of God.

And four of them were the sons of Mosiah; and their names were Ammon, and Aaron, and Omner, and Himni. These were the names of the sons of Mosiah. And they traveled throughout all the land of Zarahemla and among all the people who were under the reign of King Mosiah, zealously striving to repair all the injuries which they had done to the church, confessing all their sins, and publishing all the things which they had seen, and explaining the prophecies and the scriptures to all who desired to hear them.

And thus they were instruments in the hands of God in bringing many to the knowledge of the truth, yea, to the knowledge of their Redeemer. And how blessed are they! For they did publish peace. They did publish good tidings of good, and they did declare unto the people that the Lord reigneth. [19]

About 92 B.C.

Now it came to pass that after the sons of Mosiah had done all these things, they took a small number with them, and returned to their father, the king, and desired of him that he would grant unto them that they might, with those whom they had selected, go up to the land of Nephi, that they might preach the things which they had heard, and that they might impart the word of God to their brethren, the Lamanites; that perhaps they might bring them to the knowledge of the Lord their God, and convince them of the iniquity

---

[19] Mosiah 27: 16*-37

of their fathers, and that perhaps they might cure them of their hatred towards the Nephites; that they might also be brought to rejoice in the Lord their God, that they might become friendly to one another, and that there should be no more contentions in all the land which the Lord their God, had given them.

Now they were desirous that salvation should be declared to every creature, for they could not bear that any human soul should perish. Yea, even the very thoughts that any soul should endure endless torment did cause them to quake and tremble. And thus did the Spirit of the Lord work upon them, for they were the very vilest of sinners, and the Lord saw fit in his infinite mercy to spare them. Nevertheless, they suffered much anguish of soul because of their iniquities, and suffering much, fearing that they should be cast off forever.

And it came to pass that they did plead with their father many days that they might go up to the land of Nephi. And King Mosiah went and inquired of the Lord if he should let his sons go up among the Lamanites to preach the word.

And the Lord said unto Mosiah, Let them go up, for many shall believe on their words and they shall have eternal life. And I will deliver thy sons out of the hands of the Lamanites.

And it came to pass that Mosiah granted that they might go and do according to their request. And they took their journey into the wilderness, to go up to preach the word among the Lamanites. And I will give an account of their proceedings hereafter.

Now King Mosiah had no one to confer the kingdom upon, for there was not any of his sons who would accept of the kingdom. [20] Therefore, King Mosiah sent again among the people, yea, even a written word sent he among the people. And these were the words that were written, saying, Behold, O ye my people, or my brethren, for I esteem you as such—for I desire that ye should consider the cause which ye are called to consider, for ye are desirous to have a king.

Now I declare unto you that he to whom the kingdom doth rightly belong has declined and will not take upon him the kingdom. And now, if there should be another appointed in his

---

[20] Mosiah 28: 1-10

stead, behold, I fear there would rise contentions among you. And who knoweth but what my son, to whom the kingdom doth belong, should turn to be angry and draw away a part of this people after him, which would cause wars and contentions among you, which would be the cause of shedding much blood and perverting the way of the Lord, yea, and destroy the souls of many people.

Now I say unto you, Let us be wise and consider these things. For we have no right to destroy my son; neither should we have any right to destroy another, if he should be appointed in his stead. And if my son should turn again to his pride and vain things, he would recall the things which he had said and claim his right to the kingdom, which would cause him and also this people to commit much sin.

And now, let us be wise, and look forward to these things, and do that which will make for the peace of this people. Therefore, I will be your king the remainder of my days. Nevertheless, let us appoint judges to judge this people according to our law; and we will newly arrange the affairs of this people, for we will appoint wise men to be judges, that will judge this people according to the commandments of God.

Now it is better that a man should be judged of God than of man, for the judgments of God are always just, but the judgments of man are not always just. Now I say unto you that because all men are not just, it is not expedient that ye should have a king or kings to rule over you. [21] Therefore, choose you by the voice of this people, judges, that ye may be judged according to the laws which have been given you by our fathers, which are correct, and which were given them by the hand of the Lord.

Now it is not common that the voice of the people desireth anything contrary to that which is right. But it is common for the lesser part of the people to desire that which is not right. Therefore, this shall ye observe and make it your law to do your business by the voice of the people. And if the time comes that the voice of the people doth choose iniquity, then is the time that the judgments of God will come upon you. Yea, then is the time he

---

[21] Mosiah 29: 4-12, 16

will visit you with great destruction, even as he has hitherto visited this land.

And now, if ye have judges, and they do not judge you according to the law which has been given, ye can cause that they may be judged of a higher judge. If your higher judges do not judge righteous judgments, ye shall cause that a small number of your lower judges should be gathered together, and they shall judge your higher judges according to the voice of the people.

And I command you to do these things in the fear of the Lord. And I command you to do these things and that ye have no king, that if these people commit sins and iniquities, they shall be answered upon their own heads. For behold, I say unto you, The sins of many people have been caused by the iniquities of their kings. Therefore, their iniquities are answered upon the heads of their kings.

And now, I desire that this inequality should be no more in this land, especially among this my people. But I desire that this land be a land of liberty. And every man may enjoy his rights and privileges alike, so long as the Lord sees fit, that we may live and inherit the land, yea, even as long as any of our posterity remains upon the face of the land. [22]

And now, it came to pass after King Mosiah had sent these things forth among the people, they were convinced of the truth of his words. Therefore, they relinquished their desires for a king and became exceedingly anxious that every man should have an equal chance throughout all the land. Yea, and every man expressed a willingness to answer for his own sins.

Therefore, it came to pass that they assembled themselves together in bodies throughout the land to cast in their voices concerning who should be their judges, to judge them according to the law which had been given them. And they were exceedingly rejoiced because of the liberty which had been granted unto them.

And they did wax strong in love toward Mosiah; yea, they did esteem him more than any other man. For they did not look upon him as a tyrant, who was seeking for gain, yea, for that lucre which doth corrupt the soul. For he had not exacted riches of them; neither

---

[22] Mosiah 29: 25-32

had he delighted in the shedding of blood. But he had established peace in the land, and he had granted unto his people that they should be delivered from all manner of bondage. Therefore, they did esteem him, yea, exceedingly, beyond measure.

And it came to pass that they did appoint judges to rule over them, or to judge them according to the law. And this they did throughout all the land. And it came to pass that Alma was appointed to be the chief judge, he being also the high priest, his father having conferred the office upon him and had given him the charge concerning all the affairs of the church.

And now, it came to pass that Alma did walk in the ways of the Lord, and he did keep his commandments, and he did judge righteous judgments. And there was continual peace through the land.

And thus commenced the reign of the judges throughout all the land of Zarahemla, among all the people who were called the Nephites. And Alma was the first and chief judge. And it came to pass that his father died, being eighty and two years old, having lived to fulfil the commandments of God.

And it came to pass that Mosiah died also, in the thirty and third year of his reign, being sixty and three years old, making in the whole, five hundred and nine years from the time Lehi left Jerusalem. And thus ended the reign of the kings over the people of Nephi. And thus ended the days of Alma, who was the founder of the church. [23]

---

[23] Mosiah 29: 37-47

Chapter 6

The Order of the Priesthood

About 91 B.C.

Now it came to pass that in the first year of the reign of the judges over the people of Nephi, from this time forward, King Mosiah having gone the way of all the earth, having warred a good warfare, walking uprightly before God, leaving none to reign in his stead—nevertheless, he established laws, and they were acknowledged by the people; therefore, they were obliged to abide by the laws which he had made.

And it came to pass that in the first year of the reign of Alma in the judgment seat, there was a man brought before him to be judged, a man who was large, and was noted for his much strength. And he had gone about among the people, preaching to them that which he termed to be the word of God, bearing down against the church, declaring unto the people that every priest and teacher ought to become popular, and they ought not to labor with their own hands, but that they ought to be supported by the people.

And he also testified unto the people that all mankind should be saved at the last day, and that they need not fear nor tremble, but that they might lift up their heads and rejoice, for the Lord had created all men, and had also redeemed all men, and in the end, all men should have eternal life.

And it came to pass that he did teach these things so much that many did believe on his words, even so many that they began to support him and give him money. And he began to be lifted up in the pride of his heart, and to wear very costly apparel, yea, and even began to establish a church after the manner of his preaching.

And it came to pass as he was going to preach to those who believed on his word, he met a man who belonged to the church of God, yea, even one of their teachers. And he began to contend with him sharply, that he might lead away the people of the church. But the man withstood him, admonishing him with the words of God.

Now the name of the man was Gideon, and it was he who was an instrument in the hands of God in delivering the people of

Limhi out of bondage. Now because Gideon withstood him with the words of God, he was wroth with Gideon, and drew his sword and began to smite him. Now Gideon, being stricken with many years, therefore, he was not able to withstand his blows; therefore, he was slain by the sword.

And the man who slew him was taken by the people of the church and was brought before Alma to be judged according to the crime which he had committed. And it came to pass that he stood before Alma and pled for himself with much boldness. But Alma said unto him, Behold, this is the first time that priestcraft has been introduced among this people. And behold, thou art not only guilty of priestcraft, but hast endeavored to enforce it by the sword. And were priestcraft to be enforced among this people, it would prove their entire destruction.

And thou hast shed the blood of a righteous man, yea, a man who has done much good among this people. And were we to spare thee, his blood would come upon us for vengeance. Therefore, thou art condemned to die, according to the law which has been given us by Mosiah, our last king. And it has been acknowledged by this people; therefore, this people must abide by the law.

And it came to pass that they took him; and his name was Nehor; and they carried him upon the top of the hill Manti, and there he was caused, or rather did acknowledge, between the heavens and the earth, that what he had taught to the people was contrary to the word of God. And there he suffered an ignominious death.

Nevertheless, this did not put an end to the spreading of priestcraft through the land. For there were many who loved the vain things of the world, and they went forth preaching false doctrines. And this they did for the sake of riches and honor. Nevertheless, they durst not lie, if it were known, for fear of the law. For liars were punished. Therefore, they pretended to preach according to their belief. And now, the law could have no power on any man for his belief. And they durst not steal, for fear of the law; for such were punished. Neither durst they rob nor murder; for he that murdered was punished unto death.

But it came to pass that whosoever did not belong to the church of God began to persecute those that did belong to the church of God and had taken upon them the name of Christ. Yea, they did persecute them and afflict them with all manner of words, and this because of their humility; because they were not proud in their own eyes, and because they did impart the word of God, one with another, without money and without price.

And when the priests left their labor to impart the word of God unto the people, the people also left their labors to hear the word of God. And when the priest had imparted unto them the word of God, they all returned again diligently unto their labors. And the priest, not esteeming himself above his hearers, for the preacher was no better than the hearer, neither was the teacher any better than the learner. And thus they were all equal, and they did all labor, every man according to his strength. [1]

And now, because of the steadiness of the church, they began to be exceeding rich, having abundance of all things whatsoever they stood in need, an abundance of flocks, and herds, and fatlings of every kind, and also abundance of grain, and of gold, and of silver, and of precious things, and abundance of silk and fine twined linen, and all manner of good homely cloth.

And thus in their prosperous circumstances they did not send away any who were naked, or that were hungry, or that were athirst, or that were sick, or that had not been nourished. And they did not set their hearts upon riches. Therefore, they were liberal to all, both old and young, both bond and free, both male and female, whether out of the church or in the church, having no respect to persons, as to those who stood in need. And thus they did prosper and become far more wealthy than those who did not belong to their church.

For those who did not belong to their church did indulge themselves in sorceries, and in idolatry or idleness, and in babblings, and in envyings and strife, and wearing costly apparel, being lifted up in the pride of their own eyes, persecuting, lying, thieving, robbing, committing whoredoms, and murdering, and all

---

[1] Alma 1: 1-20, 26

manner of wickedness. Nevertheless, the law was put in force upon all those who did transgress it, inasmuch as it were possible. [2]

And it came to pass in the commencement of the fifth year of their reign, there began to be a contention among the people, for a certain man, being called Amlici, he being a very cunning man, yea, a wise man, as to the wisdom of the world, he being after the order of the man that slew Gideon by the sword, who was executed according to the law. Now this Amlici had, by his cunning, drawn away much people after him, even so much that they began to be very powerful. And they began to endeavor to establish Amlici to be a king over the people. Now this was alarming to the people of the church, and also to all those who had not been drawn away after the persuasions of Amlici; for they knew that according to their law that such things must be established by the voice of the people. Therefore, if it were possible that Amlici should gain the voice of the people, he, being a wicked man, would deprive them of their rights and privileges of the church, etc. For it was his intent to destroy the church of God.

And it came to pass that the people assembled themselves together throughout all the land, every man according to his mind, whether it were for or against Amlici, in separate bodies, having much dispute and wonderful contentions one with another. And thus they did assemble themselves together to cast in their voices concerning the matter. And they were laid before the judges.

And it came to pass that the voice of the people came against Amlici, that he was not made king over the people. Now this did cause much joy in the hearts of those who were against him; but Amlici did stir up those who were in his favor to anger against those who were not in his favor. And it came to pass that they gathered themselves together and did consecrate Amlici to be their king. Now when Amlici was made king over them, he commanded them that they should take up arms against their brethren; and this he did that he might subject them to him.

Now the people of Amlici were distinguished by the name of Amlici, being called Amlicites. And the remainder were called Nephites, or the people of God. Therefore, the people of the

Nephites were aware of the intent of the Amlicites; and, therefore, they did prepare to meet them. Yea, they did arm themselves with swords, and with cimeters, and with bows, and with arrows, and with stones, and with slings, and with all manner of weapons of war of every kind. And thus they were prepared to meet the Amlicites at the time of their coming. And there were appointed captains, and higher captains, and chief captains, according to their numbers.

And it came to pass that Amlici did arm his men with all manner of weapons of war of every kind. And he also appointed rulers and leaders over his people, to lead them to war against their brethren. And it came to pass that the Amlicites came upon the hill of Amnihu, which was east of the river Sidon, which ran by the land of Zarahemla. And there they began to make war with the Nephites.

Now Alma, being the chief judge and the governor of the people of Nephi, therefore, he went up with his people, yea, with his captains and chief captains, yea, at the head of his armies, against the Amlicites to battle. And they began to slay the Amlicites upon the hill east of Sidon. And the Amlicites did contend with the Nephites with great strength, insomuch that many of the Nephites did fall before the Amlicites. Nevertheless, the Lord did strengthen the hand of the Nephites, that they slew the Amlicites with a great slaughter, that they began to flee before them.

And it came to pass that the Nephites did pursue the Amlicites all that day and did slay them with much slaughter; insomuch that there was slain of the Amlicites twelve thousand five hundred thirty and two souls; and there was slain of the Nephites six thousand five hundred sixty and two souls.

And it came to pass that when Alma could pursue the Amlicites no longer, he caused that his people should pitch their tents in the valley of Gideon, the valley being called after that Gideon who was slain by the hand of Nehor with the sword. And in this valley the Nephites did pitch their tents for the night. And Alma sent spies to follow the remnant of the Amlicites, that he might know of their plans and their plots, whereby he might guard himself against them, that he might preserve his people from being destroyed. [3]

And it came to pass that on the morrow they returned into the camp of the Nephites in great haste, being greatly astonished and struck with much fear, saying, Behold, we followed the camp of the Amlicites; and to our great astonishment, in the land of Minon, above the land of Zarahemla, in the course of the land of Nephi, we saw a numerous host of the Lamanites. And behold, the Amlicites have joined them, and they are upon our brethren in that land; and they are fleeing before them, with their flocks, and their wives, and their children, towards our city. And except we make haste, they obtain possession of our city; and our fathers, and our wives, and our children be slain.

And it came to pass that the people of Nephi took their tents and departed out of the valley of Gideon towards their city, which was the city of Zarahemla. And behold, as they were crossing the river Sidon, the Lamanites and the Amlicites, being as numerous almost, as it were, as the sands of the sea, came upon them to destroy them.

Nevertheless, the Nephites, being strengthened by the hand of the Lord, having prayed mightily to him that he would deliver them out of the hands of their enemies, therefore, the Lord did hear their cries and did strengthen them; and the Lamanites and Amlicites did fall before them.

And it came to pass that Alma fought with Amlici with the sword, face to face; and they did contend mightily one with another. And it came to pass that Alma, being a man of God, being exercised with much faith, cried, saying, O Lord, have mercy and spare my life, that I may be an instrument in thy hands to save and protect this people. Now when Alma had said these words, he contended again with Amlici. And he was strengthened, insomuch that he slew Amlici with the sword. And he also contended with the king of the Lamanites; but the king of the Lamanites fled back from before Alma and sent his guards to contend with Alma, but

---

[3] Alma 2: 1-21

Alma with his guards contended with the guards of the king of the Lamanites until he slew and drove them back. [4]

And it came to pass that when they had all crossed the river Sidon, that the Lamanites and the Amlicites began to flee before them, notwithstanding they were so numerous that they could not be numbered. And they fled before the Nephites towards the wilderness, which was west and north, away beyond the borders of the land. And the Nephites did pursue them with their might and did slay them. [5]

And now, as many of the Lamanites and the Amlicites who had been slain upon the bank of the river Sidon were cast into the waters of Sidon. And behold, their bones are in the depths of the sea, and they are many. And the Amlicites were distinguished from the Nephites, for they had marked themselves with red in their foreheads after the manner of the Lamanites; nevertheless, they had not shorn their heads like unto the Lamanites. [6]

Now the Amlicites knew not that they were fulfilling the words of God when they began to mark themselves in their foreheads. Nevertheless, they had come out in open rebellion against God; therefore, it was expedient that the curse should fall upon them. Now I would that ye should see that they brought upon themselves the curse, and even so doth every man that is cursed bring upon himself his own condemnation.

Now it came to pass that not many days after the battle which was fought in the land of Zarahemla by the Lamanites and the Amlicites, that there was another army of the Lamanites came in upon the people of Nephi in the same place where the first army met the Amlicites. And it came to pass that there was an army sent to drive them out of their land.

Now Alma, himself, being afflicted with a wound, did not go up to battle at this time against the Lamanites; but he sent up a numerous army against them. And they went up, and slew many of the Lamanites, and drove the remainder of them out of the borders of their land. And then they returned again and began to

---

[4] Alma 2: 23-33
[5] Alma 2: 35-36
[6] Alma 3: 3-4

establish peace in the land, being troubled no more for a time with their enemies.

Now all these things were done, yea, all these wars and contentions were commenced and ended in the fifth year of the reign of the judges. And in one year were thousands and tens of thousands of souls sent to the eternal world, that they might reap their rewards according to their works, whether they were good or whether they were bad, to reap eternal happiness or eternal misery, according to the spirit which they listed to obey, whether it be a good spirit or a bad one. For every man receiveth wages of him whom he listeth to obey, and this according to the words of the spirit of prophecy. Therefore, let it be according to the truth. And thus ended the fifth year of the reign of the judges. [7]

Now it came to pass in the sixth year of the reign of the judges over the people of Nephi, there were no contentions nor wars in the land of Zarahemla; but the people were afflicted, yea, greatly afflicted for the loss of their brethren, and also for the loss of their flocks and herds, and also for the loss of their fields of grain, which were trodden underfoot and destroyed by the Lamanites. And so great were their afflictions that every soul had cause to mourn. And they believed that it was the judgments of God sent upon them because of their wickedness and their abominations. Therefore, they were awakened to a remembrance of their duty.

And they began to establish the church more fully. Yea, and many were baptized in the waters of Sidon and were joined to the church of God. Yea, they were baptized by the hand of Alma, who had been consecrated the high priest over the people of the church by the hand of his father Alma.

And it came to pass in the seventh year of the reign of the judges, there were about three thousand five hundred souls that united themselves to the church of God and were baptized. And thus ended the seventh year of the reign of the judges over the people of Nephi. And there was continual peace in all that time.

---

[7] Alma 3: 18-27

About 83 B.C.

And it came to pass in the eighth year of the reign of the judges, that the people of the church began to wax proud because of their exceeding riches, and their fine silks, and their fine twined linen, and because of their many flocks and herds, and their gold, and their silver, and all manner of precious things which they had obtained by their industry. And in all these things were they lifted up in the pride of their eyes, for they began to wear very costly apparel.

Now this was the cause of much affliction to Alma, yea, and to many of the people whom Alma had consecrated to be teachers, and priests, and elders over the church, for they saw and beheld with great sorrow that the people of the church began to be lifted up in the pride of their eyes and to set their hearts upon riches and upon the vain things of the world, that they began to be scornful, one towards another. And they began to persecute those that did not believe according to their own will and pleasure.

And thus in this eighth year of the reign of the judges, there began to be great contentions among the people of the church. Yea, there were envyings, and strifes, and malice, and persecutions, and pride, even to exceed the pride of those who did not belong to the church of God. And the wickedness of the church was a great stumbling block to those who did not belong to the church. And thus the church began to fail in its progress.

And it came to pass in the commencement of the ninth year, Alma saw the wickedness of the church; and he saw also that the example of the church began to lead those who were unbelievers on from one piece of iniquity to another, thus bringing on the destruction of the people. Yea, he saw great inequality among the people; some lifting themselves up with their pride, despising others, turning their backs upon the needy, and the naked, and those who were hungry, and those who were athirst, and those who were sick and afflicted; while others were abasing themselves, succoring those who stood in need of their succor, such as imparting their substance to the poor and the needy, feeding the hungry, and suffering all manner of afflictions for Christ's sake. [8]

And now, it came to pass that Alma, having seen the afflictions of the humble followers of God, and the persecutions which were heaped upon them by the remainder of his people, and seeing all their inequality, began to be very sorrowful. Nevertheless, the Spirit of the Lord did not fail him. And he selected a wise man who was among the elders of the church and gave him power according to the voice of the people, that he might have power to enact laws, according to the laws which had been given, and to put them in force according to the wickedness and the crimes of the people. Now this man's name was Nephihah, and he was appointed chief judge. And he sat in the judgment seat to judge and to govern the people.

Now Alma did not grant unto him the office of being high priest over the church, but he retained the office of high priest unto himself. But he delivered the judgment seat unto Nephihah. And this he did, that he himself might go forth among his people, or among the people of Nephi, that he might preach the word of God unto them, to stir them up in remembrance of their duty, and that he might pull down, by the word of God, all the pride and craftiness and all the contentions which were among his people, seeing no way that he might reclaim them, save it were in bearing down in pure testimony against them. [9]

Now it came to pass that Alma began to deliver the word of God unto the people, first in the land of Zarahemla and from thence throughout all the land. And these are the words which he spake to the people in the church which was established in the city of Zarahemla, according to his own record, saying:

I, Alma, having been consecrated by my father, Alma, to be a high priest over the church of God, he having power and authority from God to do these things, behold, I say unto you, that he began to establish a church in the land which was in the borders of Nephi, yea, the land which was called the land of Mormon. Yea, and he did baptize his brethren in the waters of Mormon.

---

[8] Alma 4: 1-13*
[9] Alma 4: 15-19

And behold, I say unto you, They were delivered out of the hands of the people of King Noah by the mercy and power of God. And behold, after that, they were brought into bondage by the hands of the Lamanites in the wilderness. Yea, I say unto you, They were in captivity, and again the Lord did deliver them out of bondage by the power of his word. And we were brought into this land. And here we began to establish the church of God throughout this land also.

And now, behold, I say unto you, my brethren, you that belong to this church, Have you sufficiently retained in remembrance the captivity of your fathers? Yea, and have you sufficiently retained in remembrance his mercy and long-suffering towards them? And moreover, have ye sufficiently retained in remembrance that he has delivered their souls from hell?

Behold, he changed their hearts; yea, he awaked them out of a deep sleep, and they awoke unto God. Behold, they were in the midst of darkness; nevertheless, their souls were illuminated by the light of the everlasting word. And I say unto you that they are saved. [10]

And now, I ask of you, On what conditions are they saved? Yea, what grounds had they to hope for salvation? Behold, I can tell you—Did not my father Alma believe in the words which were delivered by the mouth of Abinadi? And was he not a holy prophet? Did he not speak the words of God, and my father Alma believe them? And according to his faith there was a mighty change wrought in his heart. And behold, he preached the word unto your fathers, and a mighty change was also wrought in their hearts, and they humbled themselves and put their trust in the true and living God. [11]

And now, behold, I ask of you, my brethren of the church, Have ye spiritually been born of God? Have ye received his image in your countenances? Have ye experienced this mighty change in your hearts? Do ye exercise faith in the redemption of him who created you? Do you look forward with an eye of faith and view this mortal body raised in immortality, and this corruption raised

---

[10] Alma 5: 1-7*, 9*
[11] Alma 5: 10*-12*, 13*

in incorruption, to stand before God to be judged according to the deeds which have been done in the mortal body?

I say unto you, Can you imagine to yourselves that ye hear the voice of the Lord saying unto you in that day, Come unto me, ye blessed, for behold, your works have been the works of righteousness upon the face of the earth?

Or otherwise, can ye imagine yourselves brought before the tribunal of God, with your souls filled with guilt and remorse, having a remembrance of all your guilt, yea, a perfect remembrance of all your wickedness, yea, a remembrance that ye have set at defiance the commandments of God? [12]

And now, behold, I say unto you, my brethren, If ye have experienced a change of heart, and if ye have felt to sing the song of redeeming love, I would ask, Can ye feel so now?

Have ye walked, keeping yourselves blameless before God? Could ye say, if ye were called to die at this time, within yourselves, that ye have been sufficiently humble, that your garments have been cleansed and made white, through the blood of Christ, who will come to redeem his people from their sins?

Behold, are ye stripped of pride? I say unto you, If ye are not, ye are not prepared to meet God. Behold, ye must prepare quickly, for the kingdom of heaven is soon at hand, and such an one hath not eternal life.

Behold, I say, Is there one among you who is not stripped of envy? I say unto you that such an one is not prepared; and I would that he should prepare quickly; for the hour is close at hand, and he knoweth not when the time shall come; for such an one is not found guiltless.

And again I say unto you, Is there one among you that doth make a mock of his brother or that heapeth upon him persecutions? Wo unto such an one, for he is not prepared; and the time is at hand that he must repent, or he cannot be saved. Yea, even wo unto all ye workers of iniquity; repent, repent for the Lord God hath spoken it!

---

[12] Alma 5: 14-16, 18

Behold, he sendeth an invitation unto all men; for the arms of mercy are extended towards them. And he saith, Repent and I will receive you. Yea, he saith, Come unto me, and ye shall partake of the fruit of the tree of life. Yea, ye shall eat and drink of the bread and the waters of life freely. Yea, come unto me, and bring forth works of righteousness, and ye shall not be hewn down and cast into the fire. For behold, the time is at hand that whosoever bringeth forth not good fruit, or whosoever doeth not the works of righteousness, the same have cause to wail and mourn.

O ye workers of iniquity, ye that are puffed up in the vain things of the world, ye that have professed to have known the ways of righteousness, nevertheless, have gone astray, as sheep having no shepherd, notwithstanding a shepherd hath called after you and is still calling after you. But ye will not hearken unto his voice. And if ye will not hearken unto the voice of the good shepherd, to the name by which ye are called, behold, ye are not the sheep of the good shepherd. [13]

And now, my brethren, I would that ye should hear me, for I speak in the energy of my soul. For behold, I have spoken unto you plain, that ye cannot err, or have spoken according to the commandments of God, for I am called to speak after this manner, according to the holy order of God, which is in Christ Jesus. Yea, I am commanded to stand and testify unto this people the things which have been spoken by our fathers concerning the things which are to come. [14]

Behold, I have fasted and prayed many days that I might know these things of myself. And now, I do know of myself that they are true, for the Lord God hath made them manifest unto me by his Holy Spirit. And this is the spirit of revelation which is in me.

Yea, thus saith the Spirit, Repent, all ye ends of the earth, for the kingdom of heaven is soon at hand. Yea, the Son of God cometh in his glory, in his might, majesty, power, and dominion.

Yea, my beloved brethren, I say unto you that the Spirit saith, Behold, the glory of the King of all the earth and also the King of heaven shall very soon shine forth among all the children of men.

---

[13] Alma 5: 26-38*
[14] Alma 5: 43-44

And also the Spirit saith unto me, yea, crieth unto me with a mighty voice saying, Go forth and say unto this people, Repent; for except ye repent, ye can in no wise inherit the kingdom of heaven. [15]

And now, my beloved brethren, I say unto you, Yea, will ye persist in supposing that ye are better one than another? Yea, will ye persist in the persecutions of your brethren, who humble themselves and do walk after the holy order of God, wherewith they have been brought into this church, having been sanctified by the Holy Spirit? And they do bring forth works which are meet for repentance. Yea, and will you persist in turning your backs upon the poor and the needy and in withholding your substance from them?

And finally, all ye that will persist in your wickedness, I say unto you that these are they who shall be hewn down and cast into the fire, except they speedily repent. [16] For the names of the righteous shall be written in the book of life. And unto them will I grant an inheritance at my right hand.

And now, my brethren, What have ye to say against this? I say unto you, If ye speak against it, it matters not, for the word of God must be fulfilled.

For what shepherd is there among you, having many sheep, doth not watch over them, that the wolves enter not and devour his flock? And behold, if a wolf enter his flock, doth he not drive him out? Yea, and at the last, if he can, he will destroy him.

And now, I say unto you that the good shepherd doth call after you. And if you will hearken unto his voice, he will bring you into his fold and ye are his sheep. And he commandeth you that ye suffer no ravenous wolf to enter among you, that ye may not be destroyed.

And now, I, Alma, do command you in the language of him who hath commanded me, that ye observe to do the words which I have spoken unto you. I speak by way of command unto you that belong to the church; and unto those who do not belong to the church, I speak by way of invitation, saying, Come, and be

---

[15] Alma 5: 46*, 50-51
[16] Alma 5: 53*-56

baptized unto repentance, that ye also may be partakers of the fruit of the tree of life. [17]

And now, it came to pass that after Alma had made an end of speaking unto the people of the church which was established in the city of Zarahemla, he ordained priests and elders, by laying on his hands according to the order of God, to preside and watch over the church.

And it came to pass that whosoever did not belong to the church, who repented of their sins, were baptized unto repentance and were received into the church.

And it also came to pass that whosoever did belong to the church, that did not repent of their wickedness and humble themselves before God, I mean those who were lifted up in the pride of their hearts, the same were rejected, and their names were blotted out, that their names were not numbered among those of the righteous. And thus they began to establish the order of the church in the city of Zarahemla.

Now I would that ye should understand that the word of God was liberal unto all, that none were deprived of the privilege of assembling themselves together to hear the word of God. Nevertheless, the children of God were commanded that they should gather themselves together oft and join in fasting and mighty prayer in behalf of the welfare of the souls of those who knew not God.

And now, it came to pass that when Alma had made these regulations, he departed from them, yea, from the church which was in the city of Zarahemla, and went over upon the east of the river Sidon, into the valley of Gideon, there having been a city built which was called the city of Gideon, which was in the valley that was called Gideon, being called after the man who was slain by the hand of Nehor with the sword.

And Alma went and began to declare the word of God unto the church which was established in the valley of Gideon, according to the revelation of the truth of the word which had been spoken by his fathers, and according to the spirit of prophecy which was in him, according to the testimony of Jesus Christ, the

---

[17] Alma 5: 58-62

Son of God, who should come to redeem his people from their sins, and the holy order by which he was called. [18]

The words of Alma which he delivered to the people in Gideon, according to his own record:

Behold, my beloved brethren, seeing that I have been permitted to come unto you, therefore, I have come, having great hopes and much desire that I should find that ye had humbled yourselves before God and that ye had continued in the supplicating of his grace, that I should find that ye were blameless before him.[19]

I trust that ye are not lifted up in the pride of your hearts. Yea, I trust that ye have not set your hearts upon riches and the vain things of the world. Yea, I trust that you do not worship idols, but that ye do worship the true and the living God, and that ye look forward for the remission of your sins with an everlasting faith.

For behold, I say unto you, There be many things to come; and behold, there is one thing which is of more importance than they all. For behold, the time is not far distant that the Redeemer liveth, and cometh among his people. [20]

But behold, the Spirit hath said this much unto me, saying: Cry unto this people, saying, Repent ye, repent ye, and prepare the way of the Lord, and walk in his paths, which are straight. For behold, the kingdom of heaven is at hand, and the Son of God cometh upon the face of the earth.

And behold, he shall be born of Mary at Jerusalem, which is the land of our forefathers. She being a virgin, a precious and chosen vessel, who shall be overshadowed and conceive by the power of the Holy Ghost, and bring forth a son, yea, even the Son of God.

And he shall go forth, suffering pains, and afflictions, and temptations of every kind, and this that the word might be fulfilled which saith, He will take upon him the pains and the sicknesses of his people. And he will take upon him death, that he may loose the bands of death which bind his people.

---

[18] Alma 6: 1-8*
[19] Alma 7: 1*,3*
[20] Alma 7: 6*-7

And he will take upon him their infirmities, that his bowels may be filled with mercy, according to the flesh, that he may know according to the flesh how to succor his people according to their infirmities.

Now the Spirit knoweth all things, nevertheless, the Son of God suffereth according to the flesh, that he might take upon him the sins of his people, that he might blot out their transgressions, according to the power of his deliverance. And now, behold, this is the testimony which is in me. [21]

And now, my beloved brethren, do you believe these things? Behold, I say unto you, Yea, I know that ye believe them, and the way that I know that ye believe them is by the manifestation of the Spirit which is in me.

And now, because your faith is strong concerning that, yea, concerning the things which I have spoken, great is my joy, for I perceive that ye are in the paths of righteousness. I perceive that ye are in the path which leads to the kingdom of God. Yea, I perceive that ye are making his paths straight.

I perceive that it has been made known unto you by the testimony of his word that he cannot walk in crooked paths, neither doth he vary from that which he hath said. Neither hath he a shadow of turning from the right to the left, nor from that which is right to that which is wrong. Therefore, his course is one eternal round.

And he doth not dwell in unholy temples, neither can filthiness nor anything which is unclean be received into the kingdom of God. Therefore, I say unto you, the time shall come, yea, and it shall be at the last day, that he who is filthy shall remain in his filthiness.

And now, my beloved brethren, I have said these things unto you that I might awaken you to a sense of your duty to God, that ye may walk blameless before him, that ye may walk after the holy order of God, after which ye have been received. And now, I would that ye should be humble, and be submissive, and gentle, easy to be entreated, full of patience and long-suffering, being temperate in all things, being diligent in keeping the

---

[21] Alma 7: 9-13

commandments of God at all times, asking for whatsoever things ye stand in need, both spiritual and temporal, always returning thanks unto God for whatsoever things ye do receive.

And see that ye have faith, hope, and charity, and then ye will always abound in good works. And may the Lord bless you and keep your garments spotless, that ye may at last be brought to sit down with Abraham, Isaac, and Jacob, and the holy prophets who have been, ever since the world began, having your garments spotless, even as their garments are spotless in the kingdom of heaven, to go no more out.

And now, my beloved brethren, I have spoken these words unto you according to the Spirit which testifieth in me. And my soul doth exceedingly rejoice because of the exceeding diligence and heed which ye have given unto my word. And now, may the peace of God rest upon you, and upon your houses and lands, and upon your flocks and herds, and all that you possess, your women and your children, according to your faith and good works, from this time forth and forever. And thus I have spoken. Amen. [22]

About 78 B.C.

And now, it came to pass that as Alma was journeying from the land of Gideon southward, away to the land of Manti, behold, to his astonishment, he met the sons of Mosiah journeying towards the land of Zarahemla.

Now these sons of Mosiah were with Alma at the time the angel first appeared unto him, therefore Alma did rejoice exceedingly to see his brethren. And what added more to his joy, they were still his brethren in the Lord; yea, and they had waxed strong in the knowledge of the truth, for they were men of a sound understanding, and they had searched the scriptures diligently, that they might know the word of God. But this is not all. They had given themselves to much prayer and fasting; therefore, they had the spirit of prophecy and the spirit of revelation. And when they taught, they taught with power and authority, even as with the power and authority of God. And they

---

[22] Alma 7: 17, 19-27

had been teaching the word of God for the space of fourteen years among the Lamanites, having had much success in bringing many to the knowledge of the truth. Yea, by the power of their words, many were brought before the altar of God, to call on his name and confess their sins before him. [23]

Now these were their journeyings:

Having taken leave of their father Mosiah in the first year of the reign of the judges, they departed out of the land of Zarahemla and took their swords, and their spears, and their bows, and their arrows, and their slings; and this they did that they might provide food for themselves while in the wilderness. And thus they departed into the wilderness with their numbers which they had selected, to go up to the land of Nephi to preach the word of God unto the Lamanites. [24] And it came to pass when they had arrived in the borders of the land of the Lamanites, that they separated themselves and departed one from another, trusting in the Lord that they should meet again at the close of their harvest; for they supposed that great was the work which they had undertaken.

And assuredly it was great, for they had undertaken to preach the word of God to a wild, and a hardened, and a ferocious people, a people who delighted in murdering the Nephites, and robbing, and plundering them. And their hearts were set upon riches, or upon gold, and silver, and precious stones. Yet they sought to obtain these things by murdering and plundering, that they might not labor for them with their own hands. Thus they were a very indolent people, many of whom did worship idols. And the curse of God had fallen upon them because of the traditions of their fathers; notwithstanding, the promises of the Lord were extended unto them on the conditions of repentance.

Therefore, this was the cause for which the sons of Mosiah had undertaken the work, that perhaps they might bring them unto repentance, that perhaps they might bring them to know of the plan of redemption. Therefore, they separated themselves one from another and went forth among them, every man alone, according

---

[23] Alma 17: 1-4
[24] Alma 17: 6-8

to the word and power of God which was given unto him. [25]

And as Ammon entered the land of Ishmael, the Lamanites took him and bound him, as was their custom to bind all`the Nephites who fell into their hands and carry them before the king. And thus it was left to the pleasure of the king to slay them, or to retain them in captivity, or to cast them into prison, or to cast them out of his land according to his will and pleasure.

And thus Ammon was carried before the king who was over the land of Ishmael. And his name was Lamoni, and he was a descendant of Ishmael. And the king inquired of Ammon if it were his desire to dwell in the land among the Lamanites, or among his people.

And Ammon said unto him, Yea, I desire to dwell among this people for a time, yea, and perhaps until the day I die.

And it came to pass that King Lamoni was much pleased with Ammon and caused that his bands should be loosed. And he would that Ammon should take one of his daughters to wife, but Ammon said unto him, Nay, but I will be thy servant. Therefore, Ammon became a servant to King Lamoni.

And it came to pass that he was set among other servants to watch the flocks of Lamoni, according to the custom of the Lamanites. And after he had been in the service of the king three days, as he was with the Lamanitish servants going forth with their flocks to the place of water, which was called the water of Sebus, and all the Lamanites drive their flocks hither that they may have water; therefore, as Ammon and the servants of the king were driving forth their flocks to this place of water, behold, a certain number of the Lamanites, who had been with their flocks to water, stood and scattered the flocks of Ammon and the servants of the king. And they scattered them insomuch that they fled many ways.

Now the servants of the king began to murmur, saying, Now the king will slay us, as he has our brethren, because their flocks were scattered by the wickedness of these men. And they began to weep exceedingly, saying, Behold, our flocks are scattered already. Now they wept because of the fear of being slain.

---

[25] Alma 17: 13-17

Now when Ammon saw this, his heart was swollen within him with joy; for, said he, I will show forth my power unto these, my fellow servants, or the power which is in me, in restoring these flocks unto the king, that I may win the hearts of these, my fellow servants, that I may lead them to believe in my words. [26]

And it came to pass that he flattered them by his words, saying, My brethren, be of good cheer, and let us go in search of the flocks; and we will gather them together and bring them back unto the place of water; and thus we will reserve the flocks unto the king, and he will not slay us.

And it came to pass that they went in search of the flocks, and they did follow Ammon. And they rushed forth with much swiftness, and did head the flocks of the king, and did gather them together again to the place of water.

And those men again stood to scatter their flocks, but Ammon said unto his brethren, Encircle the flocks round about that they flee not; and I go and contend with these men who do scatter our flocks. Therefore, they did as Ammon commanded them, and he went forth and stood to contend with those who stood by the waters of Sebus. And they were in number not a few. [27]

But Ammon stood forth and began to cast stones at them with his sling; yea, with mighty power he did sling stones amongst them. And thus he slew a certain number of them, insomuch that they began to be astonished at his power. Nevertheless, they were angry because of the slain of their brethren, and they were determined that he should fall. Therefore, seeing that they could not hit him with their stones, they came forth with clubs to slay him.

But behold, every man that lifted his club to smite Ammon, he smote off their arms with his sword; for he did withstand their blows by smiting their arms with the edge of his sword, insomuch that they began to be astonished and began to flee before him.

And when he had driven them afar off, he returned, and they watered their flocks, and returned them to the pasture of the king, and then went in unto the king, bearing the arms, which had been

---

[26] Alma 17: 20-29
[27] Alma 17: 31-34

smitten off by the sword of Ammon, of those who sought to slay him. And they were carried in unto the king for a testimony of the things which they had done. [28]

And it came to pass that King Lamoni caused that his servants should stand forth and testify to all the things which they had seen concerning the matter. And when they had all testified to the things which they had seen, and he had learned of the faithfulness of Ammon in preserving his flocks, and also of his great power in contending against those who sought to slay him, he was astonished exceedingly and said, Surely this is more than a man. Behold, is not this the Great Spirit who doth send such great punishments upon this people because of their murders?

Now this was the tradition of Lamoni, which he had received from his father, that there was a Great Spirit. Notwithstanding they believed in a Great Spirit, they supposed that whatsoever they did was right. Nevertheless, Lamoni began to fear exceedingly with fear, lest he had done wrong in slaying his servants. [29]

And it came to pass that King Lamoni inquired of his servants, saying, Where is this man that has such great power? And they said unto him, Behold, he is feeding thy horses. Now the king had commanded his servants, previous to the time of the watering of their flocks, that they should prepare his horses and chariots and conduct him forth to the land of Nephi. For there had been a great feast appointed at the land of Nephi by the father of Lamoni, who was king over all the land.

Now when King Lamoni heard that Ammon was preparing his horses and his chariots, he was more astonished because of the faithfulness of Ammon, saying, Surely there has not been any servant among all my servants that has been so faithful as this man, for even he doth remember all my commandments to execute them. Now I surely know that this is the Great Spirit, and I would desire him that he come in unto me, but I durst not.

And it came to pass that when Ammon had made ready the horses and the chariots for the king and his servants, he went in unto the king. And he saw that the countenance of the king was

---

[28] Alma 17: 36-37*, 39
[29] Alma 18: 1-2, 5

changed; therefore, he was about to return out of his presence. And one of the king's servants said unto him, Rabbanah, which is being interpreted, powerful or great king, considering their kings to be powerful. And thus he said unto him, Rabbanah, the king desireth thee to stay.

Therefore, Ammon turned himself unto the king and said unto him, What wilt thou that I should do for thee, O King? And the king answered him not for the space of an hour, according to their time, for he knew not what he should say unto him.

And it came to pass that Ammon, being filled with the Spirit of God, therefore, he perceived the thoughts of the king, and he said unto him, Is it because thou hast heard that I defended thy servants and thy flocks, and slew seven of their brethren with the sling and with the sword, and smote off the arms of others in order to defend thy flocks and thy servants? Behold, is it this that causeth thy marvelings? [30]

King Lamoni did open his mouth and said unto him, Who art thou? Art thou that Great Spirit who knows all things?

Ammon answered and said unto him, I am not.

And the king said, How knowest thou the thoughts of my heart? Thou mayest speak boldly and tell me concerning these things, and also tell me by what power ye slew and smote off the arms of my brethren that scattered my flocks. And now, if thou wilt tell me concerning these things, whatsoever thou desirest, I will give unto thee. And if it were needed, I would guard thee with my armies, but I know that thou art more powerful than all they. Nevertheless, whatsoever thou desirest of me, I will grant it unto thee. [31]

And Ammon began to speak unto him with boldness and said unto him, Believest thou that there is a God?

And he answered and said unto him, I do not know what that meaneth.

And then Ammon said, Believest thou that there is a Great Spirit? And he said, Yea.

---

[30] Alma 18: 8-14, 16
[31] Alma 18: 18*-21

And Ammon said, This is God. And Ammon said unto him again, Believest thou that this Great Spirit, who is God, created all things which are in heaven and in the earth?

And he said, Yea, I believe that he created all things which are in the earth, but I do not know the heavens.

And Ammon said unto him, The heavens is a place where God dwells, and all his holy angels.

And King Lamoni said, Is it above the earth?

And Ammon said, Yea, and he looketh down upon all the children of men; and he knows all the thoughts and intents of the heart, for by his hand were they all created from the beginning.

And King Lamoni said, I believe all these things which thou hast spoken. Art thou sent from God?

Ammon said unto him, I am a man; and man in the beginning was created after the image of God. And I am called by his Holy Spirit to teach these things unto this people, that they may be brought to a knowledge of that which is just and true. And a portion of that Spirit dwelleth in me, which giveth me knowledge and also power, according to my faith and desires which are in God.

Now when Ammon had said these words, he began at the creation of the world, and also the creation of Adam, and told him all the things concerning the fall of man, and rehearsed and laid before him the records and the holy scriptures of the people, which had been spoken by the prophets, even down to the time that their father Lehi left Jerusalem. [32] And he also rehearsed unto them concerning the rebellions of Laman, and Lemuel, and the sons of Ishmael; yea, all their rebellions did he relate unto them. But this is not all, for he expounded unto them the plan of redemption, which was prepared from the foundation of the world. And he also made known unto them concerning the coming of Christ, and all the works of the Lord did he make known unto them. And it came to pass that after he had said all these things and expounded them to the king, that the king believed all his words.

---

[32] Alma 18: 24-36

And he began to cry unto the Lord, saying, O Lord, have mercy, according to thy abundant mercy which thou hast had upon the people of Nephi, have upon me and my people.

And now, when he had said this, he fell unto the earth as if he were dead. And it came to pass that his servants took him, and carried him in unto his wife, and laid him upon a bed. And he lay as if he were dead for the space of two days and two nights. And his wife, and his sons, and his daughters mourned over him after the manner of the Lamanites, greatly lamenting his loss. [33]

Now the queen, having heard of the fame of Ammon, therefore, she sent and desired that he should come in unto her. And it came to pass that Ammon did as he was commanded, and went in unto the queen, and desired to know what she would that he should do.

And she said unto him, The servants of my husband have made it known unto me that thou art a prophet of a holy God and that thou hast power to do many mighty works in his name. Therefore, if this is the case, I would that ye should go in and see my husband, for he has been laid upon his bed for the space of two days and two nights. And some say that he is not dead; but others say that he is dead, and that he stinketh, and that he ought to be placed in a sepulcher. But as for myself, to me he doth not stink.

Now this was what Ammon desired, for he knew that King Lamoni was under the power of God. He knew that the dark veil of unbelief being cast away from his mind, and the light which did light up his mind —which was the light of the glory of God, which was a marvelous light of his goodness —yea, this light had infused such joy into his soul, the cloud of darkness having been dispelled, and that the light of everlasting light was lit up in his soul; yea, he knew that this had overcome his natural frame, and he was carried away in God. Therefore, what the queen desired of him was his only desire. Therefore, he went in to see the king according as the queen had desired him. And he saw the king, and he knew that he was not dead.

---

[33] Alma 18: 38*-43

And he said unto the queen, He is not dead, but he sleepeth in God. And on the morrow he shall rise again; therefore, bury him not. [34] And it came to pass that she watched over the bed of her husband from that time even until that time on the morrow which Ammon had appointed that he should rise.

And it came to pass that he arose according to the words of Ammon. And as he arose, he stretched forth his hand unto the woman and said, Blessed be the name of God, and blessed art thou! For as sure as thou livest, behold, I have seen my Redeemer. And he shall come forth and be born of a woman, and he shall redeem all mankind who believe on his name.

Now when he had said these words, his heart was swollen within him, and he sank again with joy; and the queen also sank down, being overpowered by the Spirit.

Now Ammon, seeing the Spirit of the Lord poured out according to his prayers upon the Lamanites, his brethren, who had been the cause of so much mourning among the Nephites, or among all the people of God, because of their iniquities and their traditions, he fell upon his knees and began to pour out his soul in prayer and thanksgiving to God for what he had done for his brethren. And he was also overpowered with joy, and thus they all three had sunk to the earth.

Now when the servants of the king had seen that they had fallen, they also began to cry unto God; for the fear of the Lord had come upon them also. For it was they who had stood before the king and testified unto him concerning the great power of Ammon.

And it came to pass that they did call on the name of the Lord in their might, even till they had all fallen to the earth, save it were one of the Lamanitish women, whose name was Abish, she, having been converted unto the Lord for many years on account of a remarkable vision of her father, thus having been converted to the Lord, never had made it known. Therefore, when she saw that all the servants of Lamoni had fallen to the earth, and also her mistress, the queen, and the king, and Ammon lay prostrate upon the earth, she knew that it was the power of God. And supposing that this opportunity, by making known unto the people what had

---

[34] Alma 19: 2-8

happened among them, that by beholding this scene it would cause them to believe in the power of God, therefore, she ran forth from house to house, making it known unto the people. And they began to assemble themselves together unto the house of the king. And there came a multitude. And to their astonishment, they beheld the king, and the queen, and their servants prostrate upon the earth. And they all lay there as though they were dead. And they also saw Ammon, and behold, he was a Nephite. [35]

Now one of them, whose brother had been slain with the sword of Ammon, being exceeding angry with Ammon, drew his sword and went forth that he might let it fall upon Ammon to slay him. And as he lifted the sword to smite him, behold, he fell dead.

And it came to pass that when the multitude beheld that the man had fallen dead, who lifted the sword to slay Ammon, fear came upon them all, and they durst not put forth their hands to touch him or any of those who had fallen. And they began to marvel again among themselves what could be the cause of this great power, or what all these things could mean.

And it came to pass that there were many among them who said that Ammon was the Great Spirit, and others said he was sent by the Great Spirit. But others rebuked them all, saying that he was a monster, who had been sent from the Nephites to torment them.[36] And thus the contention began to be exceeding sharp among them.

And while they were thus contending, the woman servant who had caused the multitude to be gathered together came, and when she saw the contention which was among the multitude, she was exceeding sorrowful, even unto tears. And it came to pass that she went and took the queen by the hand, that perhaps she might raise her from the ground. And as soon as she touched her hand, she arose, and stood upon her feet, and cried with a loud voice, saying, O blessed Jesus, who has saved me from an awful hell! O blessed God, have mercy upon this people!

And when she had said this, she clapped her hands, being filled with joy, speaking many words which were not understood. And when she had done this, she took the king Lamoni by the

---

[35] Alma 19: 11-18
[36] Alma 19: 22, 24-26

hand. And behold, he arose and stood upon his feet, and he immediately, seeing the contention among his people, went forth and began to rebuke them and to teach them the words which he had heard from the mouth of Ammon. And as many as heard his words believed and were converted unto the Lord. But there were many among them who would not hear his words; therefore, they went their way.

And it came to pass that when Ammon arose, he also administered unto them, and also did all the servants of Lamoni. And they did all declare unto the people the selfsame thing, that their hearts had been changed, that they had no more desire to do evil. And behold, many did declare unto the people that they had seen angels and had conversed with them, and thus they had told them things of God, and of his righteousness.

And it came to pass that there were many that did believe in their words; and as many as did believe were baptized. And they became a righteous people, and they did establish a church among them. And thus the work of the Lord did commence among the Lamanites. Thus the Lord did begin to pour out his Spirit upon them. And we see that his arm is extended to all people who will repent and believe on his name. [37]

And thousands were brought to the knowledge of the Lord, yea, thousands were brought to believe in the traditions of the Nephites, and they were taught the records and the prophecies which were handed down, even to the present time.

And as sure as the Lord liveth, so sure as many as believed, or as many as were brought to the knowledge of the truth through the preaching of Ammon and his brethren, according to the spirit of revelation, and of prophecy, and the power of God working miracles in them, yea, I say unto you, as the Lord liveth, as many of the Lamanites as believed in their preaching and were converted unto the Lord, never did fall away, for they became a righteous people. They did lay down the weapons of their rebellion, that they did not fight against God anymore, neither against any of their brethren.

Now these are they who were converted unto the Lord: the

---

[37] Alma 19: 28-36

people of the Lamanites who were in the land of Ishmael, and also of the people of the Lamanites who were in the land of Middoni, and also of the people of the Lamanites who were in the city of Nephi, and also of the people of the Lamanites who were in the land of Shilom, and who were in the land of Shemlon, and in the city of Lemuel, and in the city of Shimnilon. And these are the names of the cities of the Lamanites which were converted unto the Lord. And these are they that laid down the weapons of their rebellion, yea, all their weapons of war; and they were all Lamanites.

And the Amalekites were not converted, save only one; neither were any of the Amulonites. But they did harden their hearts and also the hearts of the Lamanites in that part of the land wheresoever they dwelt, yea, and all their villages and all their cities. Therefore, we have named all the cities of the Lamanites in which they did repent and come to the knowledge of the truth and were converted. [38] And it came to pass that they called their name Anti-Nephi-Lehis. And they were called by this name and were no more called Lamanites. And they began to be a very industrious people. Yea, and they were friendly with the Nephites, therefore, they did open a correspondence with them. And the curse of God did no more follow them. [39]

About 76 B.C.

And it came to pass that the Amalekites, and the Amulonites, and the Lamanites in the land of Amulon, and also in the land of Helam, and who were in the land of Jerusalem, and in fine, in all the land round about, who had not been converted, and had not taken upon them the name of Anti-Nephi-Lehi, were stirred up by the Amalekites and by the Amulonites to anger against their brethren. And their hatred became exceeding sore against them, even insomuch that they began to rebel against their king, insomuch that they would not that he should be their king;

---

[38] Alma 23: 5-15
[39] Alma 23: 17-18

therefore, they took up arms against the people of Anti-Nephi-Lehi. [40]

Now when Ammon, and his brethren, and all those who had come up with him saw the preparations of the Lamanites to destroy their brethren, they came forth to the land of Midian, and there Ammon met all his brethren. And from thence they came to the land of Ishmael, that they might hold a council with Lamoni, and also with his brother, what they should do to defend themselves against the Lamanites.

Now there was not one soul among all the people who had been converted unto the Lord that would take up arms against their brethren. Nay, they would not even make any preparations for war. Yea, and also their king commanded them that they should not. [41] And this they did, it being in their view a testimony to God, and also to men, that they never would use weapons again for the shedding of man's blood. And this they did, vouching and covenanting with God that rather than shed the blood of their brethren, they would give up their own lives. And rather than take away from a brother, they would give unto him. And rather than spend their days in idleness, they would labor abundantly with their hands.

And thus we see that when these Lamanites were brought to believe and to know the truth, they were firm and would suffer even unto death, rather than commit sin. And thus we see that they buried the weapons of peace, or they buried the weapons of war for peace.

And it came to pass that their brethren, the Lamanites, made preparations for war and came up to the land of Nephi for the purpose of destroying the king, and to place another in his stead, and also of destroying the people of Anti-Nephi-Lehi out of the land.

Now when the people saw that they were coming against them, they went out to meet them, and prostrated themselves before them to the earth, and began to call on the name of the Lord. And thus they were in this attitude when the Lamanites

---

[40] Alma 24: 1*-2
[41] Alma 24: 5*-6

began to fall upon them and began to slay them with the sword. And thus without meeting any resistance, they did slay a thousand and five of them. And we know that they are blessed, for they have gone to dwell with their God.

Now when the Lamanites saw that their brethren would not flee from the sword, neither would they turn aside to the right hand or to the left, but that they would lie down, and perish, and praise God, even in the very act of perishing under the sword — now when the Lamanites saw this, they did forbear from slaying them. And there were many whose hearts had swollen in them for those of their brethren who had fallen under the sword, for they repented of the things which they had done.

And it came to pass that they threw down their weapons of war, and they would not take them again, for they were stung for the murders which they had committed. And they came down even as their brethren, relying upon the mercies of those whose arms were lifted to slay them.

And it came to pass that the people of God were joined that day by more than the number who had been slain. And those who had been slain were righteous people, therefore, we have no reason to doubt but what they are saved. And there was not a wicked man slain among them. But there were more than a thousand brought to the knowledge of the truth. Thus we see that the Lord worketh in many ways to the salvation of his people.

Now the greatest number of those of the Lamanites who slew so many of their brethren were Amalekites and Amulonites, the greatest number of whom were after the order of the Nehors. [42]

And behold now it came to pass that those Lamanites were more angry because they had slain their brethren; therefore they swore vengeance upon the Nephites. And they did no more attempt to slay the people of Anti-Nephi-Lehi; but they took their armies, and went over into the borders of the land of Zarahemla, and fell upon the people who were in the land of Ammonihah and destroyed them. And after that they had many battles with the Nephites, in the which they were driven and slain. [43]

---

[42] Alma 24: 18-28
[43] Alma 25: 1*-3

And thus there was a tremendous battle, yea, even such an one as never had been known among all the people in the land from the time Lehi left Jerusalem. Yea, and tens of thousands of the Lamanites were slain and scattered abroad. Yea, and also there was a tremendous slaughter among the people of Nephi. Nevertheless, the Lamanites were driven and scattered, and the people of Nephi returned again to their land.

And now, this was a time that there was a great mourning and lamentation heard throughout all the land among all the people of Nephi, yea, the cry of widows mourning for their husbands, and also of fathers mourning for their sons, and the daughter for the brother, yea, the brother for the father. And thus the cry of mourning was heard among every one of them, mourning for their kindred who had been slain. And now, surely this was a sorrowful day, yea, a time of solemnity and a time of much fasting and prayer. And thus ended the fifteenth year of the reign of the judges of the people of Nephi. [44]

And from the first year to the fifteenth has brought to pass the destruction of many thousand lives. Yea, and many thousands are mourning the loss of their kindred, because they have reason to fear, according to the promises of the Lord, that they are consigned to a state of endless wo. While many thousands of others truly mourn for the loss of their kindred, yet they rejoice and exult in the hope, and even know, according to the promises of the Lord, that they are raised to dwell at the right hand of God, in a state of never-ending happiness.

And thus we see how great the inequality of man is, because of sin, and transgression, and the power of the devil, which comes by the cunning plans which he hath devised to ensnare the hearts of men. And thus we see the great call of the diligence of men to labor in the vineyards of the Lord. And thus we see the great reason of sorrow and also of rejoicing—sorrow because of death and destruction among men, and joy because of the light of Christ unto life. [45]

---

[44] Alma 28: 2-7
[45] Alma 28: 10, 11*-14

Chapter 7

The Cause of Christians

About 75 B.C.

And it came to pass that the Amalekites, because of their loss, were exceeding angry. And when they saw that they could not seek revenge from the Nephites, they began to stir up the people in anger against their brethren, the people of Anti-Nephi-Lehi; therefore, they began again to destroy them. Now this people again refused to take their arms, and they suffered themselves to be slain according to the desires of their enemies.

Now when Ammon and his brethren saw this work of destruction among those whom they so dearly beloved, and among those who had so dearly beloved them—for they were treated as though they were angels sent from God to save them from everlasting destruction—therefore, when Ammon and his brethren saw this great work of destruction, they were moved with compassion, and they said unto the king, Let us gather together this people of the Lord, and let us go down to the land of Zarahemla, to our brethren, the Nephites, and flee out of the hands of our enemies, that we be not destroyed.

But the king said unto them, Behold, the Nephites will destroy us because of the many murders and sins we have committed against them.

And Ammon said, I will go and inquire of the Lord; and if he saith unto us, go down unto our brethren, will ye go?

And the king said unto him, Yea, if the Lord saith unto us, go, we will go down unto our brethren, and we will be their slaves until we repair unto them the many murders and sins which we have committed against them.

But Ammon said unto him, It is against the law of our brethren, which was established by my father, that there should be any slaves among them. Therefore, let us go down and rely upon the mercies of our brethren.

But the king said unto him, Inquire of the Lord; and if he saith unto us, go, we will go; otherwise, we will perish in the land.

And it came to pass that Ammon went and inquired of the Lord, and the Lord said unto him, Get this people out of this land, that they perish not; for Satan has great hold on the hearts of the Amalekites, who do stir up the Lamanites to anger against their brethren to slay them; therefore, get thee out of this land. And blessed are this people in this generation, for I will preserve them.

And now, it came to pass that Ammon went and told the king all the words which the Lord had said unto him. And they gathered together all their people, yea, all the people of the Lord, and did gather together all their flocks and herds, and departed out of the land, and came into the wilderness which divided the land of Nephi from the land of Zarahemla, and came over near the borders of the land.

And it came to pass that Ammon said unto them, Behold, I and my brethren will go forth into the land of Zarahemla, and ye shall remain here until we return. And we will try the hearts of our brethren, whether they will that ye shall come into their land.

And it came to pass that as Ammon was going forth into the land, that he and his brethren met Alma, over in the place of which has been spoken. And behold, this was a joyful meeting. [1]

And now, it came to pass that Alma conducted his brethren back to the land of Zarahemla, even to his own house. And they went and told the chief judge all the things that had happened unto them in the land of Nephi among their brethren, the Lamanites. And it came to pass that the chief judge sent a proclamation throughout all the land, desiring the voice of the people concerning the admitting their brethren, who were the people of Anti-Nephi-Lehi.

And it came to pass that the voice of the people came, saying, Behold, we will give up the land of Jershon, which is on the east by the sea, which joins the land Bountiful. And behold, we will set our armies between the land Jershon and the land Nephi, that we may protect our brethren in the land Jershon. [2] And we will guard them from their enemies with our armies, on conditions they will

---

[1] Alma 27: 2*-16
[2] Alma 27: 20-22*, 23*

give us a portion of their substance to assist us, that we may
maintain our armies.

And they went down into the land of Jershon and took
possession of the land of Jershon. And they were called by the
Nephites the people of Ammon. Therefore, they were
distinguished by that name ever after. And they were among the
people of Nephi, and also numbered among the people who were
of the church of God. And they were also distinguished for their
zeal towards God and also towards men. For they were perfectly
honest and upright in all things, and they were firm in the faith of
Christ, even unto the end. [3]

And it came to pass in the seventeenth year of the reign of the
judges there was continual peace. But it came to pass in the latter
end of the seventeenth year, there came a man into the land of
Zarahemla, and he was antichrist. For he began to preach unto the
people against the prophecies which had been spoken by the
prophets concerning the coming of Christ.

Now there was no law against a man's belief, for it was
strictly contrary to the commands of God that there should be a
law which should bring men onto unequal grounds. For thus saith
the scripture, Choose ye this day whom ye will serve. [4]

Now if a man desired to serve God, it was his privilege, or
rather, if he believed in God, it was his privilege to serve him. But
if he did not believe in him, there was no law to punish him. But if
he murdered, he was punished unto death; and if he robbed, he
was also punished; and if he stole, he was also punished; and if he
committed adultery, he was also punished; yea, for all this
wickedness they were punished. For there was a law that men
should be judged according to their crimes, nevertheless, there
was no law against a man's belief. Therefore, a man was punished
only for the crimes which he had done. Therefore, all men were on
equal grounds.

And this antichrist, whose name was Korihor—and the law
could have no hold upon him, began to preach unto the people
that there should be no Christ. And after this manner did he

---

[3] Alma 27: 24*, 26*-27
[4] Joshua 24: 14-15

preach, saying, O ye that are bound down under a foolish and a vain hope, why do ye yoke yourselves with such foolish things? Why do ye look for a Christ? For no man can know of anything which is to come.

Behold, these things which ye call prophecies, which ye say are handed down by holy prophets, behold, they are foolish traditions of your fathers. How do ye know of their surety? Behold, ye cannot know of things which ye do not see, therefore, ye cannot know that there shall be a Christ.

Ye look forward and say that ye see a remission of your sins; but behold, it is the effect of a frenzied mind. And this derangement of your minds comes because of the traditions of your fathers, which lead you away into a belief of things which are not so.

And many more such things did he say unto them, telling them that there could be no atonement made for the sins of men, but every man fared in this life according to the management of the creature. Therefore, every man prospered according to his genius, and that every man conquered according to his strength. And whatsoever a man did was no crime. And thus he did preach unto them, leading away the hearts of many, causing them to lift up their heads in their wickedness, yea, leading away many women and also men to commit whoredoms, telling them that when a man was dead, that was the end thereof. [5]

Now when the high priest and the chief judge saw the hardness of his heart, yea, when they saw that he would revile even against God, they would not make any reply to his words, but they caused that he should be bound. And they delivered him up into the hands of the officers and sent him to the land of Zarahemla, that he might be brought before Alma and the chief judge, who was governor over all the land.

And it came to pass that when he was brought before Alma and the chief judge, he did go on in the same manner as he did in the land of Gideon. Yea, he went on to blaspheme, and he did rise up in great swelling words before Alma and did revile against the priests and teachers, accusing them of leading away the people

---

[5] Alma 30: 5-18

after the silly traditions of their fathers, for the sake of glutting in the labors of the people.

Now Alma said unto him, Thou knowest that we do not glut ourselves upon the labors of this people. For behold, I have labored, even from the commencement of the reign of the judges until now, with mine own hands for my support, notwithstanding my many travels round about the land to declare the word of God unto my people. [6]

And now, if we do not receive anything for our labors in the church, what doth it profit us to labor in the church, save it were to declare the truth, that we may have rejoicings in the joy of our brethren? And now believest thou that we deceive this people? That causes such joy in their hearts?

And Korihor answered him, Yea.

And Alma said unto him: Believest thou that there is a God?

And he answered, Nay.

Now Alma said unto him, Will ye deny again that there is a God and also deny the Christ? For behold, I say unto you, I know there is a God and also that Christ shall come. And now, what evidence have ye that there is no God, or that Christ cometh not? I say unto you that ye have none, save it be your word only. But behold, I have all things as a testimony that these things are true. And ye also have all things as a testimony unto you that they are true. And will ye deny them? [7]

And now, Korihor said unto Alma, If thou wilt show me a sign, that I may be convinced that there is a God, yea, show unto me that he hath power, and then will I be convinced of the truth of thy words.

But Alma said unto him, Thou hast had signs enough. Will ye tempt your God? Will ye say, Show unto me a sign, when ye have the testimony of all these thy brethren, and also all the holy prophets? The scriptures are laid before thee. Yea, and all things denote there is a God, yea, even the earth and all things that are upon the face of it, yea, and its motion. Yea, and also all the planets which move in their regular form do witness that there is a

---

[6] Alma 30: 29-32
[7] Alma 30: 34-41*

Supreme Creator. And yet do ye go about, leading away the hearts of this people, testifying unto them there is no God? And yet will ye deny against all these witnesses?

And he said, Yea, I will deny, except ye shall show me a sign.

And now, it came to pass that Alma said unto him, Behold, I am grieved because of the hardness of your heart, yea, that ye will still resist the spirit of the truth, that thy soul may be destroyed. But behold, it is better that thy soul should be lost than that thou shouldest be the means of bringing many souls down to destruction by thy lying and by thy flattering words. Therefore, if thou shalt deny again, behold, God shall smite thee that thou shalt become dumb, that thou shalt never open thy mouth any more, that thou shalt not deceive this people any more.

Now Korihor said unto him, I do not deny the existence of a God, but I do not believe that there is a God. And I say also that ye do not know that there is a God. And except ye show me a sign, I will not believe.

Now Alma said unto him, This will I give unto thee for a sign, that thou shalt be struck dumb according to my words. And I say that in the name of God ye shall be struck dumb, that ye shall no more have utterance.

Now when Alma had said these words, Korihor was struck dumb, that he could not have utterance, according to the words of Alma. And now, when the chief judge saw this, he put forth his hand and wrote unto Korihor, saying, Art thou convinced of the power of God? In whom did ye desire that Alma should show forth his sign? Would ye that he should afflict others to show unto thee a sign? Behold, he has showed unto you a sign. And now, will ye dispute more?

And Korihor put forth his hand and wrote, saying, I know that I am dumb, for I cannot speak; and I know that nothing, save it were the power of God, could bring this upon me. Yea, and I also knew that there was a God; but behold, the devil hath deceived me; for he appeared unto me in the form of an angel and said unto me, Go and reclaim this people, for they have all gone astray after an unknown god. And he said unto me, There is no God. Yea, and he taught me that which I should say.

And I have taught his words. And I taught them because they were pleasing unto the carnal mind. And I taught them, even until I had much success, insomuch that I verily believed that they were true. And for this cause I withstood the truth, even until I have brought this great curse upon me.

Now when he had said this, he besought that Alma should pray unto God that the curse might be taken from him. But Alma said unto him, If this curse should be taken from thee, thou wouldest again lead away the hearts of this people. Therefore, it shall be unto thee, even as the Lord will.

And it came to pass that the curse was not taken off of Korihor; but he was cast out, and went about from house to house, begging for his food. Now the knowledge of what had happened unto Korihor was immediately published throughout all the land. Yea, the proclamation was sent forth by the chief judge to all the people in the land, declaring unto those who had believed in the words of Korihor that they must speedily repent, lest the same judgments would come unto them. And it came to pass that they were all convinced of the wickedness of Korihor, therefore, they were all converted again unto the Lord. And this put an end to the iniquity after the manner of Korihor.

And Korihor did go about from house to house, begging food for his support. And it came to pass that as he went forth among a people, who had separated themselves from the Nephites, and called themselves Zoramites, being led by a man whose name was Zoram, behold, he was run upon and trodden down, even until he was dead. And thus we see the end of him who perverteth the ways of the Lord. And thus we see that the devil will not support his children at the last day, but doth speedily drag them down to hell. [8]

About 74 B.C.

Now it came to pass that after the end of Korihor, Alma, having received tidings that the Zoramites were perverting the ways of the Lord, and that Zoram, who was their leader, was

---

[8] Alma 30: 42-59*, 60

leading the hearts of the people to bow down to dumb idols, etc., his heart again began to sicken because of the iniquity of the people.

Now the Zoramites had gathered themselves together in a land which they called Antionum, which was east of the land of Zarahemla, which lay nearly bordering upon the seashore, which was south of the land of Jershon, which also bordered upon the wilderness south, which wilderness was full of the Lamanites. Now the Nephites greatly feared that the Zoramites would enter into a correspondence with the Lamanites and that it would be the means of great loss on the part of the Nephites.

And now, as the preaching of the word had had a greater tendency to lead the people to do that which was just, yea, it had had more powerful effect upon the minds of the people than the sword or anything else which had happened unto them, there-fore, Alma thought it was expedient that they should try the virtue of the word of God. Therefore, he took Ammon, and Aaron, and Omner. And Himni he did leave in the church in Zarahemla. But the former three he took with him, and also Amulek and Zeezrom, who were at Melek. And he also took two of his sons. [9]

And it came to pass that they did go forth and began to preach the word of God unto the people, entering into their synagogues and into their houses. Yea, and even they did preach the word in their streets. And it came to pass that after much labor among them, they began to have success among the poor class of people. For behold, they were cast out of the synagogues because of the coarseness of their apparel. Therefore, they were not permitted to enter into their synagogues to worship God, being esteemed as filthiness. Therefore, they were poor; yea, they were esteemed by their brethren as dross. Therefore, they were poor as to things of the world, and also they were poor in heart.

Now as Alma was teaching and speaking unto the people upon the hill Onidah, there came a great multitude unto him, who were those of whom we have been speaking, who were poor in heart, because of their poverty as to the things of the world. And they came unto Alma, and the one who was the foremost among

---

[9] Alma 31: 1, 3-6

them said unto him, Behold, what shall these my brethren do? For
they are despised of all men because of their poverty; yea, and
more especially by our priests, for they have cast us out of our
synagogues, which we have labored abundantly to build with our
own hands. And they have cast us out because of our exceeding
poverty, and we have no place to worship our God. And behold,
what shall we do?

And now, when Alma heard this, he turned him about, his
face immediately towards him, and he beheld with great joy, for
he beheld that their afflictions had truly humbled them and that
they were in a preparation to hear the word. Therefore, he did say
no more to the other multitude, but he stretched forth his hand
and cried unto those whom he beheld, who were truly penitent.

And said unto them, I behold that ye are lowly in heart, and
if so, blessed are ye. Behold, thy brother hath said, What shall we
do? For we are cast out of our synagogues, that we cannot
worship our God.

Behold, I say unto you, Do ye suppose that ye cannot
worship God, save it be in your synagogues only? And moreover,
I would ask, Do ye suppose that ye must not worship God only
once in a week? [10]

Behold, I say unto you, If ye suppose that ye cannot worship
God, ye do greatly err, and ye ought to search the scriptures. If ye
suppose that they have taught you this, ye do not understand
them. Do ye remember to have read what Zenos, the prophet of
old, has said concerning prayer or worship?

For he said, Thou art merciful, O God, for thou hast heard my
prayer, even when I was in the wilderness. [11] Yea, O God, and
thou wast merciful unto me when I did cry unto thee in my field.
And again, O God, when I did turn to my house thou didst hear
me in my prayer. And when I did turn unto my closet, O Lord,
and prayed unto thee, thou didst hear me. Yea, thou art merciful
unto thy children when they cry unto thee to be heard of thee, and
not of men. And thou wilt hear them.

---

[10] Alma 32: 1-11
[11] Alma 33: 2*-4*

And thou didst hear me because of mine afflictions and my sincerity. And it is because of thy Son, that thou hast been thus merciful unto me. Therefore, I will cry unto thee in all mine afflictions; for in thee is my joy. For thou hast turned thy judgments away from me because of thy Son. [12]

Now, behold my brethren, I would ask if ye have read the scriptures? If ye have, how can ye disbelieve on the Son of God? Behold, he was spoken of by Moses; yea, and behold, a type was raised up in the wilderness, that whosoever would look upon it might live. And many did look and live. [13] But few understood the meaning of those things, and this because of the hardness of their hearts. There were many who were so hardened that they would not look, therefore, they perished. O my brethren, if ye could be healed by merely casting about your eyes, that ye might be healed, would ye not behold quickly? [14]

And now, behold, I say unto you, and I would that ye should remember, that God is merciful unto all who believe on his name. Therefore, he desireth, in the first place that ye should believe, yea, even on his word.

And now, he imparteth his word by angels unto men—yea, not only men, but women also. Now this is not all. Little children do have words given unto them many times, which confound the wise and the learned.

And now, my beloved brethren, as ye have desired to know of me what ye shall do because ye are afflicted and cast out, [15] behold, if ye will awake, and arouse your faculties, even to an experiment upon my words, and exercise a particle of faith, yea, even if ye can no more than desire to believe, let this desire work in you, even until ye believe in a manner that ye can give place for a portion of my words. [16] Faith is not to have a perfect knowledge of things. Therefore, if ye have faith, ye hope for things which are not seen, which are true. [17]

---

[12] Alma 33: 5*-8, 11
[13] Alma 33: 14,19 (Compare Numbers 21: 5-9)
[14] Alma 33: 20*,21*
[15] Alma 32: 22-24*
[16] Alma 32: 27*
[17] Alma 32: 21*

Yea, there are many who do say, If thou wilt show unto us a sign from heaven, then we shall know of a surety, then we shall believe. Now I ask, Is this faith? Behold, I say unto you, Nay. For if a man knoweth a thing, he hath no cause to believe, for he knoweth it. And now, how much more cursed is he that knoweth the will of God and doeth it not, than he that only believeth, or only hath cause to believe, and falleth into transgression? Now of this thing ye must judge. Behold, I say unto you that it is on the one hand, even as it is on the other. And it shall be unto every man according to his work. [18]

Now as I said concerning faith, that it was not a perfect knowledge, even so it is with my words. Ye cannot know of their surety at first unto perfection, any more than faith is a perfect knowledge. [19]

Now we will compare the word unto a seed. Now if ye give place that a seed may be planted in your heart, behold, if it be a true seed, or a good seed, if ye do not cast it out by your unbelief, that ye will resist the Spirit of the Lord, behold, it will begin to swell within your breasts. And when you feel these swelling motions, ye will begin to say within yourselves, It must needs be that this is a good seed, or that the word is good, for it beginneth to enlarge my soul. Yea, it beginneth to enlighten my understanding. Yea, and it beginneth to be delicious to me. [20]

And now, behold, will not this strengthen your faith? Yea, it will strengthen your faith, for ye will say, I know that this is a good seed, for behold, it sprouteth and beginneth to grow. And now, behold, are ye sure that this is a good seed? I say unto you, Yea, for every seed bringeth forth unto its own likeness. [21]

---

[18] Alma 32: 17-20
[19] Alma 32: 26
[20] Alma 32: 28
[21] Alma 32: 30*-31

And now, behold, is your knowledge perfect? Yea, your knowledge is perfect in that thing, and your faith is dormant, and this because you know. For ye know that the word hath swelled your souls, and ye also know that it hath sprouted up, that your understanding doth begin to be enlightened, and your mind doth begin to expand.

Oh, then, is not this real? I say unto you, Yea, because it is light; and whatsoever is light is good because it is discernible. Therefore, ye must know that it is good.

And now, behold, after ye have tasted this light, is your knowledge perfect? Behold, I say unto you, Nay; neither must ye lay aside your faith; for ye have only exercised your faith to plant the seed, that ye might try the experiment to know if the seed was good. [22]

And now, behold, if ye nourish it with much care, it will get root, and grow up, and bring forth fruit. But if ye neglect the tree and take no thought for its nourishment, behold, it will not get any root. And when the heat of the sun cometh and scorcheth it, because it hath no root, it withers away; and ye pluck it up and cast it out. Now this is not because the seed was not good. Neither is it because the fruit thereof would not be desirable; but it is because your ground is barren and ye will not nourish the tree. Therefore, ye cannot have the fruit thereof. [23]

But if ye will nourish the word, yea, nourish the tree as it beginneth to grow, by your faith with great diligence and with patience, looking forward to the fruit thereof, it shall take root. And behold, it shall be a tree springing up unto everlasting life. Behold, by and by ye shall pluck the fruit thereof, which is most precious, which is sweet above all that is sweet, and which is white above all that is white, yea, and pure above all that is pure. And ye shall feast upon this fruit, even until ye are filled, that ye hunger not; neither shall ye thirst. [24]

And now, my brethren, I desire that ye shall plant this word in your hearts; and as it beginneth to swell, even so nourish it by

---

[22] Alma 32: 34-36
[23] Alma 32: 37*-39
[24] Alma 32: 41-42*

your faith. And behold, it will become a tree, springing up in you unto everlasting life. And then may God grant unto you that your burdens may be light, through the joy of his Son. And even all this can ye do, if ye will. Amen. [25]

And now, it came to pass that after Alma had spoken these words unto them, he sat down upon the ground. And Amulek arose and began to teach them, saying, My brethren, I think that it is impossible that ye should be ignorant of the things which have been spoken concerning the coming of Christ, who is taught by us to be the Son of God. Yea, I know that these things were taught unto you bountifully before your dissension from among us. [26]

And now, behold, I will testify unto you of myself that these things are true. Behold, I say unto you that I do know that Christ shall come among the children of men to take upon him the transgressions of his people, and that he shall atone for the sins of the world, for the Lord God has spoken it.

For it is expedient that an atonement should be made. For according to the great plan of the eternal God, there must be an atonement made, or else all mankind must unavoidably perish. Yea, all are hardened; yea, all are fallen, and are lost and must perish, except it be through the atonement, which it is expedient should be made.

For it is expedient that there should be a great and last sacrifice; yea, not a sacrifice of man, neither of beast, neither of any manner of fowl, for it shall not be a human sacrifice; but it must be an infinite and eternal sacrifice.

Now, there is not any man that can sacrifice his own blood, which will atone for the sins of another. Now, if a man murdereth, behold, will our law which is just take the life of his brother? I say unto you, Nay. But the law requireth the life of him who hath murdered. Therefore, there can be nothing, which is short of an infinite atonement, which will suffice for the sins of the world.

Therefore, it is expedient that there should be a great and last sacrifice. And then shall there be, or, it is expedient there should be, a stop to the shedding of blood. Then shall the law of Moses be

---

[25] Alma 33: 23
[26] Alma 34: 1-2

fulfilled. Yea, it shall all be fulfilled, every jot and tittle; and none shall have passed away. And behold, this is the whole meaning of the law, every whit pointing to that great and last sacrifice.

And that great and last sacrifice will be the Son of God, yea, infinite and eternal. And thus he shall bring salvation to all those who shall believe on his name; this being the intent of this last sacrifice, to bring about the bowels of mercy, which overpowereth justice, and bringeth about means unto men that they may have faith unto repentance.

And thus mercy can satisfy the demands of justice and encircles them in the arms of safety, while he that exercises no faith unto repentance is exposed to the whole law of the demands of justice. Therefore, only unto him that has faith unto repentance is brought about the great and eternal plan of redemption.

Therefore, may God grant unto you, my brethren, that ye may begin to exercise your faith unto repentance, that ye begin to call upon his holy name, that he would have mercy upon you. Yea, cry unto him for mercy; for he is mighty to save. Yea, humble yourselves, and continue in prayer unto him. [27] For behold, this life is the time for men to prepare to meet God. Yea, behold, the day of this life is the day for men to perform their labors.

And now, as I said unto you before, as ye have had so many witnesses, therefore, I beseech of you that ye do not procrastinate the day of your repentance until the end. For after this day of life, which is given us to prepare for eternity, behold, if we do not improve our time while in this life, then cometh the night of darkness, wherein there can be no labor performed.

Ye cannot say, when ye are brought to that awful crisis, that I will repent, that I will return to my God. Nay, ye cannot say this. For that same spirit which doth possess your bodies at the time that ye go out of this life, that same spirit will have power to possess your body in that eternal world.

For behold, if ye have procrastinated the day of your repentance even until death, behold, ye have become subjected to the spirit of the devil, and he doth seal you his. Therefore, the Spirit of the Lord hath withdrawn from you and hath no place in

---

[27] Alma 34: 8-19

you, and the devil hath all power over you. And this is the final state of the wicked.

And this I know because the Lord has said he dwelleth not in unholy temples; but in the hearts of the righteous doth he dwell. Yea, and he has also said that the righteous shall sit down in his kingdom to go no more out. But their garments should be made white through the blood of the Lamb.

And now my beloved brethren, I desire that ye should remember these things, and that ye should work out your salvation with fear before God. And that ye should no more deny the coming of Christ, that ye contend no more against the Holy Ghost, but that ye receive it, and take upon you the name of Christ, that ye humble yourselves even to the dust, and worship God in whatsoever place ye may be in, in spirit and in truth, and that ye live in thanksgiving daily for the many mercies and blessings which he doth bestow upon you.

Yea, and I also exhort you, my brethren, that ye be watchful unto prayer continually, that ye may not be led away by the temptation of the devil, that he may not overpower you, that ye may not become his subjects at the last day. For behold, he rewardeth you no good thing.

And now, my beloved brethren, I would exhort you to have patience, and that ye bear with all manner of afflictions; that ye do not revile against those who do cast you out because of your exceeding poverty, lest ye become sinners like unto them. But that ye have patience, and bear with those afflictions, with a firm hope, that ye shall one day rest from all your afflictions. [28]

Now it came to pass that after Amulek had made an end of these words, they withdrew themselves from the multitude and came over into the land of Jershon. Yea, and the rest of the brethren, after they had preached the word unto the Zoramites, also came over into the land of Jershon.

And it came to pass that after the more popular part of the Zoramites had consulted together concerning the words which

---

[28] Alma 34: 32-41

had been preached unto them, they were angry because of the word, for it did destroy their craft. [29]

Now their rulers, and their priests, and their teachers did not let the people know concerning their desires; therefore, they found out privily the minds of all the people; and it came to pass that after they had found out the minds of all the people, those who were in favor of the words which had been spoken by Alma and his brethren, were cast out of the land. And they were many. And they came over also into the land of Jershon. And it came to pass that Alma and his brethren did minister unto them.

Now the people of the Zoramites were angry with the people of Ammon who were in Jershon. And the chief ruler of the Zoramites, being a very wicked man, sent over unto the people of Ammon, desiring them that they should cast out of their land all those who came over from them into their land. And he breathed out many threatenings against them.

And now, the people of Ammon did not fear their words. Therefore, they did not cast them out, but they did receive all the poor of the Zoramites that came over unto them. And they did nourish them, and did clothe them, and did give unto them lands for their inheritance. And they did administer unto them according to their wants.

Now this did stir up the Zoramites to anger against the people of Ammon, and they began to mix with the Lamanites and to stir them up also to anger against them. And thus the Zoramites and the Lamanites began to make preparations for war against the people of Ammon and also against the Nephites. And thus ended the seventeenth year of the reign of the judges over the people of Nephi.

And the people of Ammon departed out of the land of Jershon, and came over into the land of Melek, and gave place in the land of Jershon for the armies of the Nephites, that they might contend with the armies of the Lamanites and the armies of the Zoramites. And thus commenced a war betwixt the Lamanites and the Nephites in the eighteenth year of the reign of the judges. And an account shall be given of their wars hereafter.

---

[29] Alma 35: 1-3*

And Alma, and Ammon, and their brethren, and also the two sons of Alma returned to the land of Zarahemla, after having been instruments in the hands of God of bringing many of the Zoramites to repentance. [30] Now we shall say no more concerning their preaching, except that they preached the word and the truth according to the spirit of prophecy and revelation; and they preached after the holy order of God, by which they were called. [31]

About 73 B.C.

And now, I return to an account of the wars between the Nephites and the Lamanites in the eighteenth year of the reign of the judges. For behold, it came to pass that the Zoramites became Lamanites. Therefore, in the commencement of the eighteenth year, the people of the Nephites saw that the Lamanites were coming upon them. Therefore, they made preparations for war; yea, they gathered together their armies in the land of Jershon. [32]

Now the leader who had been appointed to be the chief captain over the Nephites, took the command of all the armies of the Nephites; and his name was Moroni. And Moroni took all the command and the governments of their wars. And he was only twenty and five years old when he was appointed chief captain over the armies of the Nephites.

And it came to pass that he met the Lamanites in the borders of Jershon; and his people were armed with swords, and with cimeters, and all manner of weapons of war. And when the armies of the Lamanites saw that the people of Nephi, or that Moroni had prepared his people with breastplates, and with armshields, yea, and also shields to defend their heads, and with thick clothing, [33] they durst not come against the Nephites in the borders of Jershon. Therefore, they departed out of the land of Antionum into the wilderness and took their journey round about in the wilderness, away by the head of the river Sidon, that they might

---

[30] Alma 35: 5-14*
[31] Alma 43: 2
[32] Alma 43: 3-4
[33] Alma 43: 16-19*

come into the land of Manti and take possession of the land; for they did not suppose that the armies of Moroni would know whither they had gone.

But it came to pass as soon as they had departed into the wilderness, Moroni sent spies into the wilderness to watch their camp. And Moroni, also knowing of the prophecies of Alma, sent certain men unto him, desiring him that he should inquire of the Lord whither the armies of the Nephites should go to defend themselves against the Lamanites.

And it came to pass that the word of the Lord came unto Alma; and Alma informed the messenger of Moroni that the armies of the Lamanites were marching round about in the wilderness, that they might come over into the land of Manti, that they might commence an attack upon the more weak part of the people. And those messengers went and delivered the message unto Moroni.

Now Moroni, leaving a part of his army in the land of Jershon, lest by any means a part of the Lamanites should come into that land and take possession of the city, took the remainder part of his army and marched over into the land of Manti. And he caused that all the people in that quarter of the land should gather themselves together to battle against the Lamanites, to defend their lands and their country, their rights and their liberties. Therefore, they were prepared against the time of the coming of the Lamanites. [34]

And now, as Moroni knew the intention of the Lamanites, that it was their intention to destroy their brethren, or to subject them and bring them into bondage, that they might establish a kingdom unto themselves over all the land. And he, also knowing that it was the only desire of the Nephites to preserve their lands, their liberty, and their church, therefore, he thought it no sin that he should defend them by stratagem. Therefore, he found by his spies which course the Lamanites were to take.

Therefore, he divided his army, and brought a part over into the valley, and concealed them on the east and on the south of the hill Riplah. And the remainder he concealed in the west valley, on

---

[34] Alma 43: 22*-26

the west of the river Sidon, and so down into the borders of the land of Manti. And thus having placed his army according to his desire, he was prepared to meet them. And it came to pass that the Lamanites came up on the north of the hill, where a part of the army of Moroni was concealed.

And as the Lamanites had passed the hill Riplah, and come into the valley, and begun to cross the river Sidon, the army which was concealed on the south of the hill, which was led by a man whose name was Lehi, and he led his army forth and encircled the Lamanites about on the east in their rear; and it came to pass that the Lamanites, when they saw the Nephites coming upon them in their rear, turned them about and began to contend with the army of Lehi.

And the work of death commenced on both sides. But it was more dreadful on the part of the Lamanites, for their nakedness was exposed to the heavy blows of the Nephites, with their swords and their cimeters, which brought death almost at every stroke. While on the other hand, there was now and then a man fell among the Nephites by their swords and the loss of blood, they being shielded from the more vital parts of the body, or the more vital parts of the body being shielded from the strokes of the Lamanites by their breastplates, and their armshields, and their headplates. And thus the Nephites did carry on the work of death among the Lamanites. [35]

And the Lamanites did flee again before them towards the land of Manti; and they were met again by the armies of Moroni. Now in this case, the Lamanites did fight exceedingly; yea, never had the Lamanites been known to fight with such exceeding great strength and courage, no, not even from the beginning. And they were inspired by the Zoramites and the Amalekites, who were their chief captains and leaders, and by Zerahemnah, who was their chief captain, or their chief leader and commander. Yea, they did fight like dragons. And many of the Nephites were slain by their hands; yea, for they did smite in two, many of their headplates; and they did pierce many of their breastplates; and

---

[35] Alma 43: 29-38

they did smite off many of their arms; and thus the Lamanites did smite in their fierce anger.

Nevertheless, the Nephites were inspired by a better cause, for they were not fighting for monarchy nor power; but they were fighting for their homes and their liberties, their wives and their children, and their all, yea, for their rites of worship and their church. And they were doing that which they felt was the duty which they owed to their God. For the Lord had said unto them and also unto their fathers that inasmuch as ye are not guilty of the first offense, neither the second, ye shall not suffer yourselves to be slain by the hands of your enemies. [36]

And it came to pass that when the men of Moroni saw the fierceness and the anger of the Lamanites, they were about to shrink and flee from them. And Moroni, perceiving their intent, sent forth and inspired their hearts with these thoughts: yea, the thought of their lands, their liberty, yea, their freedom from bondage.

And it came to pass that they turned upon the Lamanites, and they cried with one voice unto the Lord, their God, for their liberty and their freedom from bondage. And they began to stand against the Lamanites with power. And in the selfsame hour that they cried unto the Lord for their freedom, the Lamanites began to flee before them; and they fled, even to the waters of Sidon.

Now the Lamanites were more numerous, yea, by more than double the number of the Nephites. Nevertheless, they were driven insomuch that they were gathered together in one body in the valley, upon the bank by the river Sidon. Therefore, the armies of Moroni encircled them about, yea, even on both sides of the river; for behold, on the east were the men of Lehi. [37]

And it came to pass that Moroni caused that the work of death should cease; and he took the weapons of war from the Lamanites. And after they had entered into a covenant with him of peace, they were suffered to depart into the wilderness.

Now the number of their dead were not numbered because of the greatness of the number. Yea, the number of their dead were exceeding great, both on the Nephites and on the Lamanites. And

---

[36] Alma 43: 42-46
[37] Alma 43: 48-52

it came to pass that they did cast their dead into the waters of Sidon, and they have gone forth and are buried in the depths of the sea. And the armies of the Nephites, or of Moroni, returned and came to their houses and their lands. [38]

Behold, now it came to pass that the people of Nephi were exceedingly rejoiced because the Lord had again delivered them out of the hands of their enemies. Therefore, they gave thanks unto the Lord, their God; yea, and they did fast much and pray much; and they did worship God with exceeding great joy.

About 72 B.C.

And it came to pass in the nineteenth year of the reign of the judges over the people of Nephi, that Alma came unto his son Helaman and said unto him, Believest thou the words which I spake unto thee concerning those records which have been kept?

And Helaman said unto him, Yea, I believe.

And Alma said again, Believest thou in Jesus Christ, who shall come?

And he said, Yea, I believe all the words which thou hast spoken.

And Alma said unto him again, Will ye keep my commandments?

And he said, Yea, I will keep thy commandments with all my heart.

Then Alma said unto him, Blessed art thou; and the Lord shall prosper thee in this land. [39] And now, my son Helaman, I command you that ye take the records which have been entrusted with me, and I also command you that ye keep a record of this people, according as I have done, upon the plates of Nephi, and keep all these things sacred which I have kept, and these plates of brass which contain these engravings, which have the records of the holy scriptures upon them, which have the genealogy of our forefathers, even from the beginning.

---

[38] Alma 44: 20*-23
[39] Alma 45: 1-8

And behold, it has been prophesied by our fathers that they should be kept, and handed down from one generation to another, and be kept and preserved by the hand of the Lord until they should go forth unto every nation, kindred, tongue, and people, that they shall know of the mysteries contained thereon. And now, behold, if they are kept, they must retain their brightness; yea, and they will retain their brightness, yea, and also shall all the plates which do contain that which is holy writ.

Now ye may suppose that this is foolishness in me, but behold, I say unto you that by small and simple things are great things brought to pass. And small means in many instances doth confound the wise. And the Lord God doth work by means to bring about his great and eternal purposes. And by very small means the Lord doth confound the wise and bringeth about the salvation of many souls.

And now, it has hitherto been wisdom in God that these things should be preserved. For behold, they have enlarged the memory of this people, yea, and convinced many of the error of their ways, and brought them to the knowledge of their God, unto the salvation of their souls. [40]

And now, behold, I tell you by the spirit of prophecy, that if ye transgress the commandments of God, behold, these things which are sacred shall be taken away from you by the power of God; and ye shall be delivered up unto Satan, that he may sift you as chaff before the wind. But if ye keep the commandments of God, and do with these things which are sacred, according to that which the Lord doth command you— for you must appeal unto the Lord for all things whatsoever ye must do with them — behold, no power of earth or hell can take them from you. For God is powerful to the fulfilling of all his words; for he will fulfill all his promises which he shall make unto you. For he has fulfilled his promises which he has made unto our fathers, for he promised unto them that he would reserve these things for a wise purpose in him, that he might show forth his power unto future generations.

---

[40] Alma 37: 1-8

And now, behold, one purpose hath he fulfilled, even to the restoration of many thousands of the Lamanites to the knowledge of the truth. And he hath shown forth his power in them, and he will also still show forth his power in them unto future generations. Therefore, they shall be preserved. Therefore, I command you, my son Helaman, that ye be diligent in fulfilling all my words, and that ye be diligent in keeping the commandments of God as they are written. [41]

Yea, cry unto God for all thy support. Yea, let all thy doings be unto the Lord. And whithersoever thou goest, let it be in the Lord. Yea, let thy thoughts be directed unto the Lord. Yea, let the affections of thy heart be placed upon the Lord forever. Counsel the Lord in all thy doings, and he will direct thee for good. Yea, when thou liest down at night, lie down unto the Lord, that he may watch over you in your sleep. And when thou risest in the morning, let thy heart be full of thanks unto God. And if ye do these things, ye shall be lifted up at the last day.

And now, my son, see that ye take care of these sacred things. Yea, see that ye look to God and live. Go unto this people, and declare the word, and be sober. My son, farewell. [42]

And now, when Alma had said these words, he blessed the church, yea, all those who should stand fast in the faith from that time henceforth. And when Alma had done this, he departed out of the land of Zarahemla as if to go into the land of Melek. And it came to pass that he was never heard of more. As to his death or burial, we know not of. [43]

And now, it came to pass that Helaman went forth among the people to declare the word unto them. For behold, because of their wars with the Lamanites and the many little dissensions and disturbances which had been among the people, it became expedient that the word of God should be declared among them; yea, and that a regulation should be made throughout the church. [44]

---

[41] Alma 37: 15-20
[42] Alma 37: 36-37, 47
[43] Alma 45: 17-18
[44] Alma 45: 20*-21

And now, it came to pass that after Helaman and his brethren had appointed priests and teachers over the churches, that there arose a dissension among them. And they would not give heed to the words of Helaman and his brethren, but they grew proud, being lifted up in their hearts because of their exceeding great riches. Therefore, they grew rich in their own eyes and would not walk uprightly before God. [45]

And it came to pass that as many as would not hearken to the words of Helaman and his brethren, were gathered together against their brethren. And now behold, they were exceeding wroth, insomuch that they were determined to slay them.

Now the leader of those who were wroth against their brethren was a large and a strong man, and his name was Amalickiah. And Amalickiah was desirous to be a king. And those people who were wroth were also desirous that he should be their king. And they were, the greater part of them, the lower judges of the land. And they were seeking for power and they had been led by the flatteries of Amalickiah, that if they would support him and establish him to be their king, that he would make them rulers over the people. [46] And there were many in the church who believed in the flattering words of Amalickiah; therefore, they dissented, even from the church.

And thus were the affairs of the people of Nephi exceeding precarious and dangerous, notwithstanding their great victory which they had had over the Lamanites and their great rejoicings, which they had had because of their deliverance by the hands of the Lord. Thus we see how quick the children of men do forget the Lord, their God; yea, how quick to do iniquity, and to be led away by the evil one.

Yea, and we also see the great wickedness one very wicked man can cause to take place among the children of men. Yea, we see that Amalickiah, because he was a man of cunning devices and a man of many flattering words, that he led away the hearts of many people to do wickedly; yea, and to seek to destroy the church of God, and to destroy the foundation of liberty which God

---

[45] Alma 45: 23-24
[46] Alma 46: 1-5

had granted unto them, or which blessing God had sent upon the face of the land for the righteous' sake.

And now, it came to pass that when Moroni, who was the chief commander of the armies of the Nephites, had heard of these dissensions, he was angry with Amalickiah. And it came to pass that he rent his coat. And he took a piece thereof and wrote upon it: In memory of our God, our religion, and freedom, and our peace, our wives, and our children. And he fastened it upon the end of a pole thereof. And he fastened on his headplate, and his breastplate, and his shields, and girded on his armor about his loins.

And he took the pole, which had on the end there of his rent coat, and he called it the title of liberty. And he bowed himself to the earth, and he prayed mightily unto his God for the blessings of liberty to rest upon his brethren, so long as there should a band of Christians remain to possess the land. For thus were all the true believers of Christ, who belonged to the church of God, called by those who did not belong to the church.

And those who did belong to the church were faithful. Yea, all those who were true believers in Christ took upon them gladly the name of Christ, or Christians as they were called, because of their belief in Christ who should come.

And therefore, at this time, Moroni prayed that the cause of the Christians and the freedom of the land might be favored. And it came to pass that when he had poured out his soul to God, he gave all the land which was south of the land Desolation, yea, and, in fine, all the land, both on the north and south, a chosen land, and the land of liberty. And he said, Surely God shall not suffer that we, who are despised because we take upon us the name of Christ, shall be trodden down and destroyed, until we bring it upon us by our own transgressions.

And when Moroni had said these words, he went forth among the people, waving the rent of his garment in the air, that all might see the writing which he had written upon the rent, and crying with a loud voice, saying, Behold, whosoever will maintain this title upon the land, let them come forth in the strength of the Lord, and enter into a covenant that they will maintain their rights and their religion, that the Lord God may bless them!

And it came to pass that when Moroni had proclaimed these words, behold, the people came running together, with their armor girded about their loins, rending their garments in token, or as a covenant, that they would not forsake the Lord, their God. Or in other words, if they should transgress the commandments of God, or fall into transgression, and be ashamed to take upon them the name of Christ, the Lord should rend them even as they had rent their garments. Now this was the covenant which they made. And they cast their garments at the feet of Moroni, saying, We covenant with our God that we shall be destroyed, even as our brethren in the land northward, if we shall fall into transgression. [47]

Moroni said unto them, Behold, we are a remnant of the seed of Jacob; yea, we are a remnant of the seed of Joseph, whose coat was rent by his brethren into many pieces. Yea, and now, behold, let us remember to keep the commandments of God, or our garments shall be rent by our brethren and we be cast into prison, or be sold, or be slain. Yea, let us preserve our liberty as a remnant of Joseph! [48]

And now, it came to pass that when Moroni had said these words, he went forth, and also sent forth, in all the parts of the land where there were dissensions, and gathered together all the people who were desirous to maintain their liberty, to stand against Amalickiah and those who had dissented, who were called Amalickiahites.

And it came to pass that when Amalickiah saw that the people of Moroni were more numerous than the Amalickiahites, and he also saw that his people were doubtful concerning the justice of the cause in which they had undertaken, therefore, fearing that he should not gain the point, he took those of his people who would, and departed into the land of Nephi.

Now Moroni thought it was not expedient that the Lamanites should have any more strength; therefore, he thought to cut off the people of Amalickiah, or to take them, and bring them back, and put Amalickiah to death. Yea, for he knew that they would stir up the Lamanites to anger against them and cause them to come to

---

[47] Alma 46: 7-22*
[48] Alma 46: 23-24*

battle against them. And this he knew that Amalickiah would do, that he might obtain his purposes.

And it came to pass that he took his army and marched out into the wilderness to cut off the course of Amalickiah in the wilderness. [49] And it came to pass that Amalickiah fled with a small number of his men, and the remainder were delivered up into the hands of Moroni and were taken back into the land of Zarahemla. And it came to pass that whosoever of the Amalickiahites that would not enter into a covenant to support the cause of freedom, that they might maintain a free government, he caused to be put to death. And there was but few who denied the covenant of freedom.

And it came to pass also that he caused the title of liberty to be hoisted upon every tower which was in all the land which was possessed by the Nephites. And thus Moroni planted the standard of liberty among the Nephites, and they began to have peace again in the land. And thus they did maintain peace in the land until nearly the end of the nineteenth year of the reign of the judges. And Helaman and the high priests did also maintain order in the church. Yea, even for the space of four years did they have much peace and rejoicing in the church. [50]

About 71 B.C.

Now we will return in our record to Amalickiah and those who had fled with him into the wilderness. For behold, he had taken those who went with him, and went up into the land of Nephi among the Lamanites, and did stir up the Lamanites to anger against the people of Nephi, insomuch that the king of the Lamanites sent a proclamation throughout all his land, among all his people, that they should gather themselves together again to go to battle against the Nephites.

And it came to pass that when the proclamation had gone forth among them, they were exceeding afraid. Yea, they feared to displease the king; and they also feared to go to battle against the

---

[49] Alma 46: 28-31*
[50] Alma 46: 33, 35-38

Nephites, lest they should lose their lives. And it came to pass that they would not, or the more part of them would not obey the commandments of the king.

And now, it came to pass that the king was wroth because of their disobedience; therefore, he gave Amalickiah the command of that part of his army which was obedient unto his commands, and commanded him that he should go forth and compel them to arms.

Now behold, this was the desire of Amalickiah, for he being a very subtle man to do evil, therefore, he laid the plan in his heart to dethrone the king of the Lamanites. And now he had got the command of those parts of the Lamanites who were in favor of the king; and he sought to gain favor of those who were not obedient.

Therefore, he went forward to the place which was called Onidah, for thither had all the Lamanites fled, for they discovered the army coming. And supposing that they were coming to destroy them, therefore, they fled to Onidah, to the place of arms. [51]

Now it was not Amalickiah's intention to give them battle according to the commandments of the king. But behold, it was his intention to gain favor with the armies of the Lamanites, that he might place himself at their head, and dethrone the king, and take possession of the kingdom.

And behold, it came to pass that he caused his army to pitch their tents in the valley which was near the Mount Antipas. And it came to pass that when it was night, he sent a secret embassy into the Mount Antipas, desiring that the leader of those who were upon the mount, whose name was Lehonti, that he should come down to the foot of the mount. For he desired to speak with him. [52]

And it came to pass that when Lehonti had come down with his guards to Amalickiah, that Amalickiah desired him to come down with his army in the nighttime and surround those men in their camp, over whom the king had given him command. And that he would deliver them up into Lehonti's hands, if he would make him, Amalickiah, a second leader over the whole army.

And it came to pass that Lehonti came down with his men and surrounded the men of Amalickiah, so that before they awoke

---

[51] Alma 47: 1-5
[52] Alma 47: 8-10

at the dawn of the day, they were surrounded by the armies of Lehonti. And it came to pass that when they saw they were surrounded, they pled with Amalickiah that he would suffer them to fall in with their brethren, that they might not be destroyed. [53] Now this was the thing that Amalickiah desired, that he might accomplish his designs in dethroning the king.

Now it was the custom among the Lamanites, if their chief leader was killed, to appoint the second leader to be their chief leader. Now, it came to pass that Amalickiah caused that one of his servants should administer poison by degrees to Lehonti, that he died.

Now when Lehonti was dead, the Lamanites appointed Amalickiah to be their leader and chief commander. And it came to pass that Amalickiah marched with his armies, for he had gained his desires, to the land of Nephi, to the city of Nephi, which was the chief city. And the king came out to meet him with his guards. For he supposed that Amalickiah had fulfilled his commands, and that Amalickiah had gathered together so great an army to go against the Nephites to battle.

But behold, as the king came out to meet him, Amalickiah caused that his servants should go forth to meet the king; and they went and bowed themselves before the king, as if to reverence him because of his greatness. And it came to pass that the king put forth his hand to raise them, as was the custom with the Lamanites, as a token of peace, which custom they had taken from the Nephites. And it came to pass that when he had raised the first from the ground, behold, he stabbed the king to the heart and he fell to the earth.

Now the servants of the king fled and the servants of Amalickiah raised a cry, saying, Behold, the servants of the king have stabbed him to the heart, and he has fallen, and they have fled! Behold, come and see! [54] And it came to pass that all they who loved the king, when they heard these words, came forth and pursued after the servants of the king, and the army which pursued after them returned, having pursued after them in vain.

---

[53] Alma 47: 13-15*
[54] Alma 47: 16*-26

And thus Amalickiah, by his fraud, gained the hearts of the
people. And it came to pass on the morrow, he entered the city
Nephi with his armies and took possession of the city. [55]

And it came to pass that Amalickiah sought the favor of the
queen and took her unto him to wife. And thus by his fraud, and
by the assistance of his cunning servants, he obtained the kingdom.
Yea, he was acknowledged king throughout all the land, among all
the people of the Lamanites, who were composed of the Lamanites,
and the Lemuelites, and the Ishmaelites, and all the dissenters of
the Nephites from the reign of Nephi down to the present time. [56]

And now, it came to pass that as soon as Amalickiah had
obtained the kingdom, he began to inspire the hearts of the
Lamanites against the people of Nephi. Yea, he did appoint men
to speak unto the Lamanites from their towers against the
Nephites. And thus he did inspire their hearts against the
Nephites, insomuch that in the latter end of the nineteenth year of
the reign of the judges, he, having accomplished his designs thus
far, yea, having been made king over the Lamanites, he sought
also to reign over all the land, yea, and all the people who were in
the land, the Nephites as well as the Lamanites. Therefore, he had
accomplished his design, for he had hardened the hearts of the
Lamanites, and blinded their minds, and stirred them up to anger,
insomuch that he had gathered together a numerous host to go to
battle against the Nephites. For he was determined, because of the
greatness of the number of his people, to overpower the Nephites
and to bring them into bondage.

And thus he did appoint chief captains of the Zoramites, they
being the most acquainted with the strength of the Nephites, and
their places of resort, and the weakest parts of their cities; therefore, he appointed them to be chief captains over his armies. And
it came to pass that they took their camp and moved forth
towards the land of Zarahemla in the wilderness.

Now it came to pass, that while Amalickiah had thus been
obtaining power by fraud and deceit, Moroni, on the other hand,
had been preparing the minds of the people to be faithful unto the

---

[55] Alma 47: 28, 30-31
[56] Alma 47: 35

Lord, their God. Yea, he had been strengthening the armies of the Nephites, and erecting small forts, or places of resort, throwing up banks of earth round about to enclose his armies, and also building walls of stone to encircle them about, round about their cities and the borders of their lands, yea, all round about the land.

And in their weakest fortifications he did place the greater number of men; and thus he did fortify and strengthen the land which was possessed by the Nephites. And thus he was preparing to support their liberty, their lands, their wives, and their children, and their peace; and that they might live unto the Lord their God; and that they might maintain that which was called by their enemies the cause of Christians.

And Moroni was a strong and a mighty man. He was a man of a perfect understanding; yea, a man that did not delight in bloodshed, a man whose soul did joy in the liberty and the freedom of his country and his brethren from bondage and slavery; yea, a man whose heart did swell with thanksgiving to his God for the many privileges and blessings which he bestowed upon his people, a man who did labor exceedingly for the welfare and safety of his people. Yea, and he was a man who was firm in the faith of Christ. And he had sworn with an oath to defend his people, his rights, and his country, and his religion, even to the loss of his blood. [57]

Yea, verily, verily, I say unto you, If all men had been, and were, and ever would be like unto Moroni, behold, the very powers of hell would have been shaken forever. Yea, the devil would never have power over the hearts of the children of men. Behold, he was a man like unto Ammon, the son of Mosiah; yea, and even the other sons of Mosiah; yea, and also Alma and his sons, for they were all men of God.

Now behold, Helaman and his brethren were no less serviceable unto the people than was Moroni; for they did preach the word of God, and they did baptize unto repentance all men, whosoever would hearken unto their words. And thus they went forth, and the people did humble themselves because of their words, insomuch that they were highly favored of the Lord. And

---

[57] Alma 48: 1-13

thus they were free from wars and contentions among themselves, yea, even for the space of four years.

But as I have said, in the latter end of the nineteenth year, notwithstanding their peace amongst themselves, they were compelled reluctantly to contend with their brethren, the Lamanites. Yea, and, in fine, their wars never did cease for the space of many years with the Lamanites, notwithstanding their much reluctance.

Now they were sorry to take up arms against the Lamanites because they did not delight in the shedding of blood. Yea, and this was not all. They were sorry to be the means of sending so many of their brethren out of this world into an eternal world, unprepared to meet their God. Nevertheless, they could not suffer to lay down their lives, that their wives and their children should be massacred by the barbarous cruelty of those who were once their brethren; yea, and had dissented from their church, and had left them, and had gone to destroy them by joining the Lamanites.

Yea, they could not bear that their brethren should rejoice over the blood of the Nephites, so long as there were any who should keep the commandments of God. For the promise of the Lord was if they should keep his commandments they should prosper in the land. [58]

---

[58] Alma 48: 17-25

Chapter 8

Prepare for War

About 71 B.C.

And now, it came to pass in the eleventh month of the nineteenth year, on the tenth day of the month, the armies of the Lamanites were seen approaching towards the land of Ammonihah. But behold, how great was their disappointment. For behold, the Nephites had dug up a ridge of earth round about them, which was so high that the Lamanites could not cast their stones and arrows at them that they might take effect; neither could they come upon them, save it was by their place of entrance. Now at this time, the chief captains of the Lamanites were astonished exceedingly because of the wisdom of the Nephites in preparing their places of security.

Now the leaders of the Lamanites had supposed, because of the greatness of their numbers, yea, they supposed that they should be privileged to come upon them as they had hitherto done. Yea, and they had also prepared themselves with shields and with breastplates. And they had also prepared themselves with garments of skins, yea, very thick garments, to cover their nakedness. And being thus prepared, they supposed that they should easily overpower and subject their brethren to the yoke of bondage, or slay and massacre them according to their pleasure. But behold, to their uttermost astonishment, they were prepared for them in a manner which never had been known among all the children of Lehi. [1]

Now if King Amalickiah had come down out of the land of Nephi at the head of his army, perhaps he would have caused the Lamanites to have attacked the Nephites at the city of Ammonihah; for behold, he did care not for the blood of his people. But behold, Amalickiah did not come down himself to battle. And behold, his chief captains durst not attack the Nephites at the city of Ammonihah, for Moroni had altered the

---

[1] Alma 49: 1, 4-8*

management of affairs among the Nephites, insomuch that the Lamanites were disappointed in their places of retreat, and they could not come upon them. [2] And now, it came to pass that Moroni did not stop making preparations for war, or to defend his people against the Lamanites; for he caused that his armies should commence in digging up heaps of earth round about all the cities, throughout all the land which was possessed by the Nephites.

And it came to pass that Moroni caused that his armies should go forth into the east wilderness. Yea, and they went forth and drove all the Lamanites who were in the east wilderness into their own lands, which were south of the land of Zarahemla. And the land of Nephi did run in a straight course from the east sea to the west.

And it came to pass that when Moroni had driven all the Lamanites out of the east wilderness, which was north of the lands of their own possessions, he caused that the inhabitants who were in the land of Zarahemla and in the land round about, should go forth into the east wilderness, even to the borders by the seashore, and possess the land. And he also placed armies on the south, in the borders of their possessions, and caused them to erect fortifications, that they might secure their armies and their people from the hands of their enemies.

And thus he cut off all the strongholds of the Lamanites in the east wilderness, yea, and also on the west, fortifying the line between the Nephites and the Lamanites between the land of Zarahemla and the land of Nephi, from the west sea, running by the head of the river Sidon, the Nephites possessing all the land northward, yea, even all the land which was northward of the land Bountiful, according to their pleasure. [3]

And it came to pass that the Nephites began the foundation of a city, and they called the name of the city Moroni. And it was by the east sea, and it was on the south by the line of the possessions of the Lamanites. And they also began a foundation for a city between the city of Moroni and the city of Aaron, joining the borders of Aaron and Moroni and they called the name of the

---

[2] Alma 49: 10-11
[3] Alma 50: 1*, 7-11

city, or the land, Nephihah. And they also began in that same year to build many cities on the north, one in a particular manner, which they called Lehi, which was in the north by the borders of the seashore. And thus ended the twentieth year.

And in these prosperous circumstances were the people of Nephi in the commencement of the twenty and first year of the reign of the judges over the people of Nephi. And they did prosper exceedingly, and they became exceeding rich. Yea, and they did multiply and wax strong in the land.

And thus we see how merciful and just are all the dealings of the Lord, to the fulfilling of all his words unto the children of men. Yea, we can behold that his words are verified, even at this time, which he spake unto Lehi, saying, Inasmuch as they shall keep my commandments, they shall prosper in the land. [4]

Behold, there never was a happier time among the people of Nephi, since the days of Nephi, than in the days of Moroni, yea, even at this time, in the twenty and first year of the reign of the judges. And it came to pass that the twenty and second year of the reign of the judges also ended in peace, yea, and also the twenty and third year.

And it came to pass that in the commencement of the twenty and fourth year of the reign of the judges, there would also have been peace among the people of Nephi, had it not been for a contention which took place among them, concerning the land of Lehi and the land of Morianton, which joined upon the borders of Lehi, both of which were on the borders by the seashore. For behold, the people who possessed the land of Morianton did claim a part of the land of Lehi. Therefore, there began to be a warm contention between them, insomuch that the people of Morianton took up arms against their brethren. And they were determined by the sword to slay them. [5]

And it came to pass that the army, which was sent by Moroni, which was led by a man whose name was Teancum, did meet the people of Morianton. And so stubborn were the people of Morianton, being inspired by his wickedness and his flattering

---

[4] Alma 50: 13-20*
[5] Alma 50: 23*-26

words, that a battle commenced between them, in the which
Teancum did slay Morianton, and defeat his army, and took them
prisoners, and returned to the camp of Moroni.

And thus ended the twenty and fourth year of the reign of
the judges over the people of Nephi. And thus were the people of
Morianton brought back; and upon their covenanting to keep the
peace, they were restored to the land of Morianton. And a union
took place between them and the people of Lehi, and they were
also restored to their lands.

And it came to pass that in the same year that the people of
Nephi had peace restored unto them, that Nephihah, the second
chief judge, died, having filled the judgment seat with perfect
uprightness before God. [6]

Behold, it came to pass that the son of Nephihah was
appointed to fill the judgment seat in the stead of his father. Yea,
he was appointed chief judge and governor over the people, with
an oath and sacred ordinance to judge righteously, and to keep the
peace and the freedom of the people, and to grant unto them their
sacred privileges to worship the Lord, their God, yea, to support
and maintain the cause of God all his days, and to bring the
wicked to justice according to their crime. Now behold, his name
was Pahoran. And Pahoran did fill the seat of his father, and did
commence his reign in the end of the twenty and fourth year over
the people of Nephi. [7]

And now, having commenced the twenty and fifth year in
peace, nevertheless, they did not long maintain an entire peace in
the land, for there began to be a contention among the people
concerning the chief judge, Pahoran. For behold, there was a part
of the people who desired that a few particular points of the law
should be altered. But behold, Pahoran would not alter nor suffer
the law to be altered. Therefore, he did not hearken to those who
had sent in their voices with their petitions concerning the altering
of the law.

Therefore, those who were desirous that the law should be
altered were angry with him and desired that he should no longer

---

[6] Alma 50: 35-37
[7] Alma 50: 39-40

be chief judge over the land. And it came to pass that those who were desirous that Pahoran should be dethroned from the judgment seat were called Kingmen, for they were desirous that the law should be altered in a manner to overthrow the free government and to establish a king over the land. [8]

And it came to pass that this matter of their contention was settled by the voice of the people. And it came to pass that the voice of the people came in favor of the Freemen. And Pahoran retained the judgment seat, which caused much rejoicing among the brethren of Pahoran, and also many of the people of liberty, who also put the Kingmen to silence, that they durst not oppose, but were obliged to maintain the cause of freedom. Now those who were in favor of kings were those of high birth, and they sought to be kings. And they were supported by those who sought power and authority over the people.

But behold, this was a critical time for such contentions to be among the people of Nephi. For behold, Amalickiah had again stirred up the hearts of the people of the Lamanites against the people of the Nephites, and he was gathering together soldiers from all parts of his land and arming them and preparing for war with all diligence. For he had sworn to drink the blood of Moroni. [9]

Now his armies were not so great as they had hitherto been because of the many thousands who had been slain by the hand of the Nephites. But notwithstanding their great loss, Amalickiah had gathered together a wonderful great army, insomuch that he feared not to come down to the land of Zarahemla. Yea, even Amalickiah did himself come down at the head of the Lamanites. [10]

And it came to pass that when the men who were called Kingmen had heard that the Lamanites were coming down to battle against them, they were glad in their hearts, and they refused to take up arms; for they were so wroth with the chief judge, and also with the people of liberty, that they would not take up arms to defend their country.

---

[8] Alma 51: 1*-4*, 5
[9] Alma 51: 7-9
[10] Alma 51: 11-12*

And it came to pass that when Moroni saw this and also saw that the Lamanites were coming into the borders of the land, he was exceeding wroth because of the stubbornness of those people whom he had labored with so much diligence to preserve. Yea, he was exceeding wroth. His soul was filled with anger against them.

And it came to pass that he sent a petition, with the voice of the people, unto the governor of the land, desiring that he should read it and give him, Moroni, power to compel those dissenters to defend their country, or to put them to death. For it was his first care to put an end to such contentions and dissensions among the people. For behold, this had been hitherto a cause of all their destruction.

And it came to pass that it was granted according to the voice of the people. And it came to pass that Moroni commanded that his army should go against those Kingmen, to pull down their pride and their nobility and level them with the earth, or they should take up arms and support the cause of liberty.

And it came to pass that the armies did march forth against them and they did pull down their pride and their nobility; insomuch, that as they did lift their weapons of war to fight against the men of Moroni, they were hewn down and leveled to the earth. And it came to pass that there were four thousand of those dissenters who were hewn down by the sword. And those of their leaders who were not slain in battle were taken and cast into prison, for there was no time for their trials at this period.

And the remainder of those dissenters, rather than to be smitten down to the earth by the sword, yielded to the standard of liberty, and were compelled to hoist the title of liberty upon their towers and in their cities and to take up arms in defense of their country. And thus Moroni put an end to those Kingmen, that there were not any known by the appellation of Kingmen. And thus he put an end to the stubbornness and the pride of those people who professed the blood of nobility; but they were brought down to humble themselves like unto their brethren and to fight valiantly for their freedom from bondage.

Behold, it came to pass that while Moroni was thus breaking down the wars and contentions among his own people, and subjecting them to peace and civilization, and making regulations to prepare for war against the Lamanites, behold, the Lamanites had come into the land of Moroni, which was in the borders by the seashore. And it came to pass that the Nephites were not sufficiently strong in the city of Moroni; therefore, Amalickiah did drive them, slaying many. And it came to pass that Amalickiah took possession of the city, yea, possession of all their fortifications. [11]

And thus he went on, taking possession of many cities, the city of Nephihah, and the city of Lehi, and the city of Morianton, and the city of Omner, and the city of Gid, and the city of Mulek, all of which were on the east borders by the seashore. And thus had the Lamanites obtained, by the cunning of Amalickiah, so many cities by their numberless hosts, all of which were strongly fortified after the manner of the fortifications of Moroni, all of which afforded strongholds for the Lamanites.

And it came to pass that they marched to the borders of the land Bountiful, driving the Nephites before them and slaying many. But it came to pass that they were met by Teancum, who had slain Morianton, and had headed his people in his flight. And it came to pass that he headed Amalickiah also, as he was marching forth with his numerous army that he might take possession of the land Bountiful, and also the land northward.

But behold, he met with a disappointment, by being repulsed by Teancum and his men, for they were great warriors. For every man of Teancum did exceed the Lamanites in their strength and in their skill of war, insomuch that they did gain advantage over the Lamanites.

And it came to pass that they did harass them, insomuch that they did slay them even until it was dark. And it came to pass that Teancum and his men did pitch their tents in the borders of the land Bountiful. And Amalickiah did pitch his tents in the borders on the beach by the seashore. And after this manner were they driven.

And it came to pass that when the night had come, Teancum and his servant stole forth, and went out by night, and went into the camp of Amalickiah. And behold, sleep had overpowered them because of their much fatigue, which was caused by the labors and heat of the day. And it came to pass that Teancum stole

---

[11] Alma 51: 13-23

privily into the tent of the king and put a javelin to his heart. And he did cause the death of the king immediately, that he did not awake his servants.

And he returned again privily to his own camp, and behold, his men were asleep, and he awoke them and told them all the things that he had done. And he caused that his armies should stand in readiness, lest the Lamanites had awakened and should come upon them. And thus ended the twenty and fifth year of the reign of the judges over the people of Nephi. And thus ended the days of Amalickiah. [12]

And now, it came to pass in the twenty and sixth year of the reign of the judges over the people of Nephi, behold, when the Lamanites awoke on the first morning of the first month, behold, they found Amalickiah was dead in his own tent. And they also saw that Teancum was ready to give them battle on that day. And now, when the Lamanites saw this, they were affrighted, and they abandoned their design in marching into the land northward, and retreated with all their army into the city of Mulek, and sought protection in their fortifications.

And it came to pass that the brother of Amalickiah was appointed king over the people. And his name was Ammoron; thus King Ammoron, the brother of King Amalickiah, was appointed to reign in his stead. And it came to pass that he did command that his people should maintain those cities which they had taken by the shedding of blood; for they had not taken any cities, save they had lost much blood.

And now, Teancum saw that the Lamanites were determined to maintain those cities which they had taken and those parts of the land which they had obtained possession of. And also seeing the enormity of their number, Teancum thought it was not expedient that he should attempt to attack them in their forts, but he kept his men round about, as if making preparations for war. Yea, and truly he was preparing to defend himself against them by casting up walls round about and preparing places of resort.

And it came to pass that he kept thus preparing for war until Moroni had sent a large number of men to strengthen his army.

[12] Alma 51: 26-37

And Moroni also sent orders unto him that he should retain all the prisoners who fell into his hands, for, as the Lamanites had taken many prisoners, that he should retain all the prisoners of the Lamanites, as a ransom for those whom the Lamanites had taken. And he also said unto him, I would come unto you, but behold, the Lamanites are upon us in the borders of the land by the west sea. And behold, I go against them, therefore I cannot come unto you. [13]

And it came to pass that Moroni did arrive with his army to the land of Bountiful in the latter end of the twenty and seventh year of the reign of the judges over the people of Nephi. And in the commencement of the twenty and eighth year, Moroni, and Teancum, and many of the chief captains held a council of war, what they should do to cause the Lamanites to come out against them to battle, or that they might by some means flatter them out of their strongholds, that they might gain advantage over them and take again the city of Mulek. [14]

Therefore, he caused that Teancum should take a small number of men and march down near the seashore. And Moroni and his army, by night, marched into the wilderness on the west of the city Mulek. And thus, on the morrow when the guards of the Lamanites had discovered Teancum, they ran and told it unto Jacob, their leader.

And it came to pass that the armies of the Lamanites did march forth against Teancum, supposing by their numbers to overpower Teancum because of the smallness of his numbers. And as Teancum saw the armies of the Lamanites coming out against him, he began to retreat down by the seashore northward. And it came to pass that when the Lamanites saw that he began to flee, they took courage and pursued them with vigor.

And while Teancum was thus leading away the Lamanites who were pursuing them in vain, behold, Moroni commanded that a part of his army who were with him should march forth into the city and take possession of it. And thus they did, and slew all those who had been left to protect the city, yea, all those who

---

[13] Alma 52: 1-8, 11
[14] Alma 52: 18-19

would not yield up their weapons of war. And thus Moroni had
obtained possession of the city Mulek with a part of his army,
while he marched with the remainder to meet the Lamanites when
they should return from the pursuit of Teancum.

And it came to pass that the Lamanites did pursue Teancum
until they came near the city Bountiful. And then they were met
by Lehi and a small army, which had been left to protect the city
Bountiful. And now, behold, when the chief captains of the
Lamanites had beheld Lehi with his army coming against them,
they fled in much confusion, lest perhaps they should not obtain
the city Mulek before Lehi should overtake them, for they were
wearied because of their march, and the men of Lehi were fresh.

Now the Lamanites did not know that Moroni had been in
their rear with his army; and all they feared was Lehi and his men.
Now Lehi was not desirous to overtake them till they should meet
Moroni and his army. And it came to pass that before the
Lamanites had retreated far, they were surrounded by the
Nephites, by the men of Moroni on one hand and the men of Lehi
on the other, all of whom were fresh and full of strength. But the
Lamanites were wearied because of their long march. And Moroni
commanded his men that they should fall upon them until they
had given up their weapons of war. [15]

But behold, there were many that would not, and those who
would not deliver up their swords were taken and bound, and
their weapons of war were taken from them, and they were
compelled to march with their brethren forth into the land
Bountiful. And now, the number of prisoners who were taken
exceeded more than the number of those who had been slain, yea,
more than those who had been slain on both sides. [16]

And it came to pass that they did set guards over the
prisoners of the Lamanites and did compel them to go forth and
bury their dead, yea, and also the dead of the Nephites who were
slain. And Moroni placed men over them to guard them while
they should perform their labor. And it came to pass that after the

---

[15] Alma 52: 22-32
[16] Alma 52: 39-40

Lamanites had finished burying their dead, and also the dead of the Nephites, they were marched back into the land Bountiful.

And Teancum, by the orders of Moroni, caused that they should commence laboring in digging a ditch round about the land, or the city Bountiful. And he caused that they should build a breastwork of timbers upon the inner bank of the ditch; and they cast up dirt out of the ditch against the breastwork of timbers. And thus they did cause the Lamanites to labor until they had encircled the city of Bountiful round about with a strong wall of timbers and earth to an exceeding height. And this city became an exceeding stronghold ever after. And in this city they did guard the prisoners of the Lamanites, yea, even within a wall which they had caused them to build with their own hands.

Now Moroni was compelled to cause the Lamanites to labor because it was easy to guard them while at their labor, and he desired all his forces when he should make an attack upon the Lamanites. And it came to pass that Moroni had thus gained a victory over one of the greatest of the armies of the Lamanites and had obtained possession of the city Mulek, which was one of the strongest holds of the Lamanites in the land of Nephi. And thus he had also built a stronghold to retain his prisoners.

And it came to pass that he did no more attempt a battle with the Lamanites in that year; but he did employ his men in preparing for war, yea, and in making fortifications to guard against the Lamanites; yea, and also delivering their women and their children from famine and affliction and providing food for their armies.

And now, it came to pass that the armies of the Lamanites on the west sea south, while in the absence of Moroni, had gained some ground over the Nephites, yea, insomuch that they had obtained possession of a number of their cities in that part of the land. [17]

And it came to pass that Moroni was angry with the government because of their indifference concerning the freedom of their country. [18] And it came to pass that he wrote to the governor of the land, who was Pahoran; and these are the words

---

[17] Alma 53: 1, 3-8*
[18] Alma 59: 13

which he wrote, saying:

Behold, I direct mine epistle to Pahoran, in the city of Zarahemla, who is the chief judge and the governor over the land, and also to all those who have been chosen by this people to govern and manage the affairs of this war.

And now, behold, I say unto you that myself, and also my men, have suffered exceeding great sufferings, yea, even hunger, thirst, and fatigue, and all manner of afflictions of every kind. But behold, were this all we had suffered we would not murmur nor complain. But behold, great has been the slaughter among our people. Yea, thousands have fallen by the sword, while it might have otherwise been, if ye had rendered unto our armies sufficient strength and succor for them. Yea, great has been your neglect towards us. And now, behold, we desire to know the cause of this exceeding great neglect. Yea, we desire to know the cause of your thoughtless state.

Can you think to sit upon your thrones in a state of thoughtless stupor while your enemies are spreading the work of death around you; yea, while they are murdering thousands of your brethren? [19]

But behold, this is not all! Ye have withheld your provisions from them, insomuch that many have fought and bled out their lives, because of their great desires, which they had for the welfare of this people. Yea, and this they have done when they were about to perish with hunger, because of your exceeding great neglect towards them. [20]

But why should I say much concerning this matter? We know not but what ye are also traitors to your country. Or is it that ye have neglected us because ye are in the heart of our country, and ye are surrounded by security, that ye do not cause food to be sent unto us, and also men to strengthen our armies? Have ye forgot the commandments of the Lord, your God? Yea, have ye forgot the captivity of our fathers? Have ye forgot the many times we have been delivered out of the hands of our enemies? Or do ye suppose that the Lord will still deliver us, while we sit upon our

---

[19] Alma 60: 1*, 3*-7
[20] Alma 60: 9

thrones, and do not make use of the means which the Lord has provided for us? [21]

Now I would that ye should remember that God has said that the inward vessel shall be cleansed first, and then shall the outer vessel be cleansed also. And now, except ye do repent of that which ye have done, and begin to be up and doing, and send forth food and men unto us, behold, it will be expedient that we contend no more with the Lamanites until we have first cleansed our inward vessel, yea, even the great head of our government.

And except ye grant mine epistle, and come out and show unto me a true spirit of freedom, and strive to strengthen and fortify our armies, and grant unto them food for their support, behold, I will leave a part of my freemen to maintain this part of our land, and I will leave the strength and the blessings of God upon them, that none other power can operate against them, and I will come unto you. And if there be any among you that has a desire for freedom, yea, if there be even a spark of freedom remaining, behold, I will stir up insurrections among you, even until those who have desires to usurp power and authority shall become extinct. [22]

Behold, I am Moroni, your chief captain. I seek not for power but to pull it down. I seek not for honor of the world, but for the glory of my God and the freedom and welfare of my country. And thus I close mine epistle. [23]

Behold, now it came to pass that soon after Moroni had sent his epistle unto the chief governor, he received an epistle from Pahoran, the chief governor. And these are the words which he received:

I, Pahoran, who am the chief governor of this land, do send these words unto Moroni, the chief captain over the army: Behold, I say unto you, Moroni, that I do not joy in your great afflictions. Yea, it grieves my soul. But behold, there are those who do joy in your afflictions; yea, insomuch that they have risen up in rebellion

---

[21] Alma 60: 18*-21
[22] Alma 60: 23*, 24*, 25, 27
[23] Alma 60: 36

against me and also those of my people who are Freemen. Yea, and those who have risen up are exceeding numerous.

And it is those who have sought to take away the judgment seat from me that have been the cause of this great iniquity. For they have used great flattery, and they have led away the hearts of many people, which will be the cause of sore affliction among us. They have withheld our provisions and have daunted our Freemen, that they have not come unto you.

And behold, they have driven me out before them, and I have fled to the land of Gideon with as many men as it were possible that I could get. And behold, I have sent a proclamation throughout this part of the land. And behold, they are flocking to us daily, to their arms in the defense of their country and their freedom, and to avenge our wrongs. And they have come unto us, insomuch that those who have risen up in rebellion against us are set at defiance, yea, insomuch that they do fear us and durst not come out against us to battle.

They have got possession of the land, or the city of Zarahemla. They have appointed a king over them, and he hath written unto the king of the Lamanites, in the which he hath joined an alliance with him, in the which alliance he hath agreed to maintain the city of Zarahemla, which maintenance he supposeth will enable the Lamanites to conquer the remainder of the land. And he shall be placed king over this people when they shall be conquered under the Lamanites.

And now, in your epistle you have censured me; but it mattereth not. I am not angry, but do rejoice in the greatness of your heart. I, Pahoran, do not seek for power, save only to retain my judgment seat, that I may preserve the rights and the liberty of my people. My soul standeth fast in that liberty in the which God hath made us free. And now, behold, we will resist wickedness, even unto bloodshed. [24] Therefore, my beloved brother Moroni, let us resist evil. And whatsoever evil we cannot resist with our words, yea, such as rebellions and dissensions, let us resist them with our swords, that we may retain our freedom, that we may

---

[24] Alma 61: 1-10*

rejoice in the great privilege of our church, and in the cause of our Redeemer and our God.

Therefore, come unto me speedily with a few of your men, and leave the remainder in the charge of Lehi and Teancum. Give unto them power to conduct the war in that part of the land according to the Spirit of God, which is also the spirit of freedom which is in them. Behold, I have sent a few provisions unto them, that they may not perish until ye can come unto me.

Gather together whatsoever force ye can upon your march hither, and we will go speedily against those dissenters in the strength of our God, according to the faith which is in us. And we will take possession of the city of Zarahemla, that we may obtain more food to send forth unto Lehi and Teancum. Yea, we will go forth against them in the strength of the Lord, and we will put an end to this great iniquity.

And now, Moroni, I do joy in receiving your epistle, for I was somewhat worried concerning what we should do, whether it should be just in us to go against our brethren. But ye have said, Except they repent, the Lord hath commanded you that ye should go against them.

See that ye strengthen Lehi and Teancum in the Lord. Tell them to fear not. For God will deliver them, yea, and also all those who stand fast in that liberty wherewith God hath made them free. And now, I close mine epistle to my beloved brother Moroni. [25]

And now, it came to pass that when Moroni had received this epistle, his heart did take courage and was filled with exceeding great joy because of the faithfulness of Pahoran, that he was not also a traitor to the freedom and cause of his country.

And it came to pass that Moroni took a small number of men, according to the desire of Pahoran, and gave Lehi and Teancum command over the remainder of his army, and took his march towards the land of Gideon. And he did raise the standard of liberty in whatsoever place he did enter, and gained whatsoever force he could in all his march towards the land of Gideon.

And it came to pass that thousands did flock unto his standard and did take up their swords in the defense of their

---

[25] Alma 61: 14-21

freedom, that they might not come into bondage. And thus when Moroni had gathered together whatsoever men he could in all his march, he came to the land of Gideon. And uniting his forces with that of Pahoran, they became exceeding strong, even stronger than the men of Pachus, who was the king of those dissenters, who had driven the freemen out of the land of Zarahemla and had taken possession of the land.

And it came to pass that Moroni and Pahoran went down with their armies into the land of Zarahemla, and went forth against the city, and did meet the men of Pachus, insomuch that they did come to battle. And behold, Pachus was slain, and his men were taken prisoners, and Pahoran was restored to his judgment seat.

And the men of Pachus received their trial, according to the law, and also those Kingmen who had been taken and cast into prison. And they were executed according to the law. Yea, those men of Pachus and those Kingmen, whosoever would not take up arms in the defense of their country, but would fight against it, were put to death. [26]

And thus ended the thirtieth year of the reign of the judges over the people of Nephi, Moroni and Pahoran having restored peace to the land of Zarahemla among their own people, having inflicted death upon all those who were not true to the cause of freedom.

And it came to pass in the commencement of the thirty and first year of the reign of the judges over the people of Nephi, Moroni immediately caused that provisions should be sent; and also an army of six thousand men should be sent unto Helaman to assist him in preserving that part of the land. And he also caused that an army of six thousand men, with a sufficient quantity of food, should be sent to the armies of Lehi and Teancum. And it came to pass that this was done to fortify the land against the Lamanites.

And it came to pass that Moroni and Pahoran, leaving a large body of men in the land of Zarahemla, took their march with a large body of men towards the land of Nephihah, being determined to overthrow the Lamanites in that city. And it came to pass that as they were marching towards the land, they took a

---

[26] Alma 62: 1, 3-9

large body of men of the Lamanites and slew many of them, and took their provisions and their weapons of war.

And it came to pass after they had taken them, they caused them to enter into a covenant, that they would no more take up their weapons of war against the Nephites. And when they had entered into this covenant, they sent them to dwell with the people of Ammon. And they were in number about four thousand who had not been slain. [27]

Now it came to pass that many of the Lamanites who were prisoners were desirous to join the people of Ammon and become a free people. And it came to pass that as many as were desirous, unto them it was granted according to their desires. Therefore, all the prisoners of the Lamanites did join the people of Ammon and did begin to labor exceedingly, tilling the ground, raising all manner of grain, and flocks, and herds of every kind. And thus were the Nephites relieved from a great burden, yea, insomuch that they were relieved from all the prisoners of the Lamanites.

Now it came to pass that Moroni, after he had obtained possession of the city of Nephihah, having taken many prisoners, which did reduce the armies of the Lamanites exceedingly, and having retained many of the Nephites who had been taken prisoners, which did strengthen the army of Moroni exceedingly; therefore, Moroni went forth from the land of Nephihah to the land of Lehi.

And it came to pass that when the Lamanites saw that Moroni was coming against them, they were frightened and fled before the army of Moroni. [28] Now it came to pass that Moroni marched forth on the morrow and came upon the Lamanites, insomuch that they did slay them with a great slaughter. And they did drive them out of the land. And they did flee, even that they did not return at that time against the Nephites.

And thus ended the thirty and first year of the reign of the judges over the people of Nephi. And thus they had had wars, and bloodsheds, and famine, and affliction for the space of many years. And there had been murders, and contentions, and

---

[27] Alma 62: 11-17
[28] Alma 62: 27-31

dissensions, and all manner of iniquity among the people of Nephi. Nevertheless, for the righteous' sake, yea, because of the prayers of the righteous, they were spared.

But behold, because of the exceeding great length of the war between the Nephites and the Lamanites, many had become hardened, because of the exceeding great length of the war. And many were softened because of their afflictions, insomuch that they did humble themselves before God, even in the depth of humility.

And it came to pass that after Moroni had fortified those parts of the land which were most exposed to the Lamanites, until they were sufficiently strong, he returned to the city of Zarahemla. And also Helaman returned to the place of his inheritance. And there was once more peace established among the people of Nephi. And Moroni yielded up the command of his armies into the hands of his son, whose name was Moronihah. And he retired to his own house, that he might spend the remainder of his days in peace. And Pahoran did return to his judgment seat.

And Helaman did take upon him again to preach unto the people the word of God. For because of so many wars and contentions, it had become expedient that a regulation should be made again in the church. Therefore, Helaman and his brethren went forth and did declare the word of God with much power, unto the convincing of many people of their wickedness, which did cause them to repent of their sins and to be baptized unto the Lord their God.

And it came to pass that they did establish again the church of God throughout all the land. Yea, and regulations were made concerning the law. And their judges and their chief judges were chosen. And the people of Nephi began to prosper again in the land and began to multiply and to wax exceeding strong again in the land.

And they began to grow exceeding rich; but notwithstanding their riches, or their strength, or their prosperity, they were not lifted up in the pride of their eyes; neither were they slow to remember the Lord, their God; but they did humble themselves exceedingly before him.

Yea, they did remember how great things the Lord had done for them; that he had delivered them from death, and from bonds, and from prisons, and from all manner of afflictions. And he had delivered them out of the hands of their enemies. And they did pray unto the Lord, their God, continually, insomuch that the Lord did bless them according to his word, so that they did wax strong and prosper in the land. And it came to pass that all these things were done, and Helaman died in the thirty and fifth year of the reign of the judges over the people of Nephi. [29]

And it came to pass in the commencement of the thirty and sixth year of the reign of the judges over the people of Nephi, that Shiblon, the brother of Helaman, took possession of those sacred things which had been delivered unto Helaman by Alma. And he was a just man, and he did walk uprightly before God. And he did observe to do good continually, to keep the commandments of the Lord, his God, and also did his brother.

And it came to pass that Moroni died also. And thus ended the thirty and sixth year of the reign of the judges.

About 54 B.C.

And it came to pass that in the thirty and seventh year of the reign of the judges, there was a large company of men, even to the amount of five thousand and four hundred men with their wives and their children, departed out of the land of Zarahemla into the land which was northward.

And it came to pass that Hagoth, he being an exceeding curious man, therefore, he went forth, and built him an exceeding large ship on the borders of the land Bountiful by the land Desolation, and launched it forth into the west sea, by the narrow neck which led into the land northward. And behold, there were many of the Nephites who did enter therein and did sail forth with much provisions and also many women and children. And they took their course northward. And thus ended the thirty and seventh year.

---

[29] Alma 62: 38-52

And in the thirty and eighth year this man built other ships. And the first ship did also return, and many more people did enter into it. And they also took much provisions and set out again to the land northward. And it came to pass that they were never heard of more. And we suppose that they were drowned up in the depths of the sea. And it came to pass that one other ship also did sail forth; and whither she did go we know not. And it came to pass that in this year, there were many people who went forth into the land northward. And thus ended the thirty and eighth year.

And it came to pass in the thirty and ninth year of the reign of the judges, Shiblon died also, and Corianton had gone forth to the land northward in a ship to carry forth provisions unto the people who had gone forth into that land. Therefore, it became expedient for Shiblon to confer those sacred things, before his death, upon the son of Helaman, who was called Helaman, being called after the name of his father.

Now behold, all those engravings which were in the possession of Helaman were written and sent forth among the children of men, throughout all the land, save it were those parts which had been commanded by Alma should not go forth. Nevertheless, these things were to be kept sacred and handed down from one generation to another; therefore, in this year they had been conferred upon Helaman before the death of Shiblon. And thus ended the account of Alma, and Helaman his son, and also Shiblon, who was his son. [30]

About 51 B.C.

And now, behold, it came to pass in the commencement of the fortieth year of the reign of the judges over the people of Nephi, there began to be a serious difficulty among the people of the Nephites. For behold, Pahoran had died and gone the way of all the earth. Therefore, there began to be a serious contention concerning who should have the judgment seat among the brethren who were the sons of Pahoran.

---

[30] Alma 63: 1-13, 17

Now these are their names who did contend for the judgment seat, who did also cause the people to contend: Pahoran, Paanchi, and Pacumeni. [31] Nevertheless, it came to pass that Pahoran was appointed by the voice of the people to be chief judge and a governor over the people of Nephi.

And it came to pass that Pacumeni, when he saw that he could not obtain the judgement seat, he did unite with the voice of the people. But behold, Paanchi, and that part of the people that were desirous that he should be their governor, was exceeding wroth. Therefore, he was about to flatter away those people to rise up in rebellion against their brethren. And it came to pass as he was about to do this, behold, he was taken, and was tried according to the voice of the people, and condemned unto death; for he had risen up in rebellion and sought to destroy the liberty of the people.

Now, when those people who were desirous that he should be their governor saw that he was condemned unto death, therefore, they were angry. And behold, they sent forth one Kishkumen, even to the judgment seat of Pahoran, and murdered Pahoran as he sat upon the judgment seat. And he was pursued by the servants of Pahoran. But behold, so speedy was the flight of Kishkumen that no man could overtake him.

And he went unto those that sent him and they all entered into a covenant, yea, swearing by their everlasting Maker that they would tell no man that Kishkumen had murdered Pahoran. Therefore, Kishkumen was not known among the people of Nephi, for he was in disguise at the time that he murdered Pahoran. And Kishkumen and his band, who had covenanted with him, did mingle themselves among the people in a manner that they all could not be found. But as many as were found were condemned unto death.

And now, behold, Pacumeni was appointed, according to the voice of the people, to be a chief judge and a governor over the people, to reign in the stead of his brother Pahoran. And it was according to his right. [32]

---

[31] Helaman 1: 1-3
[32] Helaman 1: 5-13*

And it came to pass in the forty and first year of the reign of the judges that the Lamanites had gathered together an innumerable army of men and armed them with swords, and with cimeters, and with bows, and with arrows, and with headplates, and with breastplates, and with all manner of shields of every kind. And they came down again, that they might pitch battle against the Nephites. And they were led by a man whose name was Coriantumr. And he was a descendant of Zarahemla, and he was a dissenter from among the Nephites, and he was a large and a mighty man. [33]

And it came to pass that because of so much contention and so much difficulty in the government, that they had not kept sufficient guards in the land of Zarahemla; for they had supposed that the Lamanites durst not come into the heart of their lands to attack that great city Zarahemla. But it came to pass that Coriantumr did march forth at the head of his numerous host and came upon the inhabitants of the city. And their march was with such exceeding great speed that there was no time for the Nephites to gather together their armies. Therefore, Coriantumr did cut down the watch by the entrance of the city, and did march forth with his whole army into the city. And they did slay everyone who did oppose them, insomuch that they did take possession of the whole city.

And it came to pass that Pacumeni, who was the chief judge, did flee before Coriantumr, even to the walls of the city. And it came to pass that Coriantumr did smite him against the wall, insomuch that he died. And thus ended the days of Pacumeni.

And now, when Coriantumr saw that he was in possession of the city of Zarahemla, and saw that the Nephites had fled before them, and that he had obtained the possession of the strongest hold in all the land, his heart took courage, insomuch that he was about to go forth against all the land, even towards the city of Bountiful. For it was his determination to go forth and cut his way through with the sword, that he might obtain the north parts of the land. [34]

---

[33] Helaman 1: 14-15
[34] Helaman 1: 18-22*, 23*

But when Moronihah had discovered this, he immediately sent forth Lehi with an army round about to head them before they should come to the land Bountiful. And he did head them and gave unto them battle, insomuch that they began to retreat back towards the land of Zarahemla. And it came to pass that Moronihah did head them in their retreat and did give unto them battle, insomuch that it became an exceeding bloody battle. Yea, many were slain, and among the number who were slain, Coriantumr was also found. [35] And thus had Coriantumr plunged the Lamanites into the midst of the Nephites, insomuch that they were in the power of the Nephites, and he himself was slain. And the Lamanites did yield themselves into the hands of the Nephites.

And it came to pass that Moronihah took possession of the city of Zarahemla again, and caused that the Lamanites who had been taken prisoners should depart out of the land in peace. And thus ended the forty and first year of the reign of the judges. [36]

And it came to pass in the forty and second year of the reign of the judges, behold, there was no one to fill the judgment seat. Therefore, there began to be a contention among the people concerning who should fill the judgment seat. And it came to pass that Helaman, who was the son of Helaman, was appointed to fill the judgment seat by the voice of the people. But behold, Kishkumen, who had murdered Pahoran, did lie in wait to destroy Helaman also. And he was upheld by his band, who had entered into a covenant that no one should know his wickedness.

For there was one Gadianton, who was exceeding expert in many words and also in his craft to carry on the secret work of murder and of robbery. Therefore, he became the leader of the band of Kishkumen. Therefore, he did flatter them, and also Kishkumen, that if they would place him in the judgment seat, he would grant unto those who belonged to his band that they should be placed in power and authority among the people. Therefore, Kishkumen sought to destroy Helaman.

And it came to pass as he went forth towards the judgment seat to destroy Helaman, behold, one of the servants of Helaman,

---

[35] Helaman 1: 28-29*, 30
[36] Helaman 1: 32-34

having been out by night, and having obtained through disguise, a knowledge of those plans, which had been laid by his band to destroy Helaman— and it came to pass that he met Kishkumen, and he gave unto him a sign. Therefore, Kishkumen made known unto him the object of his desire, desiring that he would conduct him to the judgment seat, that he might murder Helaman.

And when the servant of Helaman had known all the heart of Kishkumen, and how that it was his object to murder, and also that it was the object of all those who belonged to his band to murder, and to rob, and to gain power, and this was their secret plan and their combination, the servant of Helaman saith unto Kishkumen, Let us go forth unto the judgment seat. Now this did please Kishkumen exceedingly, for he did suppose that he should accomplish his design.

But behold, the servant of Helaman, as they were going forth unto the judgment seat, did stab Kishkumen, even to the heart, that he fell dead without a groan. And he ran and told Helaman all the things which he had seen, and heard, and done.

And it came to pass that Helaman did send forth to take this band of robbers and secret murderers, that they might be executed according to the law. But behold, when Gadianton had found that Kishkumen did not return, he feared lest that he should be destroyed. Therefore, he caused that his band should follow him. And they took their flight out of the land by a secret way into the wilderness. And thus when Helaman sent forth to take them, they could nowhere be found. And more of this Gadianton shall be spoken hereafter. And thus ended the forty and second year of the reign of the judges over the people of Nephi. [37]

About 45 B.C.

And it came to pass in the forty and sixth year there were many contentions and many dissensions, in the which there were an exceeding great many who departed out of the land of Zarahemla, and went forth unto the land northward to inherit the land. And they did travel to an exceeding great distance, insomuch that they

[37] Helaman 2: 1*-12

came to large bodies of water and many rivers. [38] And there being but little timber upon the face of the land, nevertheless, the people who went forth became exceeding expert in the working of cement. Therefore, they did build houses of cement in the which they did dwell. And it came to pass that they did multiply, and spread, and did go forth from the land southward to the land northward, and did spread insomuch that they began to cover the face of the whole earth, from the sea south to the sea north, from the sea west to the sea east. [39]

And it came to pass, as timber was exceeding scarce in the land northward, they did send forth much by the way of shipping. And thus they did enable the people in the land northward, that they might build many cities, both of wood and of cement. And it came to pass that there were many of the people of Ammon, who were Lamanites by birth, did also go forth into this land. [40]

And now, I return again to mine account. Therefore, what I have spoken had passed after there had been great contentions, and disturbances, and wars, and dissensions, among the people of Nephi. And it came to pass that there were still great contentions in the land, yea, even in the forty and seventh year, and also in the forty and eighth year. Nevertheless, Helaman did fill the judgment seat with justice and equity; yea, he did observe to keep the statutes, and the judgments, and the commandments of God. And he did do that which was right in the sight of God continually. And he did walk after the ways of his father, insomuch that he did prosper in the land.

And it came to pass that he had two sons. He gave unto the eldest the name of Nephi and unto the youngest the name of Lehi. And they began to grow up unto the Lord.

And it came to pass that the wars and contentions began to cease, in a small degree, among the people of the Nephites, in the latter end of the forty and eighth year of the reign of the judges over the people of Nephi. [41]

---

[38] Helaman 3: 3-4
[39] Helaman 3: 7-8
[40] Helaman 3: 10-12
[41] Helaman 3: 17, 19-22

And it came to pass that there was exceeding great prosperity in the church, insomuch that there were thousands who did join themselves unto the church and were baptized unto repentance. And so great was the prosperity of the church, and so many the blessings which were poured out upon the people, that even the high priests and the teachers were themselves astonished beyond measure. [42]

And in the fifty and first year of the reign of the judges there was peace also, save it were the pride which began to enter into the church; not into the church of God, but into the hearts of the people who professed to belong to the church of God. And they were lifted up in pride, even to the persecution of many of their brethren, which did cause the more humble part of the people to suffer great persecutions, and to wade through much affliction. [43] Nevertheless, they did fast and pray oft, and did wax stronger and stronger in their humility, and firmer and firmer in the faith of Christ.

And it came to pass that the fifty and second year ended in peace also, save it were the exceeding great pride which had gotten into the hearts of the people. And it was because of their exceeding great riches and their prosperity in the land. And it did grow upon them from day to day.

And it came to pass in the fifty and third year of the reign of the judges, Helaman died. And his eldest son Nephi began to reign in his stead. And it came to pass that he did fill the judgment seat with justice and equity. Yea, he did keep the commandments of God and did walk in the ways of his father. [44]

About 36 B.C.

And it came to pass in the fifty and fourth year, there were many dissensions in the church, and there was also a contention among the people. And the rebellious part were slain and driven out of the land, and they did go unto the king of the Lamanites, to

---

[42] Helaman 3: 24-25
[43] Helaman 3: 33-34*
[44] Helaman 3: 35-37

stir up the Lamanites to war against the Nephites. But behold, the Lamanites were exceeding afraid, insomuch that they would not hearken to the words of those dissenters. [45] But it came to pass in the fifty and sixth year of the reign of the judges, they succeeded in stirring them up to anger against the Nephites, and they were all that year preparing for war.

And in the fifty and seventh year they did come down against the Nephites to battle. And they did commence the work of death; yea, insomuch that in the fifty and eighth year of the reign of the judges they succeeded in obtaining possession of the land of Zarahemla, yea, and also all the lands, even unto the land which was near the land Bountiful. And the Nephites and the armies of Moronihah were driven even into the land of Bountiful. And there they did fortify against the Lamanites, from the west sea even unto the east, it being a day's journey for a Nephite on the line which they had fortified and stationed their armies to defend their north country. And thus, those dissenters of the Nephites, with the help of a numerous army of the Lamanites, had obtained all the possession of the Nephites which was in the land southward. [46]

Now this great loss of the Nephites, and the great slaughter which was among them, would not have happened had it not been for their wickedness and their abomination which was among them. Yea, and it was among those also who professed to belong to the church of God. And it was because of the pride of their hearts, because of their exceeding riches. Yea, it was because of their oppression of the poor, making a mock of that which was sacred, denying the spirit of prophecy and of revelation, lying, stealing, committing adultery, rising up in great contentions, and deserting away into the land of Nephi among the Lamanites. [47]

And because of this their great wickedness and their boastings in their own strength, they were left in their own strength. Therefore, they did not prosper, but were afflicted, and smitten, and driven before the Lamanites until they had lost possession of almost all their lands.

---

[45] Helaman 4: 1*-3*
[46] Helaman 4: 4*-8*
[47] Helaman 4: 11-12*

But behold, Moronihah did preach many things unto the people because of their iniquity. And also Nephi and Lehi, who were the sons of Helaman, did preach many things unto the people; yea, and did prophesy many things unto them concerning their iniquities, and what should come unto them if they did not repent of their sins.

And it came to pass that they did repent. And inasmuch as they did repent, they did begin to prosper. For when Moronihah saw that they did repent, he did venture to lead them forth from place to place and from city to city, even until they had retained the one-half of their property and the one-half of all their lands. [48]

And it came to pass in the sixty and second year of the reign of the judges, that Moronihah could obtain no more possessions over the Lamanites, therefore, they did abandon their design to obtain the remainder of their lands. For so numerous were the Lamanites that it became impossible for the Nephites to obtain more power over them. Therefore, Moronihah did employ all his armies in maintaining those parts which he had taken.

And it came to pass because of the greatness of the number of the Lamanites, the Nephites were in great fear, lest they should be overpowered, and trodden down, and slain, and destroyed. Yea, they began to remember the prophecies of Alma and also the words of Mosiah. And they saw that they had been a stiff-necked people, and that they had set at naught the commandments of God, and that they had altered and trampled under their feet the laws of Mosiah, or that which the Lord commanded him to give unto the people. And thus seeing that their laws had become corrupted, they had become a wicked people, even like unto the Lamanites. [49]

And because of their iniquity the church had begun to dwindle; and they began to disbelieve in the spirit of prophecy and in the spirit of revelation. And the judgments of God did stare them in the face. [50]

---

[48] Helaman 4: 13-16
[49] Helaman 4: 18-22*
[50] Helaman 4: 23

Part III

Signs

" Behold, I will send my messenger,
and he shall prepare the way before
me; and the Lord, whom ye seek,
shall suddenly come to his temple,
even the messenger of the covenant,
whom ye delight in. Behold, he shall
come, saith the Lord of hosts "

Malachi 3: 1

Chapter 9

Spiritual Battles

About 29 B.C.

And it came to pass that Nephi delivered up the judgment seat to a man whose name was Cezoram. For, as their laws and their governments were established by the voice of the people, and they who chose evil were more numerous than they who chose good, therefore, they were ripening for destruction, for the laws had become corrupted. [1]

And it came to pass that Nephi had become weary because of their iniquity. And he yielded up the judgment seat and took it upon him to preach the word of God all the remainder of his days; and his brother Lehi also, all the remainder of his days. For they remembered the words which their father Helaman spake unto them. And these are the words which he spake:

Behold my sons, I have given unto you the names of our first parents, who came out of the land of Jerusalem. And this I have done, that when ye remember your names, that ye may remember them; and when ye remember them, ye may remember their works; and when ye remember their works, ye may know how that it is said and also written that they were good. [2] Therefore, my sons, I would that ye should do that which is good, that it may be said of you, and also written, even as it has been said and written of them.

Oh, remember, remember, my sons, the words which King Benjamin spake unto his people. Yea, remember that there is no other way nor means whereby man can be saved; only through the atoning blood of Jesus Christ, who shall come. Yea, remember that he cometh to redeem the world. And remember also the words which Amulek spake, for he said that the Lord surely should come to redeem his people, but that he should not come to

---

[1] Helaman 5: 1*-2
[2] Helaman 5: 4-6*

redeem them in their sins, but to redeem them from their sins. [3]
And he hath power given unto him from the Father to redeem
them from their sins because of repentance. Therefore, he hath
sent his angels to declare the tidings of the conditions of
repentance, which bringeth unto the power of the Redeemer, unto
the salvation of their souls.

And now, my sons, remember, remember, that it is upon the
rock of our Redeemer, who is Christ, the Son of God, that ye must
build your foundation—that when the devil shall send forth his
mighty winds, yea, his shafts in the whirlwind, yea, when all his
hail and his mighty storm shall beat upon you, it shall have no
power over you, to drag you down to the gulf of misery and endless
wo, because of the rock upon which ye are built, which is a sure
foundation, a foundation whereon if men build, they cannot fall.

And it came to pass that these were the words which
Helaman taught to his sons; yea, he did teach them many things
which are not written, and also many things which are written.
And they did remember his words.

And therefore, they went forth, keeping the commandments
of God, to teach the word of God among all the people of Nephi,
beginning at the city Bountiful, and from thence forth to the city of
Gid, and from the city of Gid to the city of Mulek, and even from
one city to another, until they had gone forth among all the people
of Nephi, who were in the land southward, and from thence into
the land of Zarahemla, among the Lamanites.

And it came to pass that they did preach with great power,
insomuch that they did confound many of those dissenters who
had gone over from the Nephites; insomuch that they came forth,
and did confess their sins, and were baptized unto repentance,
and immediately returned to the Nephites to endeavor to repair
unto them the wrongs which they had done.

And it came to pass that Nephi and Lehi did preach unto the
Lamanites with such great power and authority—for they had
power and authority given unto them that they might speak, and
they also had what they should speak given unto them—
therefore, they did speak unto the great astonishment of the

---

[3] Helaman 5: 7, 9-10*

Lamanites, to the convincing them; insomuch that there were eight thousand of the Lamanites who were in the land of Zarahemla and round about baptized unto repentance, and were convinced of the wickedness of the traditions of their fathers.

And it came to pass that Nephi and Lehi did proceed from thence to go to the land of Nephi. And it came to pass that they were taken by an army of the Lamanites and cast into prison, yea, even in that same prison in which Ammon and his brethren were cast by the servants of Limhi.

And after they had been cast into prison many days without food, behold, they went forth into the prison to take them, that they might slay them. And it came to pass that Nephi and Lehi were encircled about, as if by fire, even insomuch that they durst not lay their hands upon them; for fear lest they should be burned. [4]

And it came to pass that Nephi and Lehi did stand forth and began to speak unto them, saying, Fear not, for behold, it is God that has shown unto you this marvelous thing, in the which is shown unto you that ye cannot lay your hands on us to slay us. And behold, when they had said these words, the earth shook exceedingly, and the walls of the prison did shake as if they were about to tumble to the earth. But behold, they did not fall.

And behold, they that were in the prison were Lamanites and Nephites who were dissenters. And it came to pass that they were overshadowed with a cloud of darkness, and an awful, solemn fear came upon them.

And it came to pass that there came a voice, as if it were above the cloud of darkness, saying, Repent ye, repent ye, and seek no more to destroy my servants whom I have sent unto you to declare good tidings.

And it came to pass when they heard this voice, and beheld that it was not a voice of thunder, neither was it a voice of a great tumultuous noise. But behold, it was a still voice of perfect mildness, as if it had been a whisper, and it did pierce even to the very soul. And notwithstanding the mildness of the voice, behold, the earth shook exceedingly, and the walls of the prison trembled again as if it were about to tumble to the earth. And behold, the

---

[4] Helaman 5: 11-23*

cloud of darkness which had overshadowed them did not disperse.

And behold, the voice came again, saying, Repent ye, repent ye, for the kingdom of heaven is at hand. And seek no more to destroy my servants. And it came to pass that the earth shook again, and the walls trembled. And it came to pass that the Lamanites could not flee because of the cloud of darkness which did overshadow them; yea, and also they were immovable because of the fear which did come upon them. [5]

And it came to pass that they all did begin to cry unto the voice of him who had shook the earth. Yea, they did cry even until the cloud of darkness was dispersed. And it came to pass that when they cast their eyes about and saw that the cloud of darkness was dispersed from overshadowing them, behold, they saw that they were encircled about, yea, every soul, by a pillar of fire. [6]

And behold, the Holy Spirit of God did come down from heaven and did enter into their hearts. And they were filled as if with fire, and they could speak forth marvelous words. And it came to pass that there came a voice unto them, yea, a pleasant voice, as if it were a whisper, saying, Peace, peace be unto you because of your faith in my well beloved, who was from the foundation of the world.

And now, when they heard this, they cast up their eyes as if to behold from whence the voice came. And behold, they saw the heavens open; and angels came down out of heaven and ministered unto them. And there were about three hundred souls who saw and heard these things. And they were bid to go forth and marvel not, neither should they doubt.

And it came to pass that they did go forth and did minister unto the people, declaring throughout all the regions round about all the things which they had heard and seen, insomuch that the more part of the Lamanites were convinced of them because of the greatness of the evidences which they had received.

And as many as were convinced did lay down their weapons of war, and also their hatred, and the tradition of their fathers.

---

[5] Helaman 5: 26-32, 34
[6] Helaman 5: 42-43

And it came to pass that they did yield up unto the Nephites the lands of their possession. [7]

About 27 B.C.

And it came to pass that when the sixty and second year of the reign of the judges had ended, all these things had happened. And the Lamanites had become, the more part of them, a righteous people, insomuch that their righteousness did exceed that of the Nephites, because of their firmness and their steadiness in the faith. For behold, there were many of the Nephites who had become hardened, and impenitent, and grossly wicked, insomuch that they did reject the word of God and all the preaching and prophesying which did come among them.

Nevertheless, the people of the church did have great joy because of the conversion of the Lamanites, yea, because of the church of God, which had been established among them. And they did fellowship one with another, and did rejoice one with another, and did have great joy.

And it came to pass that many of the Lamanites did come down into the land of Zarahemla, and did declare unto the people of the Nephites the manner of their conversion, and did exhort them to faith and repentance. Yea, and many did preach with exceeding great power and authority, unto the bringing down many of them into the depths of humility to be the humble followers of God and the Lamb.

And it came to pass that many of the Lamanites did go into the land northward. And also Nephi and Lehi went into the land northward to preach unto the people. And thus ended the sixty and third year.

And behold, there was peace in all the land, insomuch that the Nephites did go into whatsoever part of the land they would, whether among the Nephites or the Lamanites. And it came to pass that the Lamanites did also go whithersoever they would, whether it were among the Lamanites or among the Nephites, to

---

[7] Helaman 5: 45-52

buy and to sell, and to get gain, according to their desire. [8]

And it came to pass that they became exceedingly rich, both the Lamanites and the Nephites. And behold, there was all manner of gold in these lands, and of silver, and of precious ore of every kind. And there were also curious workmen, who did work all kinds of ore, and did refine it; and thus they did become rich. They did raise grain in abundance, both in the north and in the south. And they did flourish exceedingly, both in the north and in the south.

And they did multiply and wax exceeding strong in the land. And they did raise many flocks and herds, yea, many fatlings. Behold, their women did toil and spin and did make all manner of cloth, of fine twined linen, and cloth of every kind to clothe their nakedness. And thus the sixty and fourth year did pass away in peace.

And in the sixty and fifth year they did also have great joy and peace, yea, much preaching, and many prophecies concerning that which was to come. And thus passed away the sixty and fifth year.

About 25 B.C.

And it came to pass that in the sixty and sixth year of the reign of the judges, behold, Cezoram was murdered by an unknown hand as he sat upon the judgment seat. And it came to pass that in the same year that his son, who had been appointed by the people in his stead, was also murdered. And thus ended the sixty and sixth year.

And in the commencement of the sixty and seventh year the people began to grow exceeding wicked again. For behold, the Lord had blessed them so long with the riches of the world that they had not been stirred up to anger, to wars, nor to bloodsheds. Therefore, they began to set their hearts upon their riches. Yea, they began to seek to get gain, that they might be lifted up one

---

[8] Helaman 6: 1-8*

above another. Therefore, they began to commit secret murders, and to rob, and to plunder, that they might get gain. [9]

And now, behold, those murderers and plunderers were a band who had been formed by Kishkumen and Gadianton. And they were called Gadianton's robbers and murderers. And it was they who did murder the chief judge Cezoram and his son while in the judgment seat. And behold, they were not found. [10]

And it came to pass that they did have their signs, yea, their secret signs and their secret words; and this that they might distinguish a brother who had entered into the covenant, that whatsoever wickedness his brother should do, he should not be injured by his brother, nor by those who did belong to his band, who had taken this covenant. And thus they might murder, and plunder, and steal, and commit whoredoms and all manner of wickedness, contrary to the laws of their country, and also the laws of their God. And whosoever of those who belonged to their band, should reveal unto the world of their wickedness, and their abominations, should be tried, not according to the laws of their country, but according to the laws of their wickedness, which had been given by Gadianton and Kishkumen. [11]

Now behold, those secret oaths and covenants did not come forth unto Gadianton from the records which were delivered unto Helaman. But behold, they were put into the heart of Gadianton by that same being who did entice our first parents to partake of the forbidden fruit; yea, that same being who did plot with Cain, that if he would murder his brother Abel, it should not be known unto the world. And he did plot with Cain and his followers from that time forth. [12]

Yea, it is that same being who put it into the heart of Gadianton to still carry on the work of darkness and of secret murder. And he has brought it forth from the beginning of man, even down to this time. And behold, it is he who is the author of all sin. And behold, he doth carry on his works of darkness and

---

[9] Helaman 6: 9*, 11*-17
[10] Helaman 6: 18*-19
[11] Helaman 6: 22-24
[12] Helaman 6: 26-27

secret murder, and doth hand down their plots, and their oaths, and their covenants, and their plans of awful wickedness from generation to generation, according as he can get hold upon the hearts of the children of men.

And now, behold, he had got great hold upon the hearts of the Nephites; yea, insomuch that they had become exceeding wicked. Yea, the more part of them had turned out of the way of righteousness, and did trample under their feet the commandments of God, and did turn unto their own ways, and did build up unto themselves idols of their gold and their silver. [13]

And thus we see that the Nephites did begin to dwindle in unbelief, and grow in wickedness and abominations; while the Lamanites began to grow exceedingly in the knowledge of their God. Yea, they did begin to keep his statutes and commandments and to walk in truth and uprightness before him.

And thus we see that the Spirit of the Lord began to withdraw from the Nephites, because of the wickedness and the hardness of their hearts. And thus we see that the Lord began to pour out his Spirit upon the Lamanites, because of their easiness and willingness to believe in his word.

And it came to pass that the Lamanites did hunt the band of robbers of Gadianton. And they did preach the word of God among the more wicked part of them, insomuch that this band of robbers was utterly destroyed from among the Lamanites.

And it came to pass on the other hand, that the Nephites did build them up and support them, beginning at the more wicked part of them, until they had overspread all the land of the Nephites, and had seduced the more part of the righteous until they had come down to believe in their works, and partake of their spoils, and to join with them in their secret murders and combinations.

And thus they did obtain the sole management of the government, insomuch that they did trample under their feet, and smite, and rend, and turn their backs upon the poor, and the meek, and the humble followers of God. And thus we see that they were in an awful state, and ripening for an everlasting

---

[13] Helaman 6: 29-31

destruction. And it came to pass that thus ended the sixty and eighth year of the reign of the judges over the people of Nephi. [14]

Behold, now it came to pass in the sixty and ninth year of the reign of the judges over the people of the Nephites, that Nephi, the son of Helaman, returned to the land of Zarahemla from the land northward. For he had been forth among the people who were in the land northward, and did preach the word of God unto them, and did prophesy many things unto them. And they did reject all his words, insomuch that he could not stay among them, but returned again unto the land of his nativity.

And seeing the people in a state of such awful wickedness, and those Gadianton robbers filling the judgment seats, having usurped the power and authority of the land, laying aside the commandments of God, and not in the least aright before him; doing no justice unto the children of men, condemning the righteous because of their righteousness, letting the guilty and the wicked go unpunished because of their money; and moreover, to be held in office at the head of government, to rule and do according to their wills, that they might get gain and glory of the world; and moreover, that they might the more easily commit adultery, and steal, and kill, and do according to their own wills— now this great iniquity had come upon the Nephites in the space of not many years. And when Nephi saw it, his heart was swollen with sorrow within his breast. And he did exclaim in the agony of his soul:

Oh, that I could have had my days in the days when my father Nephi first came out of the land of Jerusalem, that I could have joyed with him in the promised land! Then were his people easy to be entreated, firm to keep the commandments of God, and slow to be led to do iniquity. And they were quick to hearken unto the words of the Lord. Yea, if my days could have been in those days, then would my soul have had joy in the righteousness of my brethren! But behold, I am consigned that these are my days, and that my soul shall be filled with sorrow because of this, the wickedness of my brethren.

---

[14] Helaman 6: 34-41

And behold, now it came to pass that it was upon a tower, which was in the garden of Nephi, which was by the highway which led to the chief market, which was in the city of Zarahemla. Therefore, Nephi had bowed himself upon the tower which was in his garden, which tower was also near unto the garden gate which led by the highway.

And it came to pass that there were certain men passing by and saw Nephi, as he was pouring out his soul unto God upon the tower. And they ran and told the people what they had seen. And the people came together in multitudes that they might know the cause of so great mourning for the wickedness of the people.

And now, when Nephi arose, he beheld the multitudes of people who had gathered together. And it came to pass that he opened his mouth and said unto them, Behold, why have ye gathered yourselves together? That I may tell you of your iniquities? [15] Oh, how could you have forgotten your God in the very day that he has delivered you?

But behold, it is to get gain, to be praised of men; yea, and that ye might get gold and silver. And ye have set your hearts upon the riches and the vain things of this world, for the which ye do murder, and plunder, and steal, and bear false witness against your neighbor, and do all manner of iniquity. And for this cause wo shall come unto you except ye shall repent.

For if ye will not repent, behold, this great city and also all those great cities which are round about, which are in the land of our possession shall be taken away, that ye shall have no place in them. For behold, the Lord will not grant unto you strength, as he has hitherto done, to withstand against your enemies. [16]

Yea, wo be unto you because of that great abomination which has come among you. And ye have united yourselves unto it, yea, to that secret band which was established by Gadianton. Yea, wo shall come unto you because of that pride which ye have suffered to enter your hearts, which has lifted you up beyond that which is good, because of your exceeding great riches.

---

[15] Helaman 7: 1-13
[16] Helaman 7: 20-22

Yea, wo be unto you because of your wickedness and abominations. And except ye repent, ye shall perish; yea, even your lands shall be taken from you, and ye shall be destroyed from off the face of the earth. Behold, now I do not say that these things shall be of myself, because it is not of myself that I know these things. But behold, I know that these things are true because the Lord God has made them known unto me. Therefore, I testify that they shall be. [17]

And now, it came to pass that when Nephi had said these words, behold, there were men who were judges, who also belonged to the secret band of Gadianton, and they were angry. And they cried out against him, saying unto the people, Why do ye not seize upon this man and bring him forth, that he may be condemned according to the crime which he has done?

And those judges were angry with him because he spake plain unto them concerning their secret works of darkness. Nevertheless, they durst not lay their own hands upon him, for they feared the people, lest they should cry out against them.[18]

Therefore, he began again to speak unto them, seeing that he had gained favor in the eyes of some. He was constrained to speak more unto them, saying, Behold, my brethren, have ye not read that God gave power unto one man, even Moses, to smite upon the waters of the Red Sea, and they parted hither and thither, insomuch that the Israelites, who were our fathers, came through upon dry ground? And the waters closed upon the armies of the Egyptians and swallowed them up.

And now, behold, if God gave unto this man such power, then why should ye dispute among yourselves and say that he hath given unto me no power, whereby I may know concerning the judgments that shall come upon you except ye repent? But behold, ye not only deny my words, but ye also deny all the words which hath been spoken by our fathers, and also the words which were spoken by this man, Moses, who had such great power given unto him, yea, the words which he hath spoken concerning the coming of the Messiah.

---

[17] Helaman 7: 25-29
[18] Helaman 8: 1, 4

Yea, did he not bear record that the Son of God should come? And as he lifted up the brazen serpent in the wilderness, even so shall he be lifted up, who should come. And as many as should look upon that serpent should live; even so as many as should look upon the Son of God with faith, having a contrite spirit, might live, even unto that life which is eternal. [19]

But behold, this is not all. Our father Lehi was driven out of Jerusalem because he testified of these things. Nephi also testified of these things, and also almost all of our fathers even down to this time. Yea, they have testified of the coming of Christ, and have looked forward, and have rejoiced in his day which is to come. And behold, he is God, and he is with them. And he did manifest himself unto them, that they were redeemed by him. And they gave unto him glory because of that which is to come.

And now, seeing ye know these things and cannot deny them, except ye shall lie, therefore, in this ye have sinned. For ye have rejected all these things, notwithstanding so many evidences which ye have received. [20] But behold, ye have rejected the truth and rebelled against your holy God. Yea, even at this time ye are ripening, because of your murders, and your fornication, and wickedness, for everlasting destruction. Yea, and except ye repent, it will come unto you soon.

Yea, behold, it is now even at your doors. Yea, go ye in unto the judgment seat and search. And behold, your judge is murdered, and he lieth in his blood. And he hath been murdered by his brother, who seeketh to sit in the judgment seat. And behold, they both belong to your secret band, whose author is Gadianton, and the evil one, who seeketh to destroy the souls of men. [21]

Behold, now it came to pass that when Nephi had spoken these words, certain men who were among them ran to the judgment seat; yea, even there were five who went. And they said among themselves as they went, Behold, now we will know of a surety whether this man be a prophet, and God hath commanded him to prophesy such marvelous things unto us. Behold, we do

---

[19] Helaman 8: 10*-15
[20] Helaman 8: 21*-24*
[21] Helaman 8: 25*-28

not believe that he hath; yea, we do not believe that he is a prophet. Nevertheless, if this thing which he has said concerning the chief judge be true, that he be dead, then will we believe that the other words which he has spoken are true.

And it came to pass that they ran in their might and came in unto the judgment seat. And behold, the chief judge had fallen to the earth and did lie in his blood. And now, behold, when they saw this, they were astonished exceedingly, insomuch that they fell to the earth. For they had not believed the words which Nephi had spoken concerning the chief judge. [22]

Now immediately when the judge had been murdered, being stabbed by his brother by a garb of secrecy, the servants ran and told the people, raising the cry of murder among them. And behold, the people did gather themselves together unto the place of the judgment seat. And behold, to their astonishment they saw those five men who had fallen to the earth. [23]

And it came to pass that they laid hold on them, and bound them, and cast them into prison. And there was a proclamation sent abroad that the judge was slain, and that the murderers had been taken and were cast into prison.

And it came to pass that on the morrow, the people did assemble themselves together to mourn and to fast at the burial of the great chief judge who had been slain. And thus, also those judges who were at the garden of Nephi, and heard his words, were also gathered together at the burial.

And it came to pass that they inquired among the people, saying, Where are the five who were sent to inquire concerning the chief judge, whether he was dead? And they answered and said, Concerning this five whom ye say ye have sent, we know not; but there are five, who are the murderers, whom we have cast into prison.

And it came to pass that the judges desired that they should be brought; and they were brought, and behold, they were the five who were sent. And behold, the judges inquired of them to know concerning the matter, and they told them all that they had done,

---

[22] Helaman 9: 1-4
[23] Helaman 9: 6*-7

saying, We ran and came to the place of the judgment seat, and when we saw all things even as Nephi had testified, we were astonished, insomuch that we fell to the earth. And when we were recovered from our astonishment, they cast us into prison. [24]

And now, it came to pass that the judges did expound the matter unto the people and did cry out against Nephi, saying, Behold, we know that this Nephi must have agreed with someone to slay the judge, and then he might declare it unto us, that he might convert us unto his faith, that he might raise himself to be a great man, chosen of God, and a prophet. And now, behold, we will detect this man, and he shall confess his fault and make known unto us the true murderer of this judge.

And it came to pass that the five were liberated on the day of the burial. Nevertheless, they did rebuke the judges in the words which they had spoken against Nephi, and did contend with them one by one, insomuch that they did confound them.

Nevertheless, they caused that Nephi should be taken, and bound, and brought before the multitude. And they began to question him in diverse ways, that they might cross him, that they might accuse him to death, saying unto him, Thou art confederate. Who is this man that has done this murder? Now tell us, and acknowledge thy fault; saying, Behold, here is money; and also, We will grant unto thee thy life, if thou wilt tell us and acknowledge the agreement which thou hast made with him.

But Nephi said unto them, O ye fools, ye uncircumcised of heart, ye blind, and ye stiff-necked people! Do ye know how long the Lord, your God, will suffer you that ye shall go on in this your way of sin? Oh, ye ought to begin to howl and mourn because of the great destruction at this time which doth await you, except ye shall repent.

Behold, ye say that I have agreed with a man that he should murder Seezoram, our chief judge. But behold, I say unto you that this is because I have testified unto you that ye might know concerning this thing; yea, even for a witness unto you that I did know the wickedness and abominations which are among you. [25]

---

[24] Helaman 9: 9-14*
[25] Helaman 9: 16-23*

And now, behold, I will show unto you another sign, and see if ye will in this thing seek to destroy me. Behold, I say unto you, Go to the house of Seantum, who is the brother of Seezoram, and say unto him, Has Nephi, the pretended prophet, who doth prophesy so much evil concerning this people, agreed with thee, in the which ye have murdered Seezoram, who is your brother? And behold, he shall say unto you, Nay.

And ye shall say unto him, Have ye murdered your brother? And he shall stand with fear and wist not what to say. And behold, he shall deny unto you; and he shall make as if he were astonished; nevertheless, he shall declare unto you that he is innocent.

But behold, ye shall examine him, and ye shall find blood upon the skirts of his cloak. And when ye have seen this ye shall say, From whence cometh this blood? Do we not know that it is the blood of your brother? And then shall he tremble and shall look pale, even as if death had come upon him.

And then shall ye say, Because of this fear and this paleness which has come upon your face, behold, we know that thou art guilty. And then shall greater fear come upon him; and then shall he confess unto you and deny no more that he has done this murder.

And then shall he say unto you that I, Nephi, knew nothing concerning the matter, save it were given unto me by the power of God. And then shall ye know that I am an honest man, and that I am sent unto you from God.

And it came to pass that they went and did, even according as Nephi had said unto them. And behold, the words which he had said were true. For according to the words, he did deny; and also according to the words, he did confess. And he was brought to prove that he himself was the very murderer, insomuch that the five were set at liberty and also was Nephi. And there were some of the Nephites who believed on the words of Nephi; and there were some also who believed, because of the testimony of the five, for they had been converted while they were in prison.

And now, there were some among the people who said that Nephi was a prophet. And there were others who said, Behold, he is a god; for except he was a god, he could not know of all things. For behold, he has told us the thoughts of our hearts and also has told us things; and even he has brought unto our knowledge the true murderer of our chief judge. [26]

And it came to pass that there arose a division among the people, insomuch that they divided hither and thither and went their ways, leaving Nephi alone as he was standing in the midst of them. And it came to pass that Nephi went his way towards his own house, pondering upon the things which the Lord had shown unto him.

And it came to pass as he was thus pondering, being much cast down because of the wickedness of the people of the Nephites, their secret works of darkness, and their murderings, and their plunderings, and all manner of iniquities— and it came to pass, as he was thus pondering in his heart, behold, a voice came unto him, saying:

Blessed art thou, Nephi, for those things which thou hast done; for I have beheld how thou hast with unwearyingness declared the word which I have given unto thee, unto this people. And thou hast not feared them, and hast not sought thine own life, but have sought my will and to keep my commandments.

And now, because thou hast done this with such unwearyingness, behold, I will bless thee forever; and I will make thee mighty in word and in deed, in faith and in works. Yea, even that all things shall be done unto thee according to thy word, for thou shalt not ask that which is contrary to my will.

Behold, thou art Nephi, and I am God. Behold, I declare it unto thee in the presence of mine angels that ye shall have power over this people, and shall smite the earth with famine, and with pestilence, and destruction, according to the wickedness of this people.

Behold, I give unto you power that whatsoever ye shall seal on earth shall be sealed in heaven; and whatsoever ye shall loose on earth shall be loosed in heaven. And thus shall ye have power among this people. [27]

And now, behold, I command you that ye shall go and declare unto this people that, Thus saith the Lord God, who is

---

[26] Helaman 9: 25-41
[27] Helaman 10: 1-7

Almighty, Except ye repent, ye shall be smitten, even unto destruction.

And behold, now it came to pass that when the Lord had spoken these words unto Nephi, he did stop, and did not go unto his own house, but did return unto the multitudes who were scattered about upon the face of the land, and began to declare unto them the word of the Lord, which had been spoken unto him concerning their destruction if they did not repent.

Now behold, notwithstanding that great miracle which Nephi had done in telling them concerning the death of the chief judge, they did harden their hearts and did not hearken unto the words of the Lord. Therefore, Nephi did declare unto them the word of the Lord, saying, Except ye repent, thus saith the Lord, Ye shall be smitten, even unto destruction.

And it came to pass that when Nephi had declared unto them the word, behold, they did still harden their hearts and would not hearken unto his words. Therefore, they did revile against him and did seek to lay their hands upon him, that they might cast him into prison. But behold, the power of God was with him and they could not take him to cast him into prison, for he was taken by the Spirit and conveyed away out of the midst of them.

And it came to pass that thus he did go forth in the Spirit, from multitude to multitude, declaring the word of God, even until he had declared it unto them all, or sent it forth among all the people. And it came to pass that they would not hearken unto his words; and there began to be contentions, insomuch that they were divided against themselves and began to slay one another with the sword. And thus ended the seventy and first year of the reign of the judges over the people of Nephi. [28]

And now, it came to pass in the seventy and second year of the reign of the judges, that the contentions did increase, insomuch that there were wars throughout all the land among all the people of Nephi. And it was this secret band of robbers who did carry on this work of destruction and wickedness. And this war did last all that year. And in the seventy and third year it did also last.

---

[28] Helaman 10: 11-19

And it came to pass that in this year, Nephi did cry unto the Lord, saying, O Lord, do not suffer that this people shall be destroyed by the sword; but, O Lord, rather let there be a famine in the land to stir them up in remembrance of the Lord, their God; and perhaps they will repent and turn unto thee.

And so it was done according to the words of Nephi, and there was a great famine upon the land among all the people of Nephi. And thus, in the seventy and fourth year, the famine did continue, and the work of destruction did cease by the sword, but became sore by famine. And this work of destruction did also continue in the seventy and fifth year. For the earth was smitten, that it was dry, and did not yield forth grain in the season of grain.

And the whole earth was smitten, even among the Lamanites as well as among the Nephites, so that they were smitten that they did perish by thousands in the more wicked parts of the land. And it came to pass that the people saw that they were about to perish by famine, and they began to remember the Lord, their God; and they began to remember the words of Nephi.

And the people began to plead with their chief judges and their leaders, that they would say unto Nephi, Behold, we know that thou art a man of God; and therefore, cry unto the Lord, our God, that he turn away from us this famine, lest all the words which thou hast spoken concerning our destruction be fulfilled.

And it came to pass that the judges did say unto Nephi according to the words which had been desired. And it came to pass that when Nephi saw that the people had repented and did humble themselves in sackcloth, he cried again unto the Lord, saying, O Lord, behold, this people repenteth, and they have swept away the band of Gadianton from amongst them, insomuch that they have become extinct. And they have concealed their secret plans in the earth.

Now, O Lord, because of this their humility, wilt thou turn away thine anger, and let thine anger be appeased in the destruction of those wicked men whom thou hast already destroyed? O Lord, wilt thou turn away thine anger, yea, thy fierce anger, and cause that this famine may cease in this land?

O Lord, wilt thou hearken unto me, and cause that it may be done according to my words, and send forth rain upon the face of the earth, that she may bring forth her fruit and her grain in the season of grain? [29] And now, O Lord, wilt thou turn away thine anger and try again if they will serve thee? And if so, O Lord, thou canst bless them according to thy words which thou hast said.

And it came to pass that in the seventy and sixth year, the Lord did turn away his anger from the people, and caused that rain should fall upon the earth, insomuch that it did bring forth her fruit in the season of her fruit. And it came to pass that it did bring forth her grain in the season of her grain.

And behold, the people did rejoice and glorify God, and the whole face of the land was filled with rejoicing. And they did no more seek to destroy Nephi, but they did esteem him as a great prophet and a man of God, having great power and authority given unto him from God. And behold, Lehi, his brother, was not a whit behind him as to things pertaining to righteousness.

And thus it did come to pass that the people of Nephi began to prosper again in the land, and began to build up their waste places, and began to multiply and spread, even until they did cover the whole face of the land, both on the northward and on the southward, from the sea west to the sea east. And it came to pass that the seventy and sixth year did end in peace.

And the seventy and seventh year began in peace; and the church did spread throughout the face of all the land. And the more part of the people, both the Nephites and the Lamanites, did belong to the church. And they did have exceeding great peace in the land; and thus ended the seventy and seventh year. [30]

About 11 B.C.

And it came to pass that in the eightieth year of the reign of the judges over the people of Nephi, there were a certain number of the dissenters from the people of Nephi, who had some years before gone over unto the Lamanites and took upon themselves the name of Lamanites, and also, a certain number who were real descendants of the Lamanites, being stirred up to anger by them,

---

[29] Helaman 11: 1-13
[30] Helaman 11: 16-21*

or by those dissenters; therefore, they commenced a war with their brethren.

And they did commit murder and plunder; and then they would retreat back into the mountains, and into the wilderness and secret places, hiding themselves that they could not be discovered, receiving daily an addition to their numbers, inasmuch as there were dissenters that went forth unto them. And thus in time, yea, even in the space of not many years, they became an exceeding great band of robbers. And they did search out all the secret plans of Gadianton; and thus they became robbers of Gadianton.

Now behold, these robbers did make great havoc, yea, even great destruction among the people of Nephi, and also among the people of the Lamanites. And it came to pass that it was expedient that there should be a stop put to this work of destruction. Therefore, they sent an army of strong men into the wilderness and upon the mountains to search out this band of robbers and to destroy them. But behold, it came to pass that in that same year they were driven back, even into their own lands. [31]

And the robbers did still increase and wax strong, insomuch that they did defy the whole armies of the Nephites and also of the Lamanites. And they did cause great fear to come unto the people upon all the face of the land. Yea, for they did visit many parts of the land and did do great destruction unto them, yea, did kill many and did carry away others captive into the wilderness, yea, and more especially their women and their children.

Now this great evil, which came unto the people because of their iniquity, did stir them up again in remembrance of the Lord, their God. [32] And thus we see that except the Lord doth chasten his people with many afflictions, yea, except he doth visit them with death, and with terror, and with famine, and with all manner of pestilences, they will not remember him.

Behold, they do not desire that the Lord, their God, who hath created them, should rule and reign over them, notwithstanding his great goodness and his mercy towards them. They do set at naught his counsels, and they will not that he should be their guide.

---

[31] Helaman 11: 24-29*
[32] Helaman 11: 32*-34

Oh, how great is the nothingness of the children of men; yea, even they are less than the dust of the earth. For behold, the dust of the earth moveth hither and thither, to the dividing asunder at the command of our great and everlasting God.

Yea, behold, at his voice doth the hills and the mountains tremble and quake; and by the power of his voice they are broken up and become smooth, yea, even like unto a valley. Yea, by the power of his voice doth the whole earth shake; yea, by the power of his voice doth the foundations rock, even to the very center. [33]

And behold, also, if he say unto the waters of the great deep, Be thou dried up, it is done. Behold, if he say unto this mountain, Be thou raised up and come over and fall upon that city, that it be buried up, behold, it is done. [34]

And behold, if the Lord shall say unto a man, Because of thine iniquities thou shalt be accursed forever, it shall be done. And if the Lord shall say, Because of thine iniquities thou shalt be cut off from my presence, he will cause that it shall be so. Therefore, blessed are they who will repent and hearken unto the voice of the Lord, their God. For these are they that shall be saved. [35]

And I would that all men might be saved. But we read that in that great and last day there are some who shall be cast out, yea, who shall be cast off from the presence of the Lord, yea, who shall be consigned to a state of endless misery, fulfilling the words which say, They that have done good shall have everlasting life, and they that have done evil shall have everlasting damnation. And thus it is. Amen. [36]

About 5 B.C.

And now, it came to pass in the eighty and sixth year, the Nephites did still remain in wickedness, yea, in great wickedness, while the Lamanites did observe strictly to keep the commandments of God according to the law of Moses.

---

[33] Helaman 12: 3, 6-12
[34] Helaman 12: 16-17
[35] Helaman 12: 20-21, 23
[36] Helaman 12: 25-26

And it came to pass that in this year, there was one Samuel, a
Lamanite, came into the land of Zarahemla and began to preach
unto the people. And it came to pass that he did preach many days
repentance unto the people. And they did cast him out, and he was
about to return to his own land, but behold, the voice of the Lord
came unto him, that he should return again and prophesy unto the
people, whatsoever things should come into his heart.

And it came to pass that they would not suffer that he should
enter into the city, therefore, he went and got upon the wall thereof, and stretched forth his hand, and cried with a loud voice. [37] And
he said unto them, Behold, I, Samuel, a Lamanite, do speak the
words of the Lord which he doth put into my heart. And behold, he
hath put it into my heart to say unto this people that the sword of
justice hangeth over this people. And four hundred years passeth
not away save the sword of justice falleth upon this people. And
nothing can save this people, save it be repentance and faith on the
Lord Jesus Christ, who surely shall come into the world, and shall
suffer many things, and shall be slain for his people. [38]

And behold, an angel of the Lord hath declared it unto me,
and he did bring glad tidings to my soul. And behold, I was sent
unto you to declare it unto you also, that ye might have glad
tidings; but behold, ye would not receive me. Therefore, thus saith
the Lord, Because of the hardness of the hearts of the people of the
Nephites, except they repent, I will take away my word from
them, and I will withdraw my Spirit from them, and I will suffer
them no longer, and I will turn the hearts of their brethren against
them. Yea, I will visit them with the sword, and with famine, and
with pestilence. [39] Yea, I will visit them in my fierce anger, and
there shall be those of the fourth generation who shall live, of your
enemies, to behold your utter destruction. And this shall surely
come, except ye repent, saith the Lord. Blessed are they who will
repent and turn unto me. But wo unto him that repenteth not. [40]

---

[37] Helaman 13: 1-4*
[38] Helaman 13: 5-6*
[39] Helaman 13: 7-9*
[40] Helaman 13: 10*-11*

Yea, wo unto this people because of this time which has
arrived, that ye do cast out the prophets, and do mock them, and
cast stones at them, and do slay them, and do all manner of
iniquity unto them, even as they did of old time.

But behold, if a man shall come among you and shall say, Do
this, and there is no iniquity; Do that, and ye shall not suffer; yea,
he will say, Walk after the pride of your own hearts, yea, Walk
after the pride of your eyes, and do whatsoever your heart
desireth—and if a man shall come among you and say this, ye will
receive him, and ye will say that he is a prophet. Yea, ye will lift
him up, and ye will give unto him of your substance. Ye will give
unto him of your gold and of your silver, and ye will clothe him
with costly apparel. And because he speaketh flattering words
unto you and he saith that all is well, then ye will not find fault
with him.

O ye wicked and ye perverse generation, ye hardened and ye
stiff-necked people! How long will ye suppose that the Lord will
suffer you? Yea, how long will ye suffer yourselves to be led by
foolish and blind guides? Yea, how long will ye choose darkness
rather than light? [41]

Behold, we are surrounded by demons, yea, we are encircled
about by the angels of him who hath sought to destroy our souls.
Behold, our iniquities are great. O Lord, canst thou not turn away
thine anger from us? — And this shall be your language in those
days.

But behold, your days of probation are past. Ye have
procrastinated the day of your salvation until it is everlastingly
too late, and your destruction is made sure. Yea, for ye have
sought all the days of your lives for that which ye could not
obtain. And ye have sought for happiness in doing iniquity, which
thing is contrary to the nature of that righteousness which is in
our great and Eternal Head.

O ye people of the land, that ye would hear my words! And I
pray that the anger of the Lord be turned away from you, and that
ye would repent and be saved. [42]

---

[41] Helaman 13: 24, 27-29
[42] Helaman 13: 37-39

Behold, I give unto you a sign, for five years more cometh, and behold, then cometh the Son of God to redeem all those who shall believe on his name. And behold, this will I give unto you for a sign at the time of his coming: For behold, there shall be great lights in heaven, insomuch that in the night before he cometh, there shall be no darkness, insomuch that it shall appear unto man as if it was day. Therefore, there shall be one day and a night and a day, as if it were one day and there were no night. And it shall be the night before he is born. [43]

And behold, there shall be a new star arise, such an one as ye never have beheld. And this also shall be a sign unto you. And behold, this is not all; there shall be many signs and wonders in heaven. And it shall come to pass that ye shall all be amazed and wonder, insomuch that ye shall fall to the earth.

And it shall come to pass that whosoever shall believe on the Son of God, the same shall have everlasting life. And behold, thus hath the Lord commanded me by his angel, that I should come and tell this thing unto you. Yea, he hath commanded that I should prophesy these things unto you. Yea, he hath said unto me, Cry unto this people, Repent and prepare the way of the Lord! [44]

And ye shall hear my words, for, for this intent I have come up upon the walls of this city, that ye might hear and know of the judgments of God which do await you because of your iniquities; and also that ye might know the conditions of repentance. And also that ye might know of the coming of Jesus Christ, the Son of God, the Father of heaven and of earth, the Creator of all things from the beginning, and that ye might know of the signs of his coming, to the intent that ye might believe on his name. And if ye believe on his name, ye will repent of all your sins, that thereby ye may have a remission of them through his merits.

And behold, again another sign I give unto you, yea, a sign of his death. For behold, he surely must die that salvation may come. Yea, it behooveth him, and becometh expedient, that he dieth to bring to pass the resurrection of the dead, that thereby men may be brought into the presence of the Lord. Yea, behold, this death

---

[43] Helaman 14: 2*-4*
[44] Helaman 14: 5-9

bringeth to pass the resurrection, and redeemeth all mankind from the first death, that spiritual death, for all mankind by the fall of Adam, being cut off from the presence of the Lord or considered as dead, both as to things temporal and to things spiritual.

But behold, the resurrection of Christ redeemeth mankind, yea, even all mankind, and bringeth them back into the presence of the Lord. Yea, and it bringeth to pass the conditions of repentance. But whosoever repenteth not is hewn down, and cast into the fire, and there cometh upon them again a spiritual death, yea, a second death, for they are cut off again as to things pertaining to righteousness. [45] Therefore, repent ye, repent ye, lest by knowing these things and not doing them, ye shall suffer yourselves to come under condemnation, and ye are brought down unto this second death.

But behold, as I said unto you concerning another sign, a sign of his death, behold, in that day that he shall suffer death, the sun shall be darkened and refuse to give his light unto you, and also the moon and the stars. And there shall be no light upon the face of this land, even from the time that he shall suffer death, for the space of three days, to the time that he shall rise again from the dead.

Yea, at the time that he shall yield up the ghost, there shall be thunderings and lightnings for the space of many hours. And the earth shall shake and tremble. And the rocks which are upon the face of the earth, which are both above the earth and beneath, which ye know at this time is solid, or the more part of it is one solid mass, shall be broken up. Yea, they shall be rent in twain, and shall ever after be found in seams, and in cracks, and in broken fragments upon the face of the whole earth, yea, both above the earth and beneath.

And behold, there shall be great tempests, and there shall be many mountains laid low, like unto a valley. And there shall be many places which are now called valleys, which shall become mountains, whose height thereof is great. And many highways shall be broken up; and many cities shall become desolate. And many graves shall be opened and shall yield up many of their dead. And many saints shall appear unto many.

---

[45] Helaman 14: 11-18*

And behold, thus hath the angel spoken unto me, for he said unto me that there should be thunderings and lightnings for the space of many hours, and that darkness should cover the face of the whole earth for the space of three days. [46]

And the angel said unto me that many shall see greater things than these, to the intent that they might believe; that these signs and these wonders should come to pass upon all the face of this land, to the intent that there should be no cause for unbelief among the children of men; and this to the intent, that whosoever will believe might be saved, and that whosoever will not believe, a righteous judgment might come upon them. And also if they are condemned, they bring upon themselves their own condemnation.

And now, remember, remember, my brethren, that whosoever perisheth, perisheth unto himself; and whosoever doeth iniquity, doeth it unto himself. For behold, ye are free. Ye are permitted to act for yourselves. For behold, God hath given unto you a knowledge, and he hath made you free.

He hath given unto you that ye might know good from evil, and he hath given unto you that ye might choose life or death. And ye can do good, and be restored unto that which is good, or have that which is good restored unto you; or ye can do evil and have that which is evil restored unto you. [47]

Yea, wo unto this people, who are called the people of Nephi, except they shall repent when they shall see all these signs and wonders, which shall be showed unto them —for behold, they have been a chosen people of the Lord, yea, the people of Nephi hath he loved, and also hath he chastened them. Yea, in the days of their iniquities hath he chastened them because he loveth them.

But behold, my brethren, the Lamanites, hath he hated because their deeds have been evil continually, and this because of the iniquity of the tradition of their fathers. But behold, salvation hath come unto them through the preaching of the Nephites. And for this intent hath the Lord prolonged their days.

And I would that ye should behold that the more part of them are in the path of their duty, and they do walk circumspectly

---

[46] Helaman 14: 19-27*
[47] Helaman 14: 28-31

before God. And they do observe to keep his commandments, and his statutes, and his judgments according to the law of Moses. Yea, I say unto you that the more part of them are doing this, and they are striving with unwearied diligence that they may bring the remainder of their brethren to the knowledge of the truth. Therefore, there are many who do add to their numbers daily. [48]

And this is according to the prophecy that they shall again be brought to the true knowledge, which is the knowledge of their Redeemer, and their great and true Shepherd, and be numbered among his sheep. Therefore, I say unto you, It shall be better for them than for you, except ye repent. For behold, had the mighty works been shown unto them which have been shown unto you, yea, unto them who have dwindled in unbelief because of the traditions of their fathers, ye can see of yourselves that they never would again have dwindled in unbelief.

Therefore, saith the Lord, I will not utterly destroy them, but I will cause that in the day of my wisdom they shall return again unto me, saith the Lord. [49]

And now, it came to pass that there were many who heard the words of Samuel, the Lamanite, which he spake upon the walls of the city. And as many as believed on his words went forth and sought for Nephi. And when they had come forth and found him, they confessed unto him their sins and denied not, desiring that they might be baptized unto the Lord.

But as many as there were, who did not believe in the words of Samuel, were angry with him. And they cast stones at him upon the wall, and also many shot arrows at him as he stood upon the wall. But the Spirit of the Lord was with him, insomuch that they could not hit him with their stones, neither with their arrows. [50] Therefore, when they saw that they could not hit him with their stones and their arrows, they cried out unto their captains, saying, Take this fellow and bind him, for behold, he hath a devil! And because of the power of the devil which is in him, we cannot hit him with our stones and our arrows; therefore, take him, and bind him,

---

[48] Helaman 15: 3-6
[49] Helman 15: 13-16
[50] Helaman 16: 1-2

and away with him!

And as they went forth to lay their hands on him, behold, he did cast himself down from the wall, and did flee out of their lands, yea, even unto his own country, and began to preach and to prophesy among his own people. And behold, he was never heard of more among the Nephites. And thus were the affairs of the people. And thus ended the eighty and sixth year of the reign of the judges over the people of Nephi. [51]

About 5 Years Later

Now it came to pass that the ninety and first year had passed away, and it was six hundred years from the time that Lehi left Jerusalem. And it was in the year that Lachoneus was the chief judge and the governor over the land. And Nephi, the son of Helaman, had departed out of the land of Zarahemla, giving charge unto his son Nephi, who was his eldest son, concerning the plates of brass, and all the records which had been kept, and all those things which had been kept sacred, from the departure of Lehi out of Jerusalem. Then he departed out of the land. And whither he went, no man knoweth. And his son Nephi did keep the record in his stead, yea, the record of this people.

And it came to pass that in the commencement of the ninety and second year, behold, the prophecies of the prophets began to be fulfilled more fully. For there began to be greater signs and greater miracles wrought among the people. But there were some who began to say that the time was past for the words to be fulfilled which were spoken by Samuel the Lamanite. [52] And it came to pass that they did make a great uproar throughout the land.

And the people who believed began to be very sorrowful, lest by any means those things which had been spoken might not come to pass. But behold, they did watch steadfastly for that day and that night and that day, which should be as one day, as if there were no night, that they might know that their faith had not been in vain.

---

[51] Helaman 16: 6*-9
[52] 3 Nephi 1: 1-5

Now it came to pass that there was a day set apart by the
unbelievers, that all those who believed in those traditions should
be put to death, except the sign should come to pass, which had
been given by Samuel the prophet. Now it came to pass that when
Nephi, the son of Nephi, saw this wickedness of his people, his
heart was exceeding sorrowful.

And it came to pass that he went out, and bowed himself
down upon the earth, and cried mightily to his God in behalf of
his people, yea, those who were about to be destroyed because of
their faith in the tradition of their fathers. And it came to pass that
he cried mightily unto the Lord all that day. And behold, the voice
of the Lord came unto him, saying:

Lift up your head and be of good cheer, for behold, the time
is at hand; and on this night shall the sign be given. And on the
morrow come I into the world to show unto the world that I will
fulfill all, that which I have caused to be spoken by the mouth of
my holy prophets.

Behold, I come unto my own to fulfill all things which I have
made known unto the children of men, from the foundation of the
world, and to do the will, both of the Father, and of the Son; of the
Father because of me, and of the Son because of my flesh. And
behold, the time is at hand, and this night shall the sign be given.

And it came to pass that the words which came unto Nephi
were fulfilled, according as they had been spoken. For behold, at
the going down of the sun there was no darkness; and the people
began to be astonished because there was no darkness when the
night came.

And there were many who had not believed the words of the
prophets, who fell to the earth and became as if they were dead. For
they knew that the great plan of destruction, which they had laid
for those who believed in the words of the prophets, had been
frustrated. For the sign which had been given was already at hand.
And they began to know that the Son of God must shortly appear.

Yea, in fine, all the people upon the face of the whole earth,
from the west to the east, both, in the land north and in the land
south, were so exceedingly astonished that they fell to the earth. For
they knew that the prophets had testified of these things for many

years, and that the sign which had been given was already at hand. And they began to fear because of their iniquity and their unbelief.

And it came to pass that there was no darkness in all that night, but it was as light as though it was midday. And it came to pass that the sun did rise in the morning again according to its proper order. And they knew that it was the day that the Lord should be born because of the sign which had been given. And it had come to pass, yea, all things, every whit, according to the words of the prophets. And it came to pass also that a new star did appear, according to the word.

And it came to pass that from this time forth, there began to be lyings sent forth among the people by Satan to harden their hearts, to the intent that they might not believe in those signs and wonders which they had seen. But notwithstanding those lyings and deceivings, the more part of the people did believe, and were converted unto the Lord. [53] And thus the ninety and second year did pass away, bringing glad tidings unto the people because of the signs which did come to pass, according to the words of the prophecy of all the holy prophets.

And it came to pass that the ninety and third year did also pass away in peace, save it were for the Gadianton robbers, who dwelt upon the mountains, who did infest the land. For so strong were their holds and their secret places that the people could not overpower them. Therefore, they did commit many murders and did do much slaughter among the people.

And it came to pass that in the ninety and fourth year, they began to increase in a great degree, because there were many dissenters of the Nephites who did flee unto them, which did cause much sorrow unto those Nephites who did remain in the land.

And there was also a cause of much sorrow among the Lamanites; for behold, they had many children who did grow up and began to wax strong in years, that they became for them-selves, and were led away by some who were Zoramites, by their lyings and their flattering words, to join those Gadianton robbers. And thus were the Lamanites afflicted also, and began to decrease as to their faith and righteousness because of the wickedness of

---

[53] 3 Nephi 1: 7-22

the rising generation. [54] And it came to pass that thus passed away the ninety and fifth year also.

And the people began to forget those signs and wonders which they had heard, and began to be less and less astonished at a sign or a wonder from heaven, insomuch that they began to be hard in their hearts and blind in their minds, and began to disbelieve all which they had heard and seen.

And thus did Satan get possession of the hearts of the people again, insomuch that he did blind their eyes and lead them away to believe that the doctrine of Christ was a foolish and a vain thing. And it came to pass that the people began to wax strong in wickedness and abominations. And they did not believe that there should be any more signs or wonders given. And Satan did go about, leading away the hearts of the people, tempting them, and causing them that they should do great wickedness in the land. [55]

And six hundred and nine years had passed away since Lehi left Jerusalem. And nine years had passed away from the time when the sign was given, which was spoken of by the prophets, that Christ should come into the world.

Now, the Nephites began to reckon their time from this period when the sign was given, or from the coming of Christ. Therefore, nine years had passed away. And Nephi, who was the father of Nephi, who had the charge of the records, did not return to the land of Zarahemla, and could nowhere be found in all the land. [56]

---

[54] 3 Nephi 1: 26-30
[55] 3 Nephi 2: 1, 2*, 3
[56] 3 Nephi 2: 6-9

Chapter 10

The Dark Before Dawn

About 12 A.D.

And it came to pass in the thirteenth year, there began to be wars and contentions throughout all the land. For the Gadianton robbers had become so numerous, and did slay so many of the people, and did lay waste so many cities, and did spread so much death and carnage throughout the land, that it became expedient that all the people, both the Nephites and the Lamanites, should take up arms against them. Therefore, all the Lamanites who had become converted unto the Lord did unite with their brethren, the Nephites, and were compelled for the safety of their lives, and their women, and their children, to take up arms against those Gadianton robbers; yea, and also to maintain their rites, and their privileges of their church, and of their worship, and their freedom, and their liberty. And it came to pass that those Lamanites who had united with the Nephites were numbered among the Nephites. [1]

And it came to pass in the commencement of the fourteenth year, the war between the robbers and the people of Nephi did continue and did become exceeding sore. Nevertheless, the people of Nephi did gain some advantage of the robbers, insomuch that they did drive them back out of their lands into the mountains and into their secret places. [2]

And now, it came to pass that in the sixteenth year from the coming of Christ, Lachoneus, the governor of the land, received an epistle from the leader and the governor of this band of robbers. And these are the words which were written, saying:

Lachoneus, most noble and chief governor of the land, behold, I write this epistle unto you and do give unto you exceeding great praise because of your firmness, and also the firmness of your people, in maintaining that which ye suppose to

---

[1] 3 Nephi: 2: 11-12, 14
[2] 3 Nephi 2: 17

be your right and liberty. Yea, ye do stand well, as if ye were supported by the hand of a God in the defense of your liberty, and your property, and your country, or that which ye do call so.

And it seemeth a pity unto me, most noble Lachoneus, that ye should be so foolish and vain as to suppose that ye can stand against so many brave men, who are at my command, who do now at this time stand in their arms, and do await with great anxiety for the word, Go down upon the Nephites and destroy them. [3]

Therefore, I write unto you, desiring that ye would yield up unto this my people your cities, your lands, and your possessions, rather than that they should visit you with the sword, and that destruction should come upon you. Or, in other words, yield yourselves up unto us, and unite with us, and become acquainted with our secret works, and become our brethren, that ye may be like unto us—not our slaves, but our brethren and partners of all our substance.

And behold, I swear unto you if ye will do this, with an oath, ye shall not be destroyed. But if ye will not do this, I swear unto you with an oath, that on the morrow month I will command that my armies shall come down against you. And they shall not stay their hand, and shall spare not, but shall slay you, and shall let fall the sword upon you, yea, even until ye shall become extinct. [4]

And I write this epistle unto you, Lachoneus, and I hope that ye will deliver up your lands and your possessions without the shedding of blood, that this my people may recover their rights and government, who have dissented away from you, because of your wickedness in retaining from them their rights of government. And except ye do this, I will avenge their wrongs. I am Giddianhi.

And now, it came to pass when Lachoneus received this epistle, he was exceedingly astonished because of the boldness of Giddianhi in demanding the possession of the land of the Nephites, and also of threatening the people, and avenging the wrongs of those that had received no wrong, save it were they had

[3] 3 Nephi 3: 1-3
[4] 3 Nephi 3: 6-8

wronged themselves, by dissenting away unto those wicked and abominable robbers.

Now behold this Lachoneus, the governor, was a just man and could not be frightened by the demands and the threatenings of a robber. Therefore, he did not hearken to the epistle of Giddianhi, the governor of the robbers, but he did cause that his people should cry unto the Lord for strength against the time that the robbers should come down against them.

Yea, he sent a proclamation among all the people that they should gather together their women and their children, their flocks and their herds, and all their substance, save it were their land, unto one place. And he caused that fortifications should be built round about them, and the strength thereof should be exceeding great.

And he caused that there should be armies placed as guards round about, to watch them and to guard them from the robbers, day and night. [5] And it came to pass that Lachoneus did appoint chief captains over all the armies of the Nephites, to command them at the time that the robbers should come down out of the wilderness against them.

Now the chiefest among all the chief captains, and the great commander of all the armies of the Nephites was appointed, and his name was Gidgiddoni. Now it was the custom among all the Nephites to appoint for their chief captains, save it were in their times of wickedness, someone that had the spirit of revelation and also prophecy. Therefore, this Gidgiddoni was a great prophet among them, as also was the chief judge.

Now the people said unto Gidgiddoni, Pray unto the Lord, and let us go up upon the mountains and into the wilderness, that we may fall upon the robbers and destroy them in their own lands. But Gidgiddoni saith unto them, The Lord forbid. For if we should go up against them, the Lord would deliver us into their hands. Therefore, we will prepare ourselves in the center of our lands, and we will gather all our armies together, and we will not go against them; but we will wait till they shall come against us.

---

[5] 3 Nephi 3: 10-14*

Therefore, as the Lord liveth, if we do this, he will deliver them into our hands.

And it came to pass in the seventeenth year, in the latter end of the year, the proclamation of Lachoneus had gone forth throughout all the face of the land. And they had taken their horses, and their chariots, and their cattle, and all their flocks, and their herds, and their grain, and all their substance, and did march forth by thousands and by tens of thousands until they had all gone forth to the place which had been appointed, that they should gather themselves together to defend themselves against their enemies.

And the land which was appointed was the land of Zarahemla and the land which was between the land of Zarahemla and the land Bountiful, yea, to the line which was between the land Bountiful and the land Desolation. [6]

And they did fortify themselves against their enemies. And they did dwell in one land and in one body, and they did fear the words which had been spoken by Lachoneus, insomuch that they did repent of all their sins. And they did put up their prayers unto the Lord, their God, that he would deliver them in the time that their enemies should come down against them to battle. And they were exceeding sorrowful because of their enemy.

And Gidgiddoni did cause that they should make weapons of war of every kind, that they should be strong with armor, and with shields, and with bucklers, after the manner of his instructions. [7]

And it came to pass that in the latter end of the eighteenth year, those armies of robbers had prepared for battle, and began to come down, and to sally forth from the hills, and out of the mountains and the wilderness, and their strongholds, and their secret places, and began to take possession of the lands both which were in the land south and which were in the land north, and began to take possession of all the lands which had been deserted by the Nephites and the cities which had been left desolate.

But behold, there were no wild beasts nor game in those lands which had been deserted by the Nephites. And there was no

---

[6] 3 Nephi 3: 17-23
[7] 3 Nephi 3: 25-26

game for the robbers, save it were in the wilderness. And the robbers could not exist, save it were in the wilderness, for the want of food. For the Nephites had left their lands desolate and had gathered their flocks, and their herds, and all their substance. And they were in one body, therefore, there was no chance for the robbers to plunder and to obtain food, save it were to come up in open battle against the Nephites; and the Nephites being in one body, and having so great a number, and having reserved for themselves provisions, and horses, and cattle, and flocks of every kind, that they might subsist for the space of seven years, in the which time they did hope to destroy the robbers from off the face of the land. And thus the eighteenth year did pass away.

And it came to pass that in the nineteenth year, Giddianhi found that it was expedient that he should go up to battle against the Nephites, for there was no way that they could subsist, save it were to plunder, and rob, and murder. [8] And it came to pass that they did come up to battle. And it was in the sixth month. And behold, great and terrible was the day that they did come up to battle.

And they were girded about after the manner of robbers, and they had a lambskin about their loins, and they were dyed in blood, and their heads were shorn, and they had headplates upon them. And great and terrible was the appearance of the armies of Giddianhi because of their armor and because of their being dyed in blood.

And it came to pass that the armies of the Nephites, when they saw the appearance of the army of Giddianhi, had all fallen to the earth and did lift their cries to the Lord, their God, that he would spare them and deliver them out of the hands of their enemies.

And it came to pass that when the armies of Giddianhi saw this, they began to shout with a loud voice because of their joy. For they had supposed that the Nephites had fallen with fear because of the terror of their armies. But in this thing they were disappointed, for the Nephites did not fear them; but they did fear their God and did supplicate him for protection.

---

[8] 3 Nephi 4: 1-5

Therefore, when the armies of Giddianhi did rush upon
them, they were prepared to meet them. Yea, in the strength of the
Lord they did receive them. And the battle commenced in this the
sixth month. And great and terrible was the battle thereof; yea,
great and terrible was the slaughter thereof, insomuch that there
never was known so great a slaughter among all the people of
Lehi since he left Jerusalem. And notwithstanding the
threatenings and the oaths which Giddianhi had made, behold,
the Nephites did beat them, insomuch that they did fall back from
before them.

And it came to pass that Gidgiddoni commanded that his
armies should pursue them as far as the borders of the wilderness
and that they should not spare any that should fall into their
hands by the way. And thus they did pursue them and did slay
them to the borders of the wilderness, even until they had fulfilled
the commandment of Gidgiddoni.

And it came to pass that Giddianhi, who had stood and
fought with boldness, was pursued as he fled. And being weary
because of his much fighting, he was overtaken and slain. And
thus was the end of Giddianhi, the robber.

And it came to pass that the armies of the Nephites did
return again to their place of security. [9] And they did rejoice and
cry again with one voice, saying, May the God of Abraham and
the God of Isaac and the God of Jacob protect this people in
righteousness, so long as they shall call on the name of their God
for protection.

And it came to pass that they did break forth, all as one, in
singing and praising their God for the great thing which he had
done for them in preserving them from falling into the hands of
their enemies. Yea, they did cry, Hosanna to the Most High God!
And they did cry, Blessed be the name of the Lord God Almighty,
the Most High God! And their hearts were swollen with joy, unto
the gushing out of many tears because of the great goodness of
God in delivering them out of the hands of their enemies. And
they knew it was because of their repentance and their humility

---

[9] 3 Nephi 4: 7-15*

that they had been delivered from an everlasting destruction. [10]

And now, it came to pass that the people of the Nephites did all return to their own lands in the twenty and sixth year, every man with his family, his flocks and his herds, his horses and his cattle, and all things whatsoever did belong unto them.

And it came to pass that they had not eaten up all their provisions; therefore, they did take with them all that they had not devoured, of all their grain of every kind, and their gold, and their silver, and all their precious things, and they did return to their own lands and their possessions, both on the north and on the south, both on the land northward and on the land southward.

And they granted unto those robbers, who had entered into a covenant to keep the peace of the land, who were desirous to remain Lamanites, lands according to their numbers, that they might have with their labors wherewith to subsist upon. And thus they did establish peace in all the land.

And they began again to prosper and to wax great. And the twenty and sixth and seventh years passed away, and there was great order in the land. And they had formed their laws according to equity and justice. And now, there was nothing in all the land to hinder the people from prospering continually, except they should fall into transgressions. And now, it was Gidgiddoni, and the judge Lachoneus, and those who had been appointed leaders, who had established this great peace in the land.

About 28 A.D.

And it came to pass that there were many cities built anew, and there were many old cities repaired. And there were many highways cast up and many roads made which led from city to city, and from land to land, and from place to place. And thus passed away the twenty and eighth year, and the people had continual peace.

But it came to pass in the twenty and ninth year, there began to be some disputings among the people. And some were lifted up unto pride and boastings because of their exceeding great riches,

---

[10] 3 Nephi 4: 30-33

yea, even unto great persecutions. For there were many merchants in the land, and also many lawyers, and many officers.

And the people began to be distinguished by ranks according to their riches and their chances for learning. Yea, some were ignorant because of their poverty, and others did receive great learning because of their riches. Some were lifted up in pride, and others were exceeding humble. Some did return railing for railing, while others would receive railing, and persecution, and all manner of afflictions, and would not turn and revile again, but were humble and penitent before God.

And thus there became a great inequality in all the land, insomuch that the church began to be broken up; yea, insomuch that in the thirtieth year the church was broken up in all the land, save it were among a few of the Lamanites who were converted unto the true faith. And they would not depart from it, for they were firm, and steadfast, and immovable, willing with all diligence to keep the commandments of the Lord.

Now the cause of this iniquity of the people was this: Satan had great power, unto the stirring up of the people to do all manner of iniquity, and to the puffing them up with pride; tempting them to seek for power, and authority, and riches, and the vain things of the world. And thus Satan did lead away the hearts of the people to do all manner of iniquity. Therefore, they had not enjoyed peace but a few years.

And thus in the commencement of the thirtieth year, the people having been delivered up for the space of a long time, to be carried about by the temptations of the devil, whithersoever he desired to carry them, and to do whatsoever iniquity he desired they should; and thus in the commencement of this, the thirtieth year, they were in a state of awful wickedness.

Now they did not sin ignorantly, for they knew the will of God concerning them, for it had been taught unto them. Therefore, they did willfully rebel against God. And now, it was in the days of Lachoneus, the son of Lachoneus; for Lachoneus did fill the seat of his father and did govern the people that year.

And there began to be men inspired from heaven and sent forth, standing among the people in all the land, preaching and testifying boldly of the sins and iniquities of the people, and testifying unto them concerning the redemption which the Lord would make for his people, or in other words the resurrection of Christ. And they did testify boldly of his death and sufferings.

Now there were many of the people who were exceeding angry because of those who testified of these things. And those who were angry were chiefly the chief judges and they who had been high priests and lawyers. Yea, all those who were lawyers were angry with those who testified of these things.

Now there was no lawyer, nor judge, nor high priest that could have power to condemn anyone to death, save their condemnation was signed by the governor of the land. Now, there were many of those who testified of the things pertaining to Christ, who testified boldly, who were taken and put to death secretly by the judges. And the knowledge of their death came not unto the governor of the land until after their death. [11]

Therefore, a complaint came unto the land of Zarahemla, to the governor of the land, against these judges who had condemned the prophets of the Lord unto death, not according to the law. Now it came to pass that they were taken and brought up before the judge to be judged of the crime which they had done, according to the law which had been given by the people.

Now it came to pass that those judges had many friends and kindreds. And the remainder, yea, even almost all the lawyers and the high priests, did gather themselves together and unite with the kindreds of those judges, who were to be tried according to the law. And they did enter into a covenant one with another; yea, even into that covenant which was given by them of old, which covenant was given and administered by the devil, to combine against all righteousness. Therefore, they did combine against the people of the Lord, and enter into a covenant to destroy them, and to deliver those who were guilty of murder from the grasp of justice, which was about to be administered according to the law.

And they did set at defiance the law and the rights of their country. And they did covenant one with another to destroy the governor, and to establish a king over the land, that the land should

---

[11] 3 Nephi 6: 1-23

no more be at liberty, but should be subject unto kings. [12]

And now, I do not write the manner of their oaths and combinations; for it hath been made known unto me that they are had among all people. And whatsoever nation shall uphold such secret combinations to get power and gain, until they shall spread over the nation, behold, they shall be destroyed. For the Lord will not suffer that the blood of his saints, which shall be shed by them, shall always cry unto him from the ground for vengeance upon them, and yet he avenge them not.

Wherefore, O ye Gentiles, it is wisdom in God that these things should be shown unto you, that thereby ye may repent of your sins and suffer not that these murderous combinations shall get above you, which are built up to get power and gain, and the work, yea, even the work of destruction come upon you. Yea, even the sword of the justice of the eternal God shall fall upon you, to your overthrow and destruction, if ye shall suffer these things to be.

Wherefore, the Lord commandeth you, when ye shall see these things come among you, that ye shall awake to a sense of your awful situation, because of this secret combination which shall be among you. Or, wo be unto it, because of the blood of them who have been slain; for they cry from the dust for vengeance upon it, and also upon those who build it up.

For it cometh to pass that whoso buildeth it up, seeketh to overthrow the freedom of all lands, nations, and countries. And it bringeth to pass the destruction of all people. For it is built up by the devil, who is the father of all lies, even that same liar who beguiled our first parents, yea, even that same liar who hath caused man to commit murder from the beginning, who hath hardened the hearts of men, that they have murdered the prophets, and stoned them, and cast them out from the beginning.

Wherefore, I am commanded to write these things, that evil may be done away, and that the time may come that Satan may have no power upon the hearts of the children of men, but that they may be persuaded to do good continually, that they may come unto the fountain of all righteousness and be saved. [13]

---

[12] 3 Nephi 6: 25-30
[13] Ether 8: 20*, 22-26*

Now behold, I will show unto you that they did not establish a king over the land. But in this same year, yea, the thirtieth year, they did destroy upon the judgment seat, yea, did murder the chief judge of the land.

And the people were divided one against another. And they did separate one from another into tribes, every man according to his family, and his kindred, and friends. And thus they did destroy the government of the land.

And every tribe did appoint a chief or a leader over them. And thus they became tribes and leaders of tribes. Now behold, there was no man among them, save he had much family and many kindreds and friends; therefore, their tribes became exceeding great. Now all this was done, and there were no wars as yet among them. And all this iniquity had come upon the people because they did yield themselves unto the power of Satan.

And the regulations of the government were destroyed because of the secret combination of the friends and kindreds of those who murdered the prophets. And they did cause a great contention in the land; yea, insomuch that there were but few righteous men among them. And thus six years had not passed away since the more part of the people had turned from their righteousness, like the dog to his vomit, or like the sow to her wallowing in the mire.

Now this secret combination, which had brought so great iniquity upon the people, did gather themselves together, and did place at their head a man whom they did call Jacob. And they did call him their king. Therefore, he became a king over this wicked band. And he was one of the chiefest who had given his voice against the prophets who testified of Jesus.

And it came to pass that they were not so strong in number as the tribes of the people, who were united together; save it were their leaders did establish their laws, every one according to his tribe. Nevertheless, they were enemies. Notwithstanding they were not a righteous people; yet they were united in the hatred of those who had entered into a covenant to destroy the government.

Therefore, Jacob, seeing that their enemies were more numerous than they, he being the king of the band, therefore, he commanded his people that they should take their flight into the

northernmost part of the land, and there build up unto themselves
a kingdom, until they were joined by dissenters, for he flattered
them that there would be many dissenters, and they become
sufficiently strong to contend with the tribes of the people.

And they did so; and so speedy was their march that it could
not be impeded until they had gone forth out of the reach of the
people. And thus ended the thirtieth year. And thus were the
affairs of the people of Nephi.

And it came to pass in the thirty and first year, that they were
divided into tribes, every man according to his family, kindred,
and friends. Nevertheless, they had come to an agreement that
they would not go to war one with another, but they were not
united as to their laws and their manner of government. For they
were established according to the minds of those who were their
chiefs and their leaders. But they did establish very strict laws that
one tribe should not trespass against another; insomuch, that in
some degree, they had peace in the land. Nevertheless, their
hearts were turned from the Lord, their God, and they did stone
the prophets and did cast them out from among them.

And it came to pass that Nephi, having been visited by angels
and also by the voice of the Lord, therefore, having seen angels,
and being eyewitness, and having had power given unto him that
he might know concerning the ministry of Christ, and also being
eyewitness to their quick return from righteousness unto their
wickedness and abominations; therefore, being grieved for the
hardness of their hearts and the blindness of their minds, went
forth among them in that same year and began to testify boldly
repentance and remission of sins through faith on the Lord Jesus
Christ.

And he did minister many things unto them. And all of them
cannot be written, and a part of them would not suffice; therefore,
they are not written in this book. And Nephi did minister with
power and with great authority.

And it came to pass that they were angry with him, even
because he had greater power than they, for it were not possible
that they could disbelieve his words. For so great was his faith on
the Lord Jesus Christ, that angels did minister unto him daily.
And in the name of Jesus did he cast out devils and unclean

spirits. And even his brother did he raise from the dead after he had been stoned and suffered death by the people. And the people saw it, and did witness of it, and were angry with him because of his power. And he did also do many more miracles in the sight of the people in the name of Jesus.

And it came to pass that the thirty and first year did pass away, and there were but few who were converted unto the Lord. But as many as were converted did truly signify unto the people that they had been visited by the power and Spirit of God, which was in Jesus Christ in whom they believed.

And as many as had devils cast out from them, and were healed of their sicknesses and their infirmities, did truly manifest unto the people that they had been wrought upon by the Spirit of God and had been healed. And they did show forth signs also, and did do some miracles among the people. Thus passed away the thirty and second year also.

About 33 A.D.

And Nephi did cry unto the people in the commencement of the thirty and third year; and he did preach unto them repentance and remission of sins. Now I would have you remember, also, that there were none who were brought unto repentance, who were not baptized with water. Therefore, there were ordained of Nephi, men unto this ministry, that all such as should come unto them should be baptized with water, and this as a witness and a testimony before God, and unto the people, that they had repented and received a remission of their sins. And there were many in the commencement of this year that were baptized unto repentance. And thus the more part of the year did pass away. [14]

And now, it came to pass that according to our record, and we know our record to be true, for behold, it was a just man who did keep the record; for he truly did many miracles in the name of Jesus, and there was not any man who could do a miracle in the name of Jesus save he were cleansed, every whit, from his iniquity.

---

[14] 3 Nephi 7: 1-26

And now, it came to pass, if there was no mistake made by this man in the reckoning of our time, the thirty and third year had passed away. And the people began to look with great earnestness for the sign which had been given by the prophet Samuel, the Lamanite, yea, for the time that there should be darkness for the space of three days over the face of the land. And there began to be great doubtings and disputations among the people, notwithstanding so many signs had been given.

And it came to pass in the thirty and fourth year, in the first month, in the fourth day of the month, there arose a great storm, such an one as never had been known in all the land. And there was also a great and terrible tempest. And there was terrible thunder, insomuch that it did shake the whole earth as if it was about to divide asunder. And there were exceeding sharp lightnings, such as never had been known in all the land.

And the city of Zarahemla did take fire; and the city of Moroni did sink into the depths of the sea, and the inhabitants thereof were drowned. And the earth was carried up upon the city of Moronihah, that in the place of the city thereof, there became a great mountain. And there was a great and terrible destruction in the land southward; but behold, there was a more great and terrible destruction in the land northward. For behold, the whole face of the land was changed because of the tempests, and the whirlwinds, and the thunderings, and the lightnings, and the exceeding great quaking of the whole earth.

And the highways were broken up, and the level roads were spoiled, and many smooth places became rough. And many great and notable cities were sunk, and many were burned. And many were shaken till the buildings thereof had fallen to the earth, and the inhabitants thereof were slain, and the places were left desolate.

And there were some cities which remained, but the damage thereof was exceeding great, and there were many in them who were slain. And there were some who were carried away in the whirlwind, and whither they went, no man knoweth, save they know that they were carried away.

And thus the face of the whole earth became deformed because of the tempests, and the thunderings, and the lightnings, and the quaking of the earth. And behold, the rocks were rent in twain. Yea, they were broken up upon the face of the whole earth, insomuch that they were found in broken fragments, and in seams, and in cracks upon all the face of the land.

And it came to pass that when the thunderings, and the lightnings, and the storm, and the tempest, and the quakings of the earth did cease—for behold, they did last for about the space of three hours, and it was said by some that the time was greater; nevertheless, all these great and terrible things were done in about the space of three hours. And then, behold, there was darkness upon the face of the land.

And it came to pass that there was thick darkness upon all the face of the land, insomuch that the inhabitants thereof, who had not fallen, could feel the vapor of darkness. And there could be no light because of the darkness, neither candles, neither torches. Neither could there be fire kindled with their fine and exceeding dry wood, so that there could not be any light at all. And there was not any light seen, neither fire, nor glimmer, neither the sun, nor the moon, nor the stars, for so great were the mists of darkness which were upon the face of the land.

And it came to pass that it did last for the space of three days, that there was no light seen. And there was great mourning, and howling, and weeping among all the people continually; yea, great were the groanings of the people because of the darkness and the great destruction which had come upon them.

And in one place they were heard to cry, saying, Oh, that we had repented before this great and terrible day, and then would our brethren have been spared, and they would not have been burned in that great city Zarahemla.

And in another place they were heard to cry and mourn, saying, Oh, that we had repented before this great and terrible day, and had not killed and stoned the prophets, and cast them out. Then would our mothers, and our fair daughters, and our children have been spared, and not have been buried up in that great city Moronihah. And thus were the howlings of the people great and terrible. [15]

---

[15] 3 Nephi 8: 1-25

And it came to pass that thus did the three days pass away. And it was in the morning, and the darkness dispersed from off the face of the land. And the earth did cease to tremble, and the rocks did cease to rend, and the dreadful groanings did cease. And all the tumultuous noises did pass away. And the earth did cleave together again, that it stood.

And the mourning, and the weeping, and the wailing of the people who were spared alive did cease. And their mourning was turned into joy and their lamentations into the praise and thanksgiving unto the Lord Jesus Christ, their Redeemer.

And thus far were the scriptures fulfilled which had been spoken by the prophets. And it was the more righteous part of the people who were saved. And it was they who received the prophets and stoned them not. And it was they who had not shed the blood of the saints who were spared. [16]

And now, whoso readeth, let him understand; he that hath the scriptures, let him search them and see and behold if all these deaths and destructions by fire, and by smoke, and by tempests, and by whirlwinds, and by the opening of the earth to receive them, and all these things are not unto the fulfilling of the prophecies of many of the holy prophets. Behold, I say unto you, Yea, many have testified of these things at the coming of Christ, and were slain, because they testified of these things. [17]

And it came to pass that in the ending of the thirty and fourth year, behold, I will show unto you that the people of Nephi who were spared, and also those who had been called Lamanites, who had been spared, did have great favors shown unto them, and great blessings poured out upon their heads, insomuch that soon after the ascension of Christ into heaven, he did truly manifest himself unto them, showing his body unto them, and ministering unto them. And an account of his ministry shall be given hereafter. Therefore, for this time I make an end of my sayings. [18]

---

[16] 3 Nephi 10: 9-12
[17] 3 Nephi 10: 14-15
[18] 3 Nephi 10: 18-19

About 34 A.D.

And now, it came to pass that there was a great multitude gathered together of the people of Nephi, round about the temple, which was in the land Bountiful. And they were marveling and wondering, one with another, and were showing one to another the great and marvelous change which had taken place. And they were also conversing about this Jesus Christ, of whom the sign had been given concerning his death.

And it came to pass that while they were thus conversing one with another, they heard a voice, as if it came out of heaven. And they cast their eyes round about, for they understood not the voice which they heard. And it was not a harsh voice, neither was it a loud voice. Nevertheless, and notwithstanding it being a small voice, it did pierce them that did hear to the center, insomuch that there was no part of their frame that it did not cause to quake. Yea, it did pierce them to the very soul and did cause their hearts to burn.

And it came to pass that again they heard the voice, and they understood it not. And again, the third time they did hear the voice, and did open their ears to hear it. And their eyes were towards the sound thereof, and they did look steadfastly towards heaven from whence the sound came. And behold, the third time they did understand the voice which they heard.

And it said unto them, Behold, my beloved Son, in whom I am well pleased, in whom I have glorified my name. Hear ye him!

And it came to pass, as they understood, they cast their eyes up again towards heaven. And behold, they saw a man descending out of heaven. And he was clothed in a white robe, and he came down and stood in the midst of them. And the eyes of the whole multitude were turned upon him. And they durst not open their mouths, even one to another, and wist not what it meant. For they thought it was an angel that had appeared unto them.

And it came to pass that he stretched forth his hand and spake unto the people, saying, Behold, I am Jesus Christ, of whom the prophets testified should come into the world. And behold, I am the light and the life of the world. And I have drunk out of that

bitter cup, which the Father hath given me, and have glorified the
Father in taking upon me the sins of the world, in the which I have
suffered the will of the Father in all things from the beginning.

And it came to pass that when Jesus had spoken these words,
the whole multitude fell to the earth, for they remembered that it
had been prophesied among them that Christ should show
himself unto them after his ascension into heaven.

And it came to pass that the Lord spake unto them, saying,
Arise and come forth unto me, that ye may thrust your hands into
my side, and also that ye may feel the prints of the nails in my
hands and in my feet, that ye may know that I am the God of
Israel, and the God of the whole earth, and have been slain for the
sins of the world.

And it came to pass that the multitude went forth, and thrust
their hands into his side, and did feel the prints of the nails in his
hands and in his feet. And this they did do, going forth one by one
until they had all gone forth, and did see with their eyes, and did
feel with their hands, and did know of a surety, and did bear
record that it was he of whom it was written by the prophets
should come.

And when they had all gone forth and had witnessed for
themselves, they did cry out with one accord, saying, Hosanna!
Blessed be the name of the Most High God! And they did fall
down at the feet of Jesus and did worship him.

And it came to pass that he spake unto Nephi, for Nephi was
among the multitude. And he commanded him that he should
come forth. And Nephi arose and went forth, and bowed himself
before the Lord, and he did kiss his feet. And the Lord
commanded him that he should arise. And he arose and stood
before him.

And the Lord said unto him, I give unto you power that ye
shall baptize this people when I am again ascended into heaven.
And again, the Lord called others and said unto them likewise,
and he gave unto them power to baptize.

And he said unto them, On this wise shall ye baptize, and
there shall be no disputations among you. Verily, I say unto you

that whoso repenteth of his sins through your words, and desireth to be baptized in my name, on this wise shall ye baptize them:

Behold, ye shall go down and stand in the water, and in my name shall ye baptize them. And now, behold, these are the words which ye shall say, calling them by name, saying, Having authority given me of Jesus Christ, I baptize you in the name of the Father, and of the Son, and of the Holy Ghost. Amen.

And then shall ye immerse them in the water, and come forth again out of the water. And after this manner shall ye baptize in my name. For behold, verily I say unto you that the Father, and the Son, and the Holy Ghost are one. And I am in the Father, and the Father in me, and the Father and I are one. [19]

And whoso believeth in me and is baptized, the same shall be saved. And they are they who shall inherit the kingdom of God. And whoso believeth not in me and is not baptized shall be damned.

Verily, verily, I say unto you that this is my doctrine, and I bear record of it from the Father. And whoso believeth in me believeth in the Father also. And unto him will the Father bear record of me. For he will visit him with fire and with the Holy Ghost. And thus will the Father bear record of me. And the Holy Ghost will bear record unto him of the Father and me, for the Father and I and the Holy Ghost are one. [20]

And again, I say unto you, Ye must repent, and be baptized in my name, and become as a little child, or ye can in no wise inherit the kingdom of God.

Verily, verily, I say unto you that this is my doctrine. And whoso buildeth upon this, buildeth upon my rock. And the gates of hell shall not prevail against them. And whoso shall declare more or less than this, and establish it for my doctrine, the same cometh of evil and is not built upon my rock, but he buildeth upon a sandy foundation. And the gates of hell standeth open to receive such when the floods come, and the winds beat upon them. Therefore, go forth unto this people, and declare the words which I have

---

[19] 3 Nephi 11: 1-27
[20] 3 Nephi 11: 33-36

spoken unto the ends of the earth. [21]

And it came to pass that when Jesus had spoken these words unto Nephi, and to those who had been called—now the number of them who had been called and received power and authority to baptize was twelve—behold, he stretched forth his hand unto the multitude and cried unto them, saying, Blessed are ye if ye shall give heed unto the words of these twelve, whom I have chosen from among you, to minister unto you, and to be your servants.

And unto them I have given power, that they may baptize you with water. And after that ye are baptized with water, behold, I will baptize you with fire and with the Holy Ghost. Therefore, blessed are ye if ye shall believe in me and be baptized, after that ye have seen me and know that I am.

And again, more blessed are they who shall believe in your words, because that ye shall testify that ye have seen me, and that ye know that I am. Yea, blessed are they who shall believe in your words, and come down into the depths of humility and be baptized. For they shall be visited with fire and with the Holy Ghost, and shall receive a remission of their sins.

Yea, blessed are the poor in spirit who come unto me, for theirs is the kingdom of heaven.

And again, blessed are all they that mourn, for they shall be comforted.

And blessed are the meek, for they shall inherit the earth.

And blessed are all they who do hunger and thirst after righteousness, for they shall be filled with the Holy Ghost.

And blessed are the merciful, for they shall obtain mercy.

And blessed are all the pure in heart, for they shall see God.

And blessed are all the peacemakers, for they shall be called the children of God.

And blessed are all they who are persecuted for my name's sake, for theirs is the kingdom of heaven.

And blessed are ye when men shall revile you and persecute and shall say all manner of evil against you falsely, for my sake. For ye shall have great joy and be exceeding glad; for great shall

---

[21] 3 Nephi 11: 38-41

be your reward in heaven. For so persecuted they the prophets who were before you.

Verily, verily, I say unto you, I give unto you to be the salt of the earth. But if the salt shall lose its savor, wherewith shall the earth be salted? The salt shall be thenceforth good for nothing, but to be cast out and to be trodden underfoot of men.

Verily, verily, I say unto you, I give unto you to be the light of this people. A city that is set on a hill cannot be hid. Behold, do men light a candle and put it under a bushel? Nay, but on a candlestick, and it giveth light to all that are in the house. Therefore, let your light so shine before this people, that they may see your good works and glorify your Father, who is in heaven.

Think not that I am come to destroy the law or the prophets. I am not come to destroy, but to fulfill. For verily, I say unto you, One jot, nor one tittle, hath not passed away from the law; but in me it hath all been fulfilled.

And behold, I have given you the law and the commandments of my Father, that ye shall believe in me, and that ye shall repent of your sins, and come unto me with a broken heart and a contrite spirit.

Behold, ye have the commandments before you, and the law is fulfilled. Therefore, come unto me and be ye saved. For verily, I say unto you, that except ye shall keep my commandments, which I have commanded you at this time, ye shall in no case enter into the kingdom of heaven.

Ye have heard that it hath been said by them of old time, and it is also written before you, that thou shalt not kill. And whosoever shall kill shall be in danger of the judgment of God. But I say unto you that whosoever is angry with his brother shall be in danger of his judgment. And whosoever shall say to his brother, Raca, shall be in danger of the council. And whosoever shall say, Thou fool, shall be in danger of hellfire.

Therefore, if ye shall come unto me, or shall desire to come unto me, and rememberest that thy brother hath aught against thee, go thy way unto thy brother, and first be reconciled to thy brother. And then come unto me, with full purpose of heart, and I will receive you.

Agree with thine adversary quickly while thou art in the way with him, lest at any time he shall get thee, and thou shalt be cast into prison. Verily, verily, I say unto thee, Thou shalt by no means come out thence until thou hast paid the uttermost senine. And while ye are in prison, can ye pay even one senine? Verily, verily, I say unto you, Nay!

Behold, it is written by them of old time that thou shalt not commit adultery. But I say unto you that whosoever looketh on a woman to lust after her hath committed adultery already in his heart. Behold, I give you a commandment that ye suffer none of these things to enter into your heart. For it is better that ye should deny yourselves of these things, wherein ye will take up your cross, than that ye should be cast into hell.

It hath been written that whosoever shall put away his wife, let him give her a writing of divorcement. Verily, verily, I say unto you that whosoever shall put away his wife, saving for the cause of fornication, causeth her to commit adultery, and whoso shall marry her who is divorced committeth adultery.

And again, it is written, Thou shalt not forswear thyself, but shalt perform unto the Lord thine oaths. But verily, verily I say unto you, Swear not at all, neither by heaven for it is God's throne, nor by the earth for it is his footstool. Neither shalt thou swear by thy head because thou canst not make one hair black or white. But let your communication be, Yea, yea; Nay, nay; for whatsoever cometh of more than these is evil.

And behold, it is written, An eye for an eye, and a tooth for a tooth. But I say unto you that ye shall not resist evil, but whosoever shall smite thee on thy right cheek, turn to him the other also.

And if any man will sue thee at the law and take away thy coat, let him have thy cloak also. And whosoever shall compel thee to go a mile, go with him twain. Give to him that asketh thee, and to him that would borrow of thee, turn thou not away.

And behold, it is written also that thou shalt love thy neighbor and hate thine enemy. But behold, I say unto you, Love your enemies. Bless them that curse you. Do good to them that hate you, and pray for them who despitefully use you and persecute you, that ye may be the children of your Father, who is in heaven. For he maketh his sun to rise on the evil and on the good.

Therefore, those things which were of old time, which were under the law, in me are all fulfilled. Old things are done away, and all things have become new. Therefore, I would that ye should be perfect, even as I, or your Father who is in heaven, is perfect. [22]

And now, it came to pass that when Jesus had spoken these words, he turned again to the multitude and did open his mouth unto them again, saying, Verily, verily I say unto you, Judge not, that ye be not judged, for with what judgment ye judge, ye shall be judged. And with what measure ye mete, it shall be measured to you again.

And why beholdest thou the mote that is in thy brother's eye, but considerest not the beam that is in thine own eye? Or, how wilt thou say to thy brother, Let me pull the mote out of thine eye; and behold, a beam is in thine own eye? Thou hypocrite, first cast the beam out of thine own eye; and then shalt thou see clearly to cast the mote out of thy brother's eye. [23]

Therefore, all things whatsoever ye would, that men should do to you, do ye even so to them; for this is the law and the prophets.

Enter ye in at the strait gate. For wide is the gate and broad is the way that leadeth to destruction, and many there be who go in thereat. Because strait is the gate, and narrow is the way which leadeth unto life, and few there be that find it.

Beware of false prophets, who come to you in sheep's clothing, but inwardly they are ravening wolves. Ye shall know them by their fruits. Do men gather grapes of thorns, or figs of thistles? Even so, every good tree bringeth forth good fruit; but a corrupt tree bringeth forth evil fruit. A good tree cannot bring forth evil fruit, neither a corrupt tree bring forth good fruit. Every tree that bringeth not forth good fruit is hewn down and cast into the fire. Wherefore, by their fruits ye shall know them.

---

[22] 3 Nephi 11: 1-48
[23] 3 Nephi 14: 1-5

Not everyone that saith unto me, Lord, Lord, shall enter into the kingdom of heaven, but he that doeth the will of my Father who is in heaven. Many will say to me in that day, Lord, Lord, have we not prophesied in thy name, and in thy name have cast out devils, and in thy name done many wonderful works? And then will I profess unto them, I never knew you; depart from me, ye that work iniquity.

Therefore, whoso heareth these sayings of mine and doeth them, I will liken him unto a wise man who built his house upon a rock. And the rain descended, and the floods came, and the winds blew, and beat upon that house; and it fell not, for it was founded upon a rock.

And everyone that heareth these sayings of mine and doeth them not, shall be likened unto a foolish man, who built his house upon the sand. And the rain descended, and the floods came, and the winds blew, and beat upon that house, and it fell, and great was the fall of it. [24]

And now, it came to pass that when Jesus had ended these sayings, he cast his eyes round about on the multitude and said unto them, Behold, ye have heard the things which I have taught before I ascended to my Father. Therefore, whoso remembereth these sayings of mine and doeth them, him will I raise up at the last day.

And it came to pass that when Jesus had said these words, he perceived that there were some among them who marveled and wondered what he would concerning the law of Moses; for they understood not the saying that old things had passed away, and that all things had become new.

And he said unto them, Marvel not that I said unto you that old things had passed away and that all things had become new. Behold, I say unto you that the law is fulfilled that was given unto Moses.

Behold, I am he that gave the law, and I am he who covenanted with my people Israel. Therefore, the law in me is fulfilled, for I have come to fulfill the law. Therefore, it hath an end.

---

[24] 3 Nephi 14: 12-27

Behold, I do not destroy the prophets, for as many as have not been fulfilled in me, verily, I say unto you, shall all be fulfilled. And because I said unto you that old things hath passed away, I do not destroy that which hath been spoken concerning things which are to come. For behold, the covenant which I have made with my people is not all fulfilled. But the law which was given unto Moses hath an end in me.

Behold, I am the law and the light! Look unto me and endure to the end, and ye shall live. For unto him that endureth to the end will I give eternal life.

Behold, I have given unto you the commandments, therefore, keep my commandments. And this is the law and the prophets, for they truly testified of me.

And now, it came to pass that when Jesus had spoken these words, he said unto those twelve whom he had chosen, Ye are my disciples; and ye are a light unto this people, who are a remnant of the house of Joseph. And behold, this is the land of your inheritance, and the Father hath given it unto you. And not at any time hath the Father given me commandment that I should tell it unto your brethren at Jerusalem. Neither at any time hath the Father given me commandment that I should tell unto them concerning the other tribes of the house of Israel, whom the Father hath led away out of the land.

This much did the Father command me that I should tell unto them: that other sheep I have, which are not of this fold; them also I must bring, and they shall hear my voice, and there shall be one fold and one shepherd. [25] And verily, I say unto you that ye are they of whom I said, Other sheep I have which are not of this fold. And they understood me not, for they supposed it had been the Gentiles. For they understood not that the Gentiles should be converted through their preaching. And they understood me not that I said, They shall hear my voice; and they understood me not that the Gentiles should not at any time hear my voice, that I should not manifest myself unto them, save it were by the Holy Ghost. But behold, ye have both heard my voice and seen me. And

---

[25] 3 Nephi 15: 1-17 (Compare John 10; 16)

ye are my sheep. And ye are numbered among those whom the Father hath given me. [26]

And I command you that ye shall write these sayings after I am gone, that if it so be that my people at Jerusalem, they who have seen me and been with me in my ministry, do not ask the Father in my name, that they may receive a knowledge of you by the Holy Ghost, and also of the other tribes whom they know not of— that these sayings, which ye shall write, shall be kept, and shall be manifested unto the Gentiles; that through the fullness of the Gentiles, the remnant of their seed, who shall be scattered forth upon the face of the earth, because of their unbelief, may be brought in, or may be brought to a knowledge of me, their Redeemer. And then will I gather them in from the four quarters of the earth. And then will I fulfill the covenant which the Father hath made unto all the people of the house of Israel. [27]

And then the words of the prophet Isaiah shall be fulfilled, which say, Thy watchmen shall lift up the voice. With the voice together shall they sing, for they shall see eye to eye, when the Lord shall bring again Zion. Break forth into joy! Sing together, ye waste places of Jerusalem! For the Lord hath comforted his people. He hath redeemed Jerusalem! The Lord hath made bare his holy arm in the eyes of all the nations. And all the ends of the earth shall see the salvation of God. [28]

Behold, now it came to pass that when Jesus had spoken these words, he looked round about again on the multitude, and he said unto them, Behold, my time is at hand. I perceive that ye are weak, that ye cannot understand all my words which I am commanded of the Father to speak unto you at this time. Therefore, go ye unto your homes, and ponder upon the things which I have said, and ask of the Father in my name that ye may understand, and prepare your minds for the morrow. And I come unto you again. [29]

And it came to pass that when Jesus had thus spoken, he cast his eyes round about again on the multitude, and beheld they

---

[26] 3 Nephi 15: 21*-24
[27] 3 Nephi 16: 4-5
[28] 3 Nephi 16: 17-20 (Compare Isaiah 52: 8-10)
[29] 3 Nephi 17: 1-3

were in tears, and did look steadfastly upon him, as if they would
ask him to tarry a little longer with them. And he said unto them,
Behold, my bowels are filled with compassion towards you. Have
ye any that are sick among you? Bring them hither.

Have ye any that are lame, or blind, or halt, or maimed, or
leprous, or that are withered, or that are deaf, or that are afflicted
in any manner? Bring them hither, and I will heal them, for I have
compassion upon you. My bowels are filled with mercy; for I
perceive that ye desire that I should show unto you what I have
done unto your brethren at Jerusalem, for I see that your faith is
sufficient that I should heal you.

And it came to pass that when he had thus spoken, all the
multitude with one accord did go forth, with their sick, and their
afflicted, and their lame, and with their blind, and with their
dumb, and with all they that were afflicted in any manner. And he
did heal them, every one, as they were brought forth unto him.

And they did all, both they who had been healed and they
who were whole, bow down at his feet and did worship him, and
as many as could come. For the multitude, did kiss his feet,
insomuch that they did bathe his feet with their tears.

And it came to pass that he commanded that their little
children should be brought. So they brought their little children
and sat them down upon the ground round about him. And Jesus
stood in the midst. And the multitude gave way till they had all
been brought unto him.

And it came to pass that when they had all been brought, and
Jesus stood in the midst, he commanded the multitude that they
should kneel down upon the ground. And it came to pass that
when they had knelt upon the ground, Jesus groaned within
himself and saith, Father, I am troubled because of the wickedness
of the people of the house of Israel. And when he had said these
words, he himself also knelt upon the earth. And behold, he
prayed unto the Father. And the things which he prayed cannot
be written, and the multitude did bear record, who heard him.

And after this manner do they bear record: The eye hath
never seen, neither hath the ear heard before, so great and
marvelous things as we saw and heard Jesus speak unto the
Father. And no tongue can speak, neither can there be written by

any man; neither can the hearts of men conceive so great and
marvelous things as we both saw and heard Jesus speak. And no
one can conceive of the joy which filled our souls at the time we
heard him pray for us unto the Father.

And it came to pass that when Jesus had made an end of
praying unto the Father, he arose. But so great was the joy of the
multitude that they were overcome. And it came to pass that Jesus
spake unto them and bade them arise. And they arose from the
earth.

And he said unto them, Blessed are ye because of your faith.
And now, behold, my joy is full. And when he had said these
words, he wept. And the multitude bear record of it.

And he took their little children, one by one, and blessed
them, and prayed unto the Father for them. And when he had
done this, he wept again. And he spake unto the multitude and
saith unto them, Behold your little ones.

And as they looked to behold, they cast their eyes towards
heaven. And they saw the heavens open, and they saw angels
descending out of heaven, as it were in the midst of fire. And they
came down and encircled those little ones about, and they were
encircled about with fire. And the angels did minister unto them.
And the multitude did see, and hear, and bear record. And they
know that their record is true; for they, all of them, did see and
hear, every man for himself. And they were in number about two
thousand and five hundred souls. And they did consist of men,
women, and children. [30]

And it came to pass that Jesus commanded his disciples that
they should bring forth some bread and wine unto him. And
while they were gone for bread and wine, he commanded the
multitude that they should sit themselves down upon the earth.

And when the disciples had come with bread and wine, he
took of the bread, and brake, and blessed it. And he gave unto the
disciples and commanded that they should eat. And when they
had eaten and were filled, he commanded that they should give
unto the multitude.

---

[30] 3 Nephi 17: 5-25

And when the multitude had eaten and were filled, he said unto the disciples, Behold, there shall one be ordained among you, and to him will I give power that he shall break bread, and bless it, and give it unto the people of my church, unto all those who shall believe, and be baptized in my name. And this shall ye always observe to do, even as I have done, even as I have broken bread, and blessed it, and given it unto you.

And this shall ye do in remembrance of my body, which I have shown unto you. And it shall be a testimony unto the Father that ye do always remember me. And if ye do always remember me, ye shall have my Spirit to be with you.

And it came to pass that when he had said these words, he commanded his disciples that they should take of the wine of the cup and drink of it, and that they should also give unto the multitude, that they might drink of it. And it came to pass that they did so, and did drink of it, and were filled. And they gave unto the multitude, and they did drink. And they were filled.

And when the disciples had done this, Jesus said unto them, Blessed are ye for this thing which ye have done, for this is fulfilling my commandments. And this doth witness unto the Father that ye are willing to do that which I have commanded you. And this shall ye always do unto those who repent and are baptized in my name. And ye shall do it in remembrance of my blood, which I have shed for you, that ye may witness unto the Father that ye do always remember me. And if ye do always remember me, ye shall have my Spirit to be with you.

And I give unto you a commandment that ye shall do these things. And if ye shall always do these things, blessed are ye, for ye are built upon my rock. But whoso among you shall do more or less than these, are not built upon my rock, but are built upon a sandy foundation. And when the rain descends, and the floods come, and the winds blow and beat upon them, they shall fall. And the gates of hell are already open to receive them. Therefore, blessed are ye if ye shall keep my commandments, which the Father hath commanded me that I should give unto you.

Verily, verily, I say unto you, Ye must watch and pray always, lest ye be tempted by the devil, and ye are led away captive by him. And, as I have prayed among you, even so shall ye pray in my church, among my people, who do repent and are baptized in my name. Behold, I am the light; I have set an example for you.

And it came to pass that when Jesus had spoken these words unto his disciples, he turned again unto the multitude and said unto them, Behold, verily, verily, I say unto you, Ye must watch and pray always, lest ye enter into temptation; for Satan desireth to have you, that he may sift you as wheat. Therefore, ye must always pray unto the Father in my name. And whatsoever ye shall ask the Father in my name, which is right, believing that ye shall receive, behold, it shall be given unto you. Pray in your families unto the Father, always in my name, that your wives and your children may be blessed.

And behold, ye shall meet together oft, and ye shall not forbid any man from coming unto you when ye shall meet together. But suffer them that they may come unto you, and forbid them not. But ye shall pray for them, and shall not cast them out. And if it so be that they come unto you oft, ye shall pray for them unto the Father in my name.

Therefore, hold up your light, that it may shine unto the world. Behold, I am the light which ye shall hold up, that which ye have seen me do.

Behold, ye see that I have prayed unto the Father, and ye all have witnessed. And ye see that I have commanded that none of you should go away, but rather have commanded that ye should come unto me, that ye might feel and see. Even so shall ye do unto the world. And whosoever breaketh this commandment suffereth himself to be led into temptation.

And now, it came to pass that when Jesus had spoken these words, he turned his eyes again upon the disciples whom he had chosen and said unto them, Behold, verily, verily, I say unto you, I give unto you another commandment, and then I must go unto my Father, that I may fulfill other commandments which he hath given me.

And now, behold, this is the commandment which I give unto you, that ye shall not suffer anyone knowingly to partake of my flesh and blood unworthily when ye shall minister it. For whoso eateth and drinketh my flesh and blood unworthily, eateth and drinketh damnation to his soul. Therefore, if ye know that a man is unworthy to eat and drink of my flesh and blood, ye shall forbid him. Nevertheless, ye shall not cast him out of your synagogues or your places of worship, for unto such shall ye continue to minister. For ye know not but what they will return, and repent, and come unto me with full purpose of heart, and I shall heal them. And ye shall be the means of bringing salvation unto them. [31]

Therefore, keep these sayings which I have commanded you, that ye come not under condemnation. For wo unto him whom the Father condemneth. And I give you these commandments because of the disputations which have been among you. And blessed are you if ye have no disputations among you.

And now, I go unto the Father, because it is expedient that I should go unto the Father for your sakes.

And it came to pass that when Jesus had made an end of these sayings, he touched with his hand the disciples whom he had chosen, one by one, and spake unto [32] the twelve whom he had chosen, as he laid his hands upon them. And he called them by name saying, Ye shall call on the Father in my name in mighty prayer. And after ye have done this, ye shall have power, that on him whom ye shall lay your hands, ye shall give the Holy Ghost. And in my name shall ye give it, for thus do mine apostles. [33]

And the multitude heard not the words which he spake, therefore, they did not bear record. But the disciples bare record that he gave them power to give the Holy Ghost. And I will show unto you hereafter that this record is true.

And it came to pass that when Jesus had touched them all, there came a cloud and overshadowed the multitude, that they could not see Jesus. And while they were overshadowed, he departed from them and ascended into heaven. And the disciples saw and did bear record that he ascended again into heaven. [34]

---

[31] 3 Nephi 18: 1-29, 32
[32] 3 Nephi 18: 34-36*
[33] Moroni 2: 1*-2
[34] 3 Nephi 18: 37-39

Chapter 11

A New Day

And now, it came to pass that when Jesus had ascended into heaven, the multitude did disperse. And every man did take his wife and his children and did return to his own home. And it was noised abroad among the people immediately, before it was yet dark, that the multitude had seen Jesus, and that he had ministered unto them, and that he would also show himself on the morrow unto the multitude. Yea, and even all the night it was noised abroad concerning Jesus, that they might be on the morrow in the place where Jesus should show himself unto the multitude. [1]

And it came to pass that on the morrow, when the multitude was gathered together, behold, Nephi and his brother, whom he had raised from the dead, whose name was Timothy, and also his son, whose name was Jonas, and also Mathoni, and Mathonihah his brother, and Kumen, and Kumenonhi, and Jeremiah, and Shemnon, and Jonas, and Zedekiah, and Isaiah— now these were the names of the disciples whom Jesus had chosen; and it came to pass that they went forth and stood in the midst of the multitude.

And behold, the multitude was so great that they did cause that they should be separated into twelve bodies. And the twelve did teach the multitude. And behold, they did cause that the multitude should kneel down upon the face of the earth and should pray unto the Father in the name of Jesus. And the disciples did pray unto the Father also, in the name of Jesus.

And it came to pass that they arose and ministered unto the people. And when they had ministered those same words which Jesus had spoken—nothing varying from the words which Jesus had spoken, behold, they knelt again and prayed to the Father in the name of Jesus. And they did pray for that which they most desired. And they desired that the Holy Ghost should be given unto them.

And when they had thus prayed, they went down unto the water's edge, and the multitude followed them. And it came to

---

[1] 3 Nephi 19: 1-3*

pass that Nephi went down into the water and was baptized. And he came up out of the water and began to baptize. And he baptized all those whom Jesus had chosen.

And it came to pass when they were all baptized and had come up out of the water, the Holy Ghost did fall upon them, and they were filled with the Holy Ghost and with fire. And behold, they were encircled about as if it were fire. And it came down from heaven, and the multitude did witness it and do bear record. And angels did come down out of heaven and did minister unto them.

And it came to pass that while the angels were ministering unto the disciples, behold, Jesus came and stood in the midst and ministered unto them. And it came to pass that he spake unto the multitude, and commanded them that they should kneel down again upon the earth, and also that his disciples should kneel down upon the earth.

And it came to pass that when they had all knelt down upon the earth, he commanded his disciples that they should pray. And behold, they began to pray. And they did pray unto Jesus, calling him their Lord and their God.

And it came to pass that Jesus departed out of the midst of them, and went a little way off from them, and bowed himself to the earth. And he said, Father, I thank thee that thou hast given the Holy Ghost unto these whom I have chosen. And it is because of their belief in me that I have chosen them out of the world.

Father, I pray thee that thou wilt give the Holy Ghost unto all them that shall believe in their words. Father, thou hast given them the Holy Ghost because they believe in me. And thou seest that they believe in me because thou hearest them, and they pray unto me. And they pray unto me because I am with them. And now, Father, I pray unto thee for them, and also for all those who shall believe on their words, that they may believe in me, that I may be in them as thou, Father, art in me, that we may be one.

And it came to pass that when Jesus had thus prayed unto the Father, he came unto his disciples. And behold, they did still continue without ceasing to pray unto him. And they did not multiply many words, for it was given unto them what they should pray. And they were filled with desire.

And it came to pass that Jesus beheld them as they did pray unto him; and his countenance did smile upon them, and the light of his countenance did shine upon them. And behold, they were as white as the countenance and also the garments of Jesus. And behold, the whiteness thereof did exceed all the whiteness; yea, even there could be nothing upon earth so white as the whiteness thereof.

And Jesus said unto them, Pray on. Nevertheless, they did not cease to pray. And he turned from them again, and went a little way off, and bowed himself to the earth, and he prayed again unto the Father, saying, Father, I thank thee that thou hast purified these whom I have chosen because of their faith. And I pray for them, and also for them who shall believe on their words, that they may be purified in me through faith on their words, even as they are purified in me. Father, I pray not for the world, but for those whom thou hast given me out of the world because of their faith, that they may be purified in me, that I may be in them as thou, Father, art in me, that we may be one, that I may be glorified in them.

And when Jesus had spoken these words, he came again unto his disciples; and behold, they did pray steadfastly without ceasing unto him. And he did smile upon them again. And behold, they were white, even as Jesus.

And it came to pass that he went again a little way off and prayed unto the Father. And tongue cannot speak the words which he prayed; neither can be written by man the words which he prayed. And the multitude did hear and do bear record. And their hearts were open, and they did understand in their hearts the words which he prayed; nevertheless, so great and marvelous were the words which he prayed that they cannot be written, neither can they be uttered by man. [2]

And it came to pass that he commanded the multitude that they should cease to pray, and also his disciples. And he commanded them that they should not cease to pray in their hearts. And he commanded them that they should arise and stand upon their feet. And they arose up and stood upon their feet.

---

[2] 3 Nephi 19: 4-34

And it came to pass that he brake bread again, and blessed it, and gave to the disciples to eat. And when they had eaten, he commanded them that they should break bread and give it unto the multitude. And when they had given unto the multitude, he also gave them wine to drink, and commanded them that they should give unto the multitude.

Now there had been no bread, neither wine, brought by the disciples, neither by the multitude; but he truly gave unto them bread to eat and also wine to drink. And he said unto them, He that eateth this bread eateth of my body to his soul; and he that drinketh of this wine drinketh of my blood to his soul; and his soul shall never hunger nor thirst but shall be filled.

Now when the multitude had all eaten and drunk, behold, they were filled with the Spirit, and they did cry out with one voice and gave glory to Jesus, whom they both saw and heard!

And it came to pass that when they had all given glory unto Jesus, he said unto them, Behold, now I finish the commandment which the Father hath commanded me concerning this people who are a remnant of the house of Israel.

Ye remember that I spake unto you and said that when the words of Isaiah should be fulfilled— behold, they are written, ye have them before you, therefore, search them, and verily, verily, I say unto you that when they shall be fulfilled, then is the fulfilling of the covenant which the Father hath made unto his people, O house of Israel. And then shall the remnants which shall be scattered abroad upon the face of the earth be gathered in from the east, and from the west, and from the south, and from the north. And they shall be brought to the knowledge of the Lord, their God, who hath redeemed them.

And the Father hath commanded me that I should give unto you this land for your inheritance. [3] And it shall come to pass that I will establish my people, O house of Israel. And behold, this people will I establish in this land, unto the fulfilling of the covenant which I made with your father Jacob. And it shall be a new Jerusalem.

---

[3] 3 Nephi 20: 1-14

And the powers of heaven shall be in the midst of this people; yea, even I will be in the midst of you. Behold, I am he of whom Moses spake, saying, A prophet shall the Lord, your God, raise up unto you of your brethren, like unto me. Him shall ye hear in all things whatsoever he shall say unto you. And it shall come to pass that every soul who will not hear that prophet shall be cut off from among the people. [4]

Verily, I say unto you, Yea, and all the prophets from Samuel, and those that follow after, as many as have spoken, have testified of me. And behold, ye are the children of the prophets; and ye are of the house of Israel. And ye are of the covenant which the Father made with your fathers, saying unto Abraham, And in thy seed shall all the kindreds of the earth be blessed. [5]

And I will remember the covenant which I have made with my people. And I have covenanted with them that I would gather them together in mine own due time, that I would give unto them again the land of their fathers for their inheritance, which is the land of Jerusalem, which is the promised land unto them forever, saith the Father.

And it shall come to pass, that the time cometh when the fullness of my gospel shall be preached unto them, and they shall believe in me, that I am Jesus Christ, the Son of God, and shall pray unto the Father in my name. Then shall their watchmen lift up their voice, and with the voice together shall they sing. For they shall see eye to eye.

Then will the Father gather them together again and give unto them Jerusalem for the land of their inheritance. Then shall they break forth into joy. Sing together ye waste places of Jerusalem! For the Father hath comforted his people; he hath redeemed Jerusalem!

The Father hath made bare his holy arm in the eyes of all the nations; and all the ends of the earth shall see the salvation of the Father. [6] And the Father and I are one!

And then shall be brought to pass that which is written, Awake, awake again, and put on thy strength, O Zion; put on thy

---

[4] Compare Deuteronomy 18: 15, 18-19
[5] 3 Nephi 20: 21-25, (Compare Genesis 22: 17-18)
[6] Compare Isaiah 52: 8-10

beautiful garments, O Jerusalem, the holy city! For henceforth there shall no more come into thee the uncircumcised and the unclean.

Shake thyself from the dust. Arise. Sit down, O Jerusalem! Loose thyself from the bands of thy neck, O captive daughter of Zion. For thus saith the Lord, Ye have sold yourselves for naught, and ye shall be redeemed without money. [7]

Verily, verily, I say unto you, that my people shall know my name; yea, in that day they shall know that I am he that doth speak.

And then shall they say, How beautiful upon the mountains are the feet of him that bringeth good tidings unto them, that publisheth peace, that bringeth good tidings unto them of good, that publisheth salvation, that saith unto Zion, Thy God reigneth! [8]

And then shall a cry go forth, Depart ye, depart ye; go ye out from thence; touch not that which is unclean! Go ye out of the midst of her! Be ye clean that bear the vessels of the Lord. For ye shall not go out with haste, nor go by flight. For the Lord will go before you; and the God of Israel shall be your rearward.

Behold, my servant shall deal prudently. He shall be exalted and extolled and be very high. As many were astonished at thee, his visage was so marred, more than any man, and his form, more than the sons of men. So shall he sprinkle many nations. The kings shall shut their mouths at him; for that which had not been told them shall they see; and that which they had not heard shall they consider. [9]

Verily, verily, I say unto you, All these things shall surely come, even as the Father hath commanded me. Then shall this covenant which the Father hath covenanted with his people be fulfilled. And then shall Jerusalem be inhabited again with my people, and it shall be the land of their inheritance. [10]

And verily, I say unto you, I give unto you a sign, that ye may know the time when these things shall be about to take place, that I shall gather in from their long dispersion my people, O house of Israel, and shall establish again among them my Zion.

---

[7] Compare Isaiah 52: 1-3
[8] Compare Isaiah 52: 6-7
[9] Compare Isaiah 52: 11-15
[10] 3 Nephi 20: 29-46

And behold, this is the thing which I will give unto you for a sign:
For verily, I say unto you that when these things which I
declare unto you, and which I shall declare unto you hereafter of
myself, and by the power of the Holy Ghost, which shall be given
unto you of the Father, shall be made known unto the Gentiles,
that they may know concerning this people who are a remnant of
the house of Jacob, and concerning this my people who shall be
scattered by them; verily, verily, I say unto you, When these
things shall be made known unto them of the Father, and shall
come forth of the Father from them unto you —for it is wisdom in
the Father that they should be established in this land, and be set
up as a free people by the power of the Father, that these things
might come forth from them unto a remnant of your seed, that the
covenant of the Father may be fulfilled, which he hath covenanted
with his people, O house of Israel; therefore, when these works
and the work which shall be wrought among you hereafter shall
come forth from the Gentiles unto your seed, which shall dwindle
in unbelief because of iniquity —for thus it behooveth the Father
that it should come forth from the Gentiles, that he may show
forth his power unto the Gentiles for this cause; that the Gentiles,
if they will not harden their hearts, that they may repent, and
come unto me, and be baptized in my name, and know of the true
points of my doctrine, that they may be numbered among my
people, O house of Israel; and when these things come to pass,
that thy seed shall begin to know these things, it shall be a sign
unto them, that they may know that the work of the Father hath
already commenced unto the fulfilling of the covenant which he
hath made unto the people who are of the house of Israel.

And when that day shall come, it shall come to pass that kings
shall shut their mouths; for that which had not been told them shall
they see; and that which they had not heard shall they consider. [11]

For in that day, for my sake, shall the Father work a work,
which shall be a great and a marvelous work among them. And
there shall be among them who will not believe it, although a man
shall declare it unto them.

---

[11] Compare Isaiah 52: 15

But behold, the life of my servant shall be in my hand; therefore, they shall not hurt him, although he shall be marred because of them. Yet I will heal him, for I will show unto them that my wisdom is greater than the cunning of the devil.

Therefore, it shall come to pass that whosoever will not believe in my words, who am Jesus Christ, whom the Father shall cause him to bring forth unto the Gentiles, and shall give unto him power that he shall bring them forth unto the Gentiles, it shall be done even as Moses said; they shall be cut off from among my people who are of the covenant.

And my people who are a remnant of Jacob shall be among the Gentiles, yea, in the midst of them as a lion among the beasts of the forest, as a young lion among the flocks of sheep, who, if he go through both treadeth down and teareth in pieces, and none can deliver. Their hand shall be lifted up upon their adversaries, and all their enemies shall be cut off.

Yea, wo be unto the Gentiles, except they repent. For it shall come to pass in that day, saith the Father, that I will cut off thy horses out of the midst of thee, and I will destroy thy chariots; and I will cut off the cities of thy land, and throw down all thy strongholds. And I will cut off witchcrafts out of thy hand, and thou shalt have no more soothsayers.

Thy graven images I will also cut off, and thy standing images out of the midst of thee. And thou shalt no more worship the works of thy hands. And I will pluck up thy groves out of the midst of thee. So will I destroy thy cities. And it shall come to pass that all lyings, and deceivings, and envyings, and strifes, and priestcrafts, and whoredoms shall be done away.

For it shall come to pass, saith the Father, that at that day, whosoever will not repent and come unto my beloved Son, them will I cut off from among my people, O house of Israel. And I will execute vengeance and fury upon them, even as upon the heathen, such as they have not heard. [12]

But if they will repent, and hearken unto my words, and harden not their hearts, I will establish my church among them. And they shall come in unto the covenant, and be numbered among this, the remnant of Jacob, unto whom I have given this

---

[12] Compare Micah 5: 8-15

land for their inheritance.

And they shall assist my people, the remnant of Jacob, and also as many of the house of Israel as shall come, that they may build a city, which shall be called the New Jerusalem. And then shall they assist my people that they may be gathered in, who are scattered upon all the face of the land, in unto the New Jerusalem.

And then shall the power of heaven come down among them. And I also will be in the midst. And then shall the work of the Father commence at that day, even when this gospel shall be preached among the remnant of this people.

Verily, I say unto you, At that day shall the work of the Father commence among all the dispersed of my people, yea, even the tribes which have been lost, which the Father hath led away out of Jerusalem. Yea, the work shall commence among all the dispersed of my people, with the Father, to prepare the way whereby they may come unto me, that they may call on the Father in my name. Yea, and then shall the work commence, with the Father, among all nations, in preparing the way whereby his people may be gathered home to the land of their inheritance. [13]

And they shall go out from all nations; and they shall not go out in haste, nor go by flight; for I will go before them, saith the Father, and I will be their rearward. [14] And then shall that which is written come to pass:

Sing, O barren, thou that didst not bear; break forth into singing, and cry aloud, thou that didst not travail with child. For more are the children of the desolate than the children of the married wife, saith the Lord. Enlarge the place of thy tent and let them stretch forth the curtains of thy habitations. Spare not! Lengthen thy cords and strengthen thy stakes! For thou shalt break forth on the right hand and on the left. And thy seed shall inherit the Gentiles and make the desolate cities to be inhabited.

Fear not, for thou shalt not be ashamed. Neither be thou confounded, for thou shalt not be put to shame; for thou shalt forget the shame of thy youth and shalt not remember the reproach of thy widowhood anymore. For thy Maker, thy husband, the Lord of hosts is his name! And thy Redeemer, the Holy One of Israel, the God of the whole earth shall he be called!

---

[13] 3 Nephi 21: 1-28
[14] 3 Nephi 21: 29 (Compare Isaiah 52: 12)

For the Lord hath called thee as a woman forsaken, and grieved in spirit, and a wife of youth when thou wast refused, saith thy God. For a small moment have I forsaken thee; but with great mercies will I gather thee. In a little wrath I hid my face from thee for a moment; but with everlasting kindness will I have mercy on thee, saith the Lord, thy Redeemer.

For this is as the waters of Noah unto me. For as I have sworn that the waters of Noah should no more go over the earth. So have I sworn that I would not be wroth with thee. For the mountains shall depart and the hills be removed; but my kindness shall not depart from thee. Neither shall the covenant of my peace be removed, saith the Lord that hath mercy on thee.

O thou afflicted, tossed with tempest and not comforted, behold, I will lay thy stones with fair colors and lay thy foundations with sapphires. And I will make thy windows of agates, and thy gates of carbuncles, and all thy borders of pleasant stones. And all thy children shall be taught of the Lord, and great shall be the peace of thy children.

In righteousness shalt thou be established. Thou shalt be far from oppression, for thou shalt not fear, and from terror, for it shall not come near thee. Behold, they shall surely gather together against thee, not by me. Whosoever shall gather together against thee shall fall for thy sake.

Behold, I have created the smith that bloweth the coals in the fire and that bringeth forth an instrument for his work; and I have created the waster to destroy. No weapon that is formed against thee shall prosper. And every tongue that shall revile against thee in judgment, thou shalt condemn. This is the heritage of the servants of the Lord; and their righteousness is of me, saith the Lord. [15]

And now, behold, I say unto you that ye ought to search these things. Yea, a commandment I give unto you, that ye search these things diligently, for great are the words of Isaiah. For surely he spake as touching all things concerning my people which are of the house of Israel. Therefore, it must needs be that he must speak also to the Gentiles. And all things that he spake hath been, and shall be, even according to the words which he spake. Therefore, give heed to my words.

---

[15] 3 Nephi 22: 1-17, (Compare Isaiah 54)

Write the things which I have told you, and according to the times and the will of the Father, they shall go forth unto the Gentiles. And whosoever will hearken unto my words, and repenteth, and is baptized, the same shall be saved. Search the prophets, for many there be that testify of these things.

And now, it came to pass that when Jesus had said these words, he said unto them, Behold, other scriptures I would that ye should write, that ye have not. [16]

And it came to pass that he commanded them that they should write the words which the Father had given unto Malachi, which he should tell unto them. And it came to pass that after they were written, he expounded them. And these are the words which he did tell unto them, saying:

Thus said the Father unto Malachi, Behold, I will send my messenger, and he shall prepare the way before me; and the Lord, whom ye seek, shall suddenly come to his temple, even the messenger of the covenant, whom ye delight in. Behold, he shall come, saith the Lord of hosts.

But who may abide the day of his coming? And who shall stand when he appeareth? For he is like a refiner's fire, and like fullers' soap. And he shall sit as a refiner and purifier of silver; and he shall purify the sons of Levi and purge them as gold and silver, that they may offer unto the Lord an offering in righteousness. Then shall the offering of Judah and Jerusalem be pleasant unto the Lord, as in the days of old, and as in former years.

And I will come near to you to judgment; and I will be a swift witness against the sorcerers, and against the adulterers, and against false swearers, and against those that oppress the hireling in his wages, the widow, and the fatherless, and that turn aside the stranger, and fear not me, saith the Lord of hosts. For I am the Lord. I change not; therefore, ye sons of Jacob are not consumed.

Even from the days of your fathers ye are gone away from mine ordinances and have not kept them. Return unto me, and I will return unto you, saith the Lord of hosts. But ye said, Wherein shall we return?

Will a man rob God? Yet ye have robbed me. But ye say, Wherein have we robbed thee? —In tithes and offerings.

[16] 3 Nephi 23: 1-6*

Ye are cursed with a curse, for ye have robbed me, even this whole nation. Bring ye all the tithes into the storehouse, that there may be meat in my house; and prove me now herewith, saith the Lord of hosts, if I will not open you the windows of heaven and pour you out a blessing, that there shall not be room enough to receive it. And I will rebuke the devourer for your sakes, and he shall not destroy the fruits of your ground; neither shall your vine cast her fruit before the time in the fields, saith the Lord of hosts. And all nations shall call you blessed, for ye shall be a delightsome land, saith the Lord of hosts.

Your words have been stout against me, saith the Lord. Yet ye say, What have we spoken against thee? – Ye have said, It is vain to serve God, and, What doth it profit that we have kept his ordinances, and that we have walked mournfully before the Lord of hosts? And now, we call the proud happy; yea, they that work wickedness are set up; yea, them that tempt God are even delivered.

Then they that feared the Lord spake often one to another; and the Lord hearkened and heard. And a book of remembrance was written before him, for them that feared the Lord, and that thought upon his name. And they shall be mine, saith the Lord of hosts, in that day when I make up my jewels. And I will spare them as a man spareth his own son that serveth him.

Then shall ye return and discern between the righteous and the wicked, between him that serveth God and him that serveth him not. [17] For behold, the day cometh that shall burn as an oven; and all the proud, yea, and all that do wickedly shall be stubble. And the day that cometh shall burn them up, saith the Lord of hosts, that it shall leave them neither root nor branch.

But unto you that fear my name, shall the Son of Righteousness arise with healing in his wings; and ye shall go forth and grow up as calves of the stall. And ye shall tread down the wicked; for they shall be ashes under the soles of your feet in the day that I shall do this, saith the Lord of hosts.

Remember ye the law of Moses, my servant, which I commanded unto him in Horeb for all Israel, with the statutes and judgments. Behold, I will send you Elijah, the prophet, before the coming of the great and dreadful day of the Lord. And he shall turn the heart of the fathers to the children, and the heart of the

---

[17] 3 Nephi 24: 1-18, (Compare Malachi 3: 1-18)

children to their fathers, lest I come and smite the earth with a curse. [18]

And now, it came to pass that when Jesus had told these things, he expounded them unto the multitude. And he did expound all things unto them, both great and small. And he saith, These scriptures which ye had not with you, the Father commanded that I should give unto you, for it was wisdom in him that they should be given unto future generations.

And he did expound all things, even from the beginning until the time that he should come in his glory; yea, even all things which should come upon the face of the earth, even until the elements should melt with fervent heat, and the earth should be wrapped together as a scroll, and the heavens and the earth should pass away, and even unto the great and last day, when all people, and all kindreds, and all nations, and tongues shall stand before God to be judged of their works, whether they be good or whether they be evil—if they be good, to the resurrection of everlasting life; and if they be evil, to the resurrection of damnation; being on a parallel, the one on the one hand, and the other on the other hand, according to the mercy, and the justice, and the holiness which is in Christ, who was before the world began.

And now, there cannot be written in this book even a hundredth part of the things which Jesus did truly teach unto the people. But behold, the plates of Nephi do contain the more part of the things which he taught the people. And these things have I written, which are a lesser part of the things which he taught the people. And I have written them to the intent that they may be brought again unto this people from the Gentiles according to the words which Jesus hath spoken.

And when they shall have received this, which is expedient that they should have first to try their faith—and if it shall so be that they shall believe these things, then shall the greater things be made manifest unto them. [19]

Behold, I was about to write them all, which were engraven upon the plates of Nephi, but the Lord forbade it, saying, I will try

---

[18] 3 Nephi 25: 1-6, (Compare Malachi 4: 1-6)
[19] 3 Nephi 26: 1-9

the faith of my people. Therefore, I, Mormon, do write the things which have been commanded me of the Lord.

And now, I, Mormon, make an end of my sayings and proceed to write the things which have been commanded me. Therefore, I would that ye should behold that the Lord truly did teach the people for the space of three days. And after that, he did show himself unto them oft, and did break bread oft, and bless it, and give it unto them.

And it came to pass that he did teach and minister unto the children of the multitude of whom hath been spoken, and he did loose their tongues. And they did speak unto their fathers great and marvelous things, even greater than he had revealed unto the people, and loosed their tongues, that they could utter.

And it came to pass that after he had ascended into heaven, the second time that he showed himself unto them, and had gone unto the Father, after having healed all their sick, and their lame, and opened the eyes of their blind, and unstopped the ears of the deaf, and even had done all manner of cures among them, and raised a man from the dead, and had shown forth his power unto them, and had ascended unto the Father—behold, it came to pass on the morrow, that the multitude gathered themselves together; and they both saw and heard these children; yea, even babes did open their mouths and utter marvelous things. And the things which they did utter were forbidden, that there should not any man write them.

And it came to pass that the disciples whom Jesus had chosen began from that time forth to baptize and to teach as many as did come unto them. And as many as were baptized in the name of Jesus were filled with the Holy Ghost. [20] And they taught and did minister one to another. And they had all things common among them, every man dealing justly one with another. And it came to pass that they did do all things even as Jesus had commanded them. And they who were baptized in the name of Jesus were called the church of Christ. [21]

---

[20] 3 Nephi 26: 11-17
[21] 3 Nephi 26: 19-21

And the church did meet together oft to fast, and to pray, and
to speak one with another concerning the welfare of their souls.
And they did meet together oft to partake of bread and wine in
remembrance of the Lord Jesus. And their meetings were
conducted by the church after the manner of the workings of the
Spirit, and by the power of the Holy Ghost. For as the power of
the Holy Ghost led them, whether to preach, or exhort, or to pray,
or to supplicate, or to sing, even so it was done. [22]

The manner of their elders and priests administering the flesh
and blood of Christ unto the church, according to the
commandments of Christ: And they did kneel down with the
church and pray to the Father in the name of Christ, saying,

O God, the eternal Father, we ask thee, in the name of thy
Son Jesus Christ, to bless and sanctify this bread to the souls of all
those who partake of it, that they may eat in remembrance of the
body of thy Son, and witness unto thee, O God, the eternal Father,
that they are willing to take upon them the name of thy Son, and
always remember him, and keep his commandments which he
hath given them, that they may always have his Spirit to be with
them. Amen. [23]

Behold, they took the cup and said,

O God, the eternal Father, we ask thee in the name of thy Son
Jesus Christ, to bless and sanctify this wine to the souls of all those
who drink of it, that they may do it in remembrance of the blood of
thy Son, which was shed for them, that they may witness unto thee,
O God, the eternal Father, that they do always remember him, that
they may have his Spirit to be with them. Amen.[24]

The manner which the disciples, who were called the elders
of the church, ordained priests and teachers: After they had
prayed unto the Father in the name of Christ, they laid their hands
upon them and said, In the name of Jesus Christ I ordain you to be
a priest; or if he be a teacher, I ordain you to be a teacher, to
preach repentance and remission of sins through Jesus Christ, by
the endurance of faith on his name to the end. Amen. And after

---

[22] Moroni 6: 5-6, 9
[23] Moroni 4: 1-3
[24] Moroni 5: 1*-2

this manner did they ordain priests and teachers, according to the gifts and callings of God unto men. And they ordained them by the power of the Holy Ghost which was in them. [25]

And now, I speak concerning baptism. Behold, elders, priests, and teachers were baptized; and they were not baptized save they brought forth fruit meet that they were worthy of it. Neither did they receive any unto baptism save they came forth with a broken heart and a contrite spirit, and witnessed unto the church that they truly repented of all their sins. And none were received unto baptism save they took upon them the name of Christ, having a determination to serve him to the end.

And after they had been received unto baptism and were wrought upon and cleansed by the power of the Holy Ghost, they were numbered among the people of the church of Christ. And their names were taken, that they might be remembered and nourished by the good word of God, to keep them in the right way, to keep them continually watchful unto prayer, relying alone upon the merits of Christ, who was the author and the finisher of their faith. [26]

And they were strict to observe that there should be no iniquity among them. And whoso was found to commit iniquity, and three witnesses of the church did condemn them before the elders, and if they repented not, and confessed not, their names were blotted out. And they were not numbered among the people of Christ. But as oft as they repented and sought forgiveness, with real intent, they were forgiven. [27]

About 35 A.D.

And it came to pass that as the disciples of Jesus were journeying, and were preaching the things which they had both heard and seen, and were baptizing in the name of Jesus, it came to pass that the disciples were gathered together, and were united in mighty prayer and fasting. And Jesus again showed himself

---

[25] Moroni 3: 1-4
[26] Moroni 6: 1-4
[27] Moroni 6: 7-8

unto them, for they were praying unto the Father in his name. And Jesus came, and stood in the midst of them, and said unto them, What will ye that I shall give unto you?

And they said unto him, Lord, we will that thou wouldest tell us the name whereby we shall call this church, for there are disputations among the people concerning this matter.

And the Lord said unto them, Verily, verily, I say unto you, Why is it that the people should murmur and dispute because of this thing? Have they not read the scriptures which say, Ye must take upon you the name of Christ, which is my name? For by this name shall ye be called at the last day. And whoso taketh upon him my name and endureth to the end, the same shall be saved at the last day. Therefore, whatsoever ye shall do, ye shall do it in my name.

Therefore, ye shall call the church in my name; and ye shall call upon the Father in my name, that he will bless the church for my sake. And how be it my church, save it be called in my name?

For if a church be called in Moses' name, then it be Moses' church; or if it be called in the name of a man, then it be the church of a man. But if it be called in my name, then it is my church, if it so be that they are built upon my gospel.

Verily, I say unto you that ye are built upon my gospel. Therefore, ye shall call whatsoever things ye do call in my name. Therefore, if ye call upon the Father for the church, if it be in my name, the Father will hear you.

And if it so be that the church is built upon my gospel, then will the Father show forth his own works in it. But if it be not built upon my gospel, and is built upon the works of men, or upon the works of the devil, verily, I say unto you, They have joy in their works for a season; and by and by the end cometh, and they are hewn down and cast into the fire, from whence there is no return. For their works do follow them, for it is because of their works that they are hewn down. Therefore, remember the things that I have told you.

Behold, I have given unto you my gospel; and this is the gospel which I have given unto you, that I came into the world to do the will of my Father because my Father sent me. And my Father sent me that I might be lifted up upon the cross; and after that I had been lifted up upon the cross, I might draw all men unto me —that as I have been lifted up by men, even so should men be lifted up by the Father to stand before me, to be judged of their works, whether they be good or whether they be evil.

And for this cause have I been lifted up. Therefore, according to the power of the Father, I will draw all men unto me, that they may be judged according to their works. And it shall come to pass that whoso repenteth and is baptized in my name shall be filled. And if he endureth to the end, behold, him will I hold guiltless before my Father at that day when I shall stand to judge the world. [28] And no unclean thing can enter into his kingdom. Therefore, nothing entereth into his rest, save it be those who have washed their garments in my blood because of their faith, and the repentance of all their sins, and their faithfulness unto the end.

Now this is the commandment: Repent, all ye ends of the earth, and come unto me, and be baptized in my name, that ye may be sanctified by the reception of the Holy Ghost, that ye may stand spotless before me at the last day.

Verily, verily, I say unto you, This is my gospel. And ye know the things that ye must do in my church. For the works which ye have seen me do, that shall ye also do. Therefore, if ye do these things, blessed are ye, for ye shall be lifted up at the last day. [29]

Write the things which ye have seen and heard, save it be those which are forbidden. Write the works of this people, which shall be, even as hath been written of that which hath been. For behold, out of the books which have been written, and which shall be written, shall this people be judged; for by them shall their works be known unto men.

And behold, all things are written by the Father. Therefore, out of the books which shall be written shall the world be judged. And know ye that ye shall be judges of this people, according to the judgment which I shall give unto you, which shall be just. Therefore, what manner of men ought ye to be? Verily, I say unto you, Even as I am.

---

[28] 3 Nephi 27: 1-16
[29] 3 Nephi 27: 19-21*, 22

And now, I go unto the Father. And verily, I say unto you, Whatsoever things ye shall ask the Father in my name, it shall be given unto you. Therefore ask, and ye shall receive; knock, and it shall be opened unto you. For he that asketh, receiveth; and unto him that knocketh, it shall be opened.

And now my joy is great, even unto fulness, because of you, and also this generation; yea, and even the Father rejoiceth, and also all the holy angels, because of you and this generation, for none of them are lost. [30]

And it came to pass that they did go forth among all the people of Nephi, and did preach the gospel of Christ unto all people on the face of the land. And they were converted unto the Lord and were united unto the church of Christ. And thus the people of that generation were blessed, according to the word of Jesus. [31]

And it came to pass in the thirty and sixth year, the people were all converted unto the Lord upon all the face of the land, both Nephites and Lamanites. And there were no contentions and disputations among them, and every man did deal justly one with another. And they had all things common among them. Therefore, they were not rich and poor, bond and free; but they were all made free and partakers of the heavenly gift. And it came to pass that the thirty and seventh year passed away also, and there still continued to be peace in the land.

And there were great and marvelous works wrought by the disciples of Jesus, insomuch that they did heal the sick, and raise the dead, and cause the lame to walk, and the blind to receive their sight, and the deaf to hear. And all manner of miracles did they work among the children of men. And in nothing did they work miracles save it were in the name of Jesus.

And thus did the thirty and eighth year pass away, and also the thirty and ninth, and the forty and first, and even until fifty and nine years had passed away. And the Lord did prosper them exceedingly in the land; yea, insomuch that they did build cities

---

[30] 3 Nephi 27: 23-30
[31] 3 Nephi 28: 23

again where there had been cities burned. Yea even that great city Zarahemla did they cause to be built again. [32]

And now, behold, it came to pass that the people of Nephi did wax strong, and did multiply exceeding fast, and became an exceeding fair and delightsome people. And they were married, and given in marriage, and were blessed according to the multitude of the promises which the Lord had made unto them. And they did not walk any more after the performances and ordinances of the law of Moses; but they did walk after the commandments which they had received from their Lord and their God, continuing in fasting, and prayer, and in meeting together oft, both to pray and to hear the word of the Lord. And it came to pass that there was no contention among all the people in all the land. [33]

And it came to pass that the seventy and first year passed away, and also the seventy and second year; yea, and, in fine, until the seventy and ninth year had passed away. Yea, even a hundred years had passed away. And it came to pass that there was no contention in the land because of the love of God which did dwell in the hearts of the people.

And there were no envyings, nor strifes, nor tumults, nor whoredoms, nor lyings, nor murders, nor any manner of lasciviousness. And surely there could not be a happier people among all the people who had been created by the hand of God.

There were no robbers, nor murderers; neither were there Lamanites nor any manner of ites; but they were in one, the children of Christ, and heirs to the kingdom of God. And how blessed were they, for the Lord did bless them in all their doings. Yea, even they were blessed and prospered until a hundred and ten years had passed away. And the first generation from Christ had passed away, and there was no contention in all the land. [34]

---

[32] 4 Nephi 2-6*
[33] 4 Nephi 10-13*
[34] 4 Nephi 14*-18

Chapter 12

The Witness

About 120 A.D.

And it came to pass that Nephi, he that kept the last record, died, and his son Amos kept it in his stead, and he kept it upon the plates of Nephi also; and he kept it eighty and four years. And there was still peace in the land, save it were a small part of the people who had revolted from the church and took upon them the name of Lamanites. Therefore, there began to be Lamanites again in the land.

And it came to pass that Amos died also, and it was a hundred and ninety and four years from the coming of Christ. And his son Amos kept the record in his stead, and he also kept it upon the plates of Nephi, which is this book. [1] And it came to pass that two hundred years had passed away, and the second generation had all passed away, save it were a few.

And now, I, Mormon, would that ye should know that the people had multiplied, insomuch that they were spread upon all the face of the land, and that they had become exceeding rich because of their prosperity in Christ.

And now, in this two hundred and first year, there began to be among them those who were lifted up in pride, such as the wearing of costly apparel and all manner of fine pearls, and of the fine things of the world. And from that time forth they did have their goods and their substance no more common among them. And they began to be divided into classes. And they began to build up churches unto themselves, to get gain, and began to deny the true church of Christ.

And it came to pass that when two hundred and ten years had passed away, there were many churches in the land. Yea, there were many churches which professed to know the Christ, and yet they did deny the more part of his gospel, insomuch that they did receive all manner of wickedness, and did administer

---

[1] 4 Nephi 19*-21*

that which was sacred unto him to whom it had been forbidden because of unworthiness. And this church did multiply exceedingly because of iniquity, and because of the power of Satan, who did get hold upon their hearts.

And again, there was another church which denied the Christ, and they did persecute the true church of Christ because of their humility and their belief in Christ. And they did despise them because of the many miracles which were wrought among them. [2]

And now, it came to pass in the two hundred and thirty and first year, there was a great division among the people. And it came to pass that there arose a people who were called the Nephites, and they were true believers in Christ. And among them there were those who were called by the Lamanites, Jacobites, and Josephites, and Zoramites. [3]

And it came to pass that they who rejected the gospel were called Lamanites, and Lemuelites, and Ishmaelites. And they did not dwindle in unbelief, but they did willfully rebel against the gospel of Christ. And they did teach their children that they should not believe, even as their fathers from the beginning did dwindle. And it was because of the wickedness and abominations of their fathers, even as it was in the beginning. And they were taught to hate the children of God, even as the Lamanites were taught to hate the children of Nephi from the beginning. And it came to pass that two hundred and forty and four years had passed away, and thus were the affairs of the people.

And the more wicked part of the people did wax strong and became exceeding more numerous than were the people of God. And they did still continue to build up churches unto themselves and adorn them with all manner of precious things. And thus did two hundred and fifty years pass away, and also two hundred and sixty years.

And it came to pass that the wicked part of the people began again to build up the secret oaths and combinations of Gadianton. And also the people who were called the people of Nephi began to be proud in their hearts, because of their exceeding riches, and

---

[2] 4 Nephi 1: 22-29
[3] 4 Nephi 1: 35*-36

became vain like unto their brethren, the Lamanites.

And from this time, the disciples began to sorrow for the sins of the world. And it came to pass that when three hundred years had passed away, both the people of Nephi and the Lamanites had become exceeding wicked, one like unto another. And it came to pass that the robbers of Gadianton did spread over all the face of the land. And there were none that were righteous, save it were the disciples of Jesus. And gold and silver did they lay up in store in abundance, and did traffic in all manner of traffic.

And it came to pass that after three hundred and five years had passed away, and the people did still remain in wickedness, Amos died, and his brother Ammoron did keep the record in his stead.

And it came to pass that when three hundred and twenty years had passed away, Ammoron, being constrained by the Holy Ghost, did hide up the records which were sacred; yea, even all the sacred records which had been handed down from generation to generation, which were sacred, even until the three hundred and twentieth year from the coming of Christ.

And he did hide them up unto the Lord, that they might come again unto the remnant of the house of Jacob, according to the prophecies and the promises of the Lord. And thus is the end of the record of Ammoron. [4]

About 320 A.D.

And now, I, Mormon, make a record of the things which I have both seen and heard and call it the book of Mormon. And about the time that Ammoron hid up the records unto the Lord, he came unto me, I being about ten years of age. And I began to be learned somewhat after the manner of the learning of my people. And Ammoron said unto me, I perceive that thou art a sober child and art quick to observe; therefore, when ye are about twenty and four years old, I would that ye should remember the things that ye have observed concerning this people. And when ye are of that age, go to the land of Antum unto a hill which shall be called

---

[4] 4 Nephi 38-49

Shim, and there have I deposited unto the Lord all the sacred engravings concerning this people. And behold, ye shall take the plates of Nephi unto yourself, and the remainder shall ye leave in the place where they are. And ye shall engrave upon the plates of Nephi all the things that ye have observed concerning this people.

And I, Mormon, being a descendant of Nephi, and my father's name was Mormon, I remembered the things which Ammoron commanded me. And it came to pass that I, being eleven years old, was carried by my father into the land southward, even to the land of Zarahemla, the whole face of the land having become covered with buildings. And the people were as numerous, almost, as it were the sand of the sea. [5]

And it came to pass that the war began to be among them in the borders of Zarahemla by the waters of Sidon. And it came to pass that the Nephites had gathered together a great number of men, even to exceed the number of thirty thousand. And it came to pass that they did have in this same year a number of battles, in the which the Nephites did beat the Lamanites and did slay many of them.

And it came to pass that the Lamanites withdrew their design, and there was peace settled in the land. And peace did remain for the space of about four years, that there was no blood shed. But wickedness did prevail upon the face of the whole land; insomuch that the Lord did take away his beloved disciples, and the work of miracles and of healing did cease because of the iniquity of the people. And there were no gifts from the Lord, and the Holy Ghost did not come upon any because of their wickedness and unbelief.

And I, being fifteen years of age and being somewhat of a sober mind, therefore, I was visited of the Lord and tasted and knew of the goodness of Jesus. And I did endeavor to preach unto this people. But my mouth was shut, and I was forbidden that I should preach unto them; for behold, they had willfully rebelled against their God. [6]

---

[5] Mormon 1: 1-7
[6] Mormon 1: 10-16*

And Gadianton robbers, who were among the Lamanites, did infest the land, insomuch that the inhabitants thereof began to hide up their treasures in the earth; and they became slippery because the Lord had cursed the land, that they could not hold them nor retain them again. And it came to pass that there were sorceries, and witchcrafts, and magics. And the power of the evil one was wrought upon all the face of the land. [7]

And it came to pass that in that same year, there began to be a war again between the Nephites and the Lamanites. And notwithstanding I being young, was large in stature. Therefore the people of Nephi appointed me that I should be their leader, or the leader of their armies. Therefore, it came to pass that in my sixteenth year I did go forth at the head of an army of the Nephites against the Lamanites. Therefore, three hundred and twenty and six years had passed away.

And it came to pass that in the three hundred and twenty and seventh year, the Lamanites did come upon us with exceeding great power, insomuch that they did frighten my armies. Therefore they would not fight and they began to retreat towards the north countries. [8] And it came to pass that we did gather in our people as fast as it were possible, that we might get them together in one body. But behold, the land was filled with robbers and with Lamanites. And notwithstanding the great destruction which hung over my people, they did not repent of their evil doings. Therefore, there was blood and carnage spread throughout all the face of the land, both on the part of the Nephites and also on the part of the Lamanites. And it was one complete revolution throughout all the face of the land.

And now, the Lamanites had a king, and his name was Aaron. And he came against us with an army of forty and four thousand. And behold, I withstood him with forty and two thousand. And it came to pass that I beat him with my army, that he fled before me. And behold, all this was done, and three hundred and thirty years had passed away.

---

[7] Mormon 1: 18*-19*
[8] Mormon 2: 1-3

And it came to pass that the Nephites began to repent of their iniquity and began to cry, even as had been prophesied by Samuel, the prophet. For behold, no man could keep that which was his own, for the thieves, and the robbers, and the murderers, and the magic art, and the witchcraft which was in the land. Thus there began to be a mourning and a lamentation in all the land because of these things, and more especially among the people of Nephi.

And it came to pass that when I, Mormon, saw their lamentations, and their mourning, and their sorrowing before the Lord, my heart did begin to rejoice within me, knowing the mercies and the long-suffering of the Lord; therefore, supposing that he would be merciful unto them, that they would again become a righteous people. But behold, this my joy was vain, for their sorrowing was not unto repentance, because of the goodness of God, but it was rather the sorrowing of the damned, because the Lord would not always suffer them to take happiness in sin. And they did not come unto Jesus with broken hearts and contrite spirits, but they did curse God and wish to die. Nevertheless, they would struggle with the sword for their lives.

And it came to pass that my sorrow did return unto me again, and I saw that the day of grace was past with them, both temporally and spiritually. For I saw thousands of them hewn down in open rebellion against their God, and heaped up as dung upon the face of the land. And thus three hundred and forty and four years had passed away. [9]

And it came to pass in the three hundred and forty and sixth year, they began to come upon us again. And it came to pass that I did speak unto my people and did urge them with great energy that they would stand boldly before the Lamanites and fight for their wives, and their children, and their houses, and their homes. And my words did arouse them somewhat to vigor, insomuch that they did not flee from before the Lamanites, but did stand with boldness against them.

And it came to pass that we did contend with an army of thirty thousand, against an army of fifty thousand. And it came to pass that we did stand before them with such firmness that they

[9] Mormon 2: 7-15

did flee from before us. And it came to pass that when they had fled, we did pursue them with our armies, and did meet them again, and did beat them. Nevertheless, the strength of the Lord was not with us. Yea, we were left to ourselves, that the Spirit of the Lord did not abide in us; therefore, we had become weak like unto our brethren.

And my heart did sorrow because of this the great calamity of my people, because of their wickedness and their abominations. But behold, we did go forth against the Lamanites and the robbers of Gadianton, until we had again taken possession of the lands of our inheritance. And the three hundred and forty and ninth year had passed away.

And in the three hundred and fiftieth year, we made a treaty with the Lamanites and the robbers of Gadianton, in which we did get the lands of our inheritance divided. And the Lamanites did give unto us the land northward, yea, even to the narrow passage which led into the land southward. And we did give unto the Lamanites all the land southward. [10]

And it came to pass that the Lamanites did not come to battle again until ten years more had passed away. And behold, I had employed my people, the Nephites, in preparing their lands and their arms against the time of battle.

About 360 A.D.

And it came to pass that the Lord did say unto me, Cry unto this people, repent ye, and come unto me and be ye baptized, and build up again my church, and ye shall be spared. And I did cry unto this people, but it was in vain; and they did not realize that it was the Lord that had spared them and granted unto them a chance for repentance. And behold, they did harden their hearts against the Lord, their God.

And it came to pass that after this tenth year had passed away, making in the whole three hundred and sixty years from the coming of Christ, the king of the Lamanites sent an epistle unto me, which gave unto me to know that they were preparing to

---

[10] Mormon 2: 22-29

come again to battle against us.

And it came to pass that I did cause my people that they should gather themselves together at the land Desolation, to a city which was in the borders by the narrow pass which led into the land southward. And there we did place our armies, that we might stop the armies of the Lamanites, that they might not get possession of any of our lands. Therefore, we did fortify against them with all our force.

And it came to pass that in the three hundred and sixty and first year, the Lamanites did come down to the city of Desolation to battle against us. And it came to pass that in that year we did beat them, insomuch that they did return to their own lands again. And in the three hundred and sixty and second year, they did come down again to battle. And we did beat them again and did slay a great number of them, and their dead were cast into the sea.

And now, because of this great thing which my people, the Nephites, had done, they began to boast in their own strength and began to swear before the heavens that they would avenge themselves of the blood of their brethren who had been slain by their enemies. And they did swear by the heavens, and also by the throne of God, that they would go up to battle against their enemies, and would cut them off from the face of the land.

And it came to pass that I, Mormon, did utterly refuse from this time forth to be a commander and a leader of this people because of their wickedness and abomination. Behold, I had led them, notwithstanding their wickedness. I had led them many times to battle and had loved them, according to the love of God which was in me, with all my heart. And my soul had been poured out in prayer unto my God, all the day long for them. Nevertheless, it was without faith because of the hardness of their hearts. And thrice have I delivered them out of the hands of their enemies, and they have repented not of their sins.

And when they had sworn, by all that had been forbidden them, by our Lord and Savior Jesus Christ, that they would go up unto their enemies to battle and avenge themselves of the blood of their brethren, behold, the voice of the Lord came unto me, saying, Vengeance is mine, and I will repay. And because this people repented not after I had delivered them, behold, they shall be cut off from the face of the earth.

And it came to pass that I utterly refused to go up against mine enemies. And I did even as the Lord had commanded me, and I did stand as an idle witness to manifest unto the world the things which I saw and heard, according to the manifestations of the Spirit which had testified of things to come.

Therefore, I write unto you Gentiles, and also unto you House of Israel, when the work shall commence, that ye shall be about to prepare to return to the land of your inheritance, yea, behold, I write unto all the ends of the earth, yea, unto you twelve tribes of Israel. [11] And these things does the Spirit manifest unto me; therefore, I write unto you all.

And for this cause I write unto you: that ye may know that ye must all stand before the judgment seat of Christ, yea, every soul who belongs to the whole human family of Adam. And ye must stand to be judged of your works, whether they be good or evil; and also that ye may believe the gospel of Jesus Christ, which ye shall have among you; and also that the Jews, the covenant people of the Lord, shall have another witness besides him whom they saw and heard, that Jesus, whom they slew, was the very Christ and the very God. And I would that I could persuade all ye ends of the earth to repent and prepare to stand before the judgment seat of Christ. [12]

About 363 A.D.

And now, it came to pass that in the three hundred and sixty and third year, the Nephites did go up with their armies to battle against the Lamanites out of the land of Desolation. And it came to pass that the armies of the Nephites were driven back again to the land of Desolation. And while they were yet weary, a fresh army of the Lamanites did come upon them. And they had a sore battle, insomuch that the Lamanites did take possession of the city Desolation, and did slay many of the Nephites and did take many prisoners. And the remainder did flee and join the inhabitants of

---

[11] Mormon 3: 1-18*
[12] Mormon 3: 20-22

the city Teancum. Now the city Teancum lay in the borders by the seashore. And it was also near the city Desolation.

And it was because the armies of the Nephites went up unto the Lamanites that they began to be smitten; for were it not for that, the Lamanites could have had no power over them. But behold, the judgments of God will overtake the wicked. And it is by the wicked that the wicked are punished. For it is the wicked that stir up the hearts of the children of men unto bloodshed.

And it came to pass that the Lamanites did make preparation to come against the city Teancum. And it came to pass in the three hundred and sixty and fourth year, the Lamanites did come against the city Teancum, that they might take possession of the city Teancum also. And it came to pass that they were repulsed and driven back by the Nephites. And when the Nephites saw that they had driven the Lamanites they did again boast of their own strength; and they went forth in their own might and took possession again of the city Desolation.

And now, all these things had been done and there had been thousands slain on both sides, both the Nephites and the Lamanites. And it came to pass that the three hundred and sixty and sixth year had passed away. And the Lamanites came again upon the Nephites to battle; and yet the Nephites repented not of the evil they had done, but persisted in their wickedness continually.

And it is impossible for the tongue to describe, or for man to write a perfect description of the horrible scene of the blood and carnage which was among the people, both of the Nephites and of the Lamanites. And every heart was hardened so that they delighted in the shedding of blood continually. And there never had been so great wickedness among all the children of Lehi, nor even among all the house of Israel, according to the words of the Lord, as was among this people.

And it came to pass that the Lamanites did take possession of the city Desolation, and this because their number did exceed the number of the Nephites. And they did also march forward against the city Teancum, and did drive the inhabitants forth out of her and did take many prisoners, both women and children, and did offer them up as sacrifices unto their idol gods.

And it came to pass that in the three hundred and sixty and seventh year, the Nephites, being angry because the Lamanites had sacrificed their women and their children, that they did go against the Lamanites with exceeding great anger, insomuch that they did beat again the Lamanites and drive them out of their lands. And the Lamanites did not come again against the Nephites until the three hundred and seventy and fifth year. And in this year they did come down against the Nephites with all their powers. And they were not numbered because of the greatness of their number. And from this time forth did the Nephites gain no power over the Lamanites, but began to be swept off by them, even as a dew before the sun. [13]

And now, I, Mormon, seeing that the Lamanites were about to overthrow the land, therefore, I did go to the hill Shim and did take up all the records which Ammoron had hid up unto the Lord. [14]

And it came to pass that I did go forth among the Nephites and did repent of the oath which I had made that I would no more assist them. And they gave me command again of their armies, for they looked upon me as though I could deliver them from their afflictions. But behold, I was without hope, for I knew the judgments of the Lord which should come upon them, for they repented not of their iniquities, but did struggle for their lives, without calling upon that being who created them.

And it came to pass that the Lamanites did come against us as we had fled to the city of Jordan; but behold, they were driven back, that they did not take the city at that time. And it came to pass that they came against us again, and we did maintain the city. And there were also other cities which were maintained by the Nephites, which strongholds did cut them off, that they could not get into the country which lay before us, to destroy the inhabitants of our land. But it came to pass that whatsoever lands we had passed by, and the inhabitants thereof were not gathered in, were destroyed by the Lamanites. And their towns, and villages, and cities were burned with fire. And thus the three hundred and seventy and ninth year passed away.

---

[13] Mormon 4: 1-18
[14] Mormon 4: 23

And it came to pass that in the three hundred and eightieth year, the Lamanites did come again against us to battle. And we did stand against them boldly. But it was all in vain, for so great were their numbers that they did tread the people of the Nephites under their feet. And it came to pass that we did again take to flight. And those whose flight was swifter than the Lamanites did escape, and those whose flight did not exceed the Lamanites were swept down and destroyed.

And now, behold, I, Mormon, do not desire to harrow up the souls of men in casting before them such an awful scene of blood and carnage as was laid before mine eyes. But I, knowing that these things must surely be made known, and that all things which are hid must be revealed upon the housetops, and also that a knowledge of these things must come unto the remnant of these people, and also unto the Gentiles, which the Lord hath said should scatter this people, and this people should be counted as naught among them; therefore, I write a small abridgment, daring not to give a full account of the things which I have seen, because of the commandment which I have received, and also that ye might not have too great sorrow, because of the wickedness of this people.

And now, behold, this I speak unto their seed, and also to the Gentiles, who have care for the house of Israel, that realize and know from whence their blessings come. For I know that such will sorrow for the calamity of the house of Israel. Yea, they will sorrow for the destruction of this people. They will sorrow that this people had not repented, that they might have been clasped in the arms of Jesus.

Now these things are written unto the remnant of the house of Jacob, and they are written after this manner, because it is known of God that wickedness will not bring them forth unto them. And they are to be hid up unto the Lord, that they may come forth in his own due time. And this is the commandment which I have received. And behold, they shall come forth according to the commandment of the Lord when he shall see fit, in his wisdom.

And behold, they shall go unto the unbelieving of the Jews. And for this intent shall they go: that they may be persuaded that Jesus is the Christ, the Son of the living God, that the Father may bring about, through his most beloved, his great and eternal purpose in restoring the Jews, or all the House of Israel, to the land of their inheritance, which the Lord, their God, hath given them, unto the fulfilling of his covenant; and also that the seed of this people may more fully believe his gospel, which shall go forth unto them from the Gentiles. [15]

For behold, the Spirit of the Lord hath already ceased to strive with their fathers, and they are without Christ and God in the world. And they are driven about as chaff before the wind. They were once a delightsome people, and they had Christ for their Shepherd. Yea, they were led, even by God, the Father. But now, behold, they are led about by Satan, even as chaff is driven before the wind, or as a vessel is tossed about upon the waves, without sail or anchor, or without anything wherewith to steer her. And even as she is, so are they. And behold, the Lord hath reserved their blessings, which they might have received in the land, for the Gentiles who shall possess the land.

But behold, it shall come to pass that they shall be driven and scattered by the Gentiles. And after they have been driven and scattered by the Gentiles, behold, then will the Lord remember the covenant which he made unto Abraham, and unto all the house of Israel. And also the Lord will remember the prayers of the righteous, which have been put up unto him for them.

And then, O ye Gentiles, how can ye stand before the power of God, except ye shall repent and turn from your evil ways? Know ye not that ye are in the hands of God? Know ye not that he hath all power, and at his great command the earth shall be rolled together as a scroll? Therefore, repent ye, and humble yourselves before him, lest he shall come out in justice against you; lest a remnant of the seed of Jacob shall go forth among you as a lion, and tear you in pieces, and there is none to deliver. [16]

---

[15] Mormon 5: 1-15*
[16] Mormon 5: 16-24

And now, we can behold the decrees of God concerning this land: that it is a land of promise; and whatsoever nation shall possess it shall serve God, or they shall be swept off when the fullness of his wrath shall come upon them. And the fullness of his wrath cometh upon them when they are ripened in iniquity.

And this cometh unto you, O ye Gentiles, that ye may know the decrees of God, that ye may repent and not continue in your iniquities until the fullness come, that ye may not bring down the fullness of the wrath of God upon you as the inhabitants of the land have hitherto done.

Behold, this is a choice land; and whatsoever nation shall possess it shall be free from bondage, and from captivity, and from all other nations under heaven--if they will but serve the God of the land, who is Jesus Christ, who hath been manifested by the things which we have written. [17]

About 383 A.D.

And now, I finish my record concerning the destruction of my people, the Nephites. And it came to pass that we did march forth before the Lamanites. And I, Mormon, wrote an epistle unto the king of the Lamanites and desired of him that he would grant unto us that we might gather together our people unto the land of Cumorah, by a hill which was called Cumorah. And there we would give them battle. And it came to pass that the king of the Lamanites did grant unto me the thing which I desired.

And it came to pass that we did march forth to the land of Cumorah, and we did pitch our tents round about the hill Cumorah. And it was in a land of many waters, rivers, and fountains. And here we had hope to gain advantage over the Lamanites. And when three hundred and eighty and four years had passed away, we had gathered in all the remainder of our people unto the land Cumorah.

And it came to pass that when we had gathered in all our people in one to the land of Cumorah, behold, I, Mormon, began to be old. And, knowing it to be the last struggle of my people,

---

[17] Ether 2: 9, 11-12

and having been commanded of the Lord that I should not suffer that the records which had been handed down by our fathers, which were sacred, to fall into the hands of the Lamanites, for the Lamanites would destroy them, therefore, I made this record out of the plates of Nephi, and hid up in the hill Cumorah all the records which had been entrusted to me by the hand of the Lord, save it were these few plates which I gave unto my son Moroni.

And it came to pass that my people, with their wives and their children, did now behold the armies of the Lamanites marching towards them. And with that awful fear of death, which fills the breasts of all the wicked, did they wait to receive them. And it came to pass that they came to battle against us, and every soul was filled with terror because of the greatness of their numbers.

And it came to pass that they did fall upon my people with the sword, and with the bow, and with the arrow, and with the ax, and with all manner of weapons of war. And it came to pass that my men were hewn down, yea, even my ten thousand who were with me; and I fell wounded in the midst. And they passed by me, that they did not put an end to my life.

And when they had gone through and hewn down all my people, save it were twenty and four of us, among whom was my son Moroni; and we, having survived the dead of our people, did behold on the morrow, when the Lamanites had returned unto their camps, from the top of the hill Cumorah, the ten thousand of my people who were hewn down, being led in the front by me. And we also beheld the ten thousand of my people who were led by my son Moroni.

And behold, the ten thousand of Gidgiddonah had fallen, and he also in the midst; and Lama had fallen with his ten thousand; and Gilgal had fallen with his ten thousand; and Limhah had fallen with his ten thousand; and Jeneum had fallen with his ten thousand; and Cumenihah, and Moronihah, and Antionum, and Shiblom, and Shem, and Josh had fallen with their ten thousand each.

And it came to pass that there were ten more who did fall by the sword with their ten thousand each. Yea, even all my people, save it were those twenty and four who were with me, and also a few who had escaped into the south countries, and a few who had deserted over unto the Lamanites, had fallen. And their flesh and bones and blood lay upon the face of the earth, being left by the hands of those who slew them, to moulder upon the land, and to crumble, and to return to their mother earth.

And my soul was rent with anguish because of the slain of my people. And I cried, O ye fair ones, how could ye have departed from the ways of the Lord! O ye fair ones, how could ye have rejected that Jesus, who stood with open arms to receive you! Behold, if ye had not done this, ye would not have fallen. But behold, ye are fallen, and I mourn your loss.

O ye fair sons and daughters, ye fathers and mothers, ye husbands and wives, ye fair ones, how is it that ye could have fallen! But behold, ye are gone, and my sorrows cannot bring your return. And the day soon cometh that your mortal must put on immortality, and these bodies which are now mouldering in corruption must soon become incorruptible bodies. And then ye must stand before the judgment seat of Christ to be judged according to your works. And if it so be that ye are righteous, then are ye blessed with your fathers who have gone before you.

Oh, that ye had repented before this great destruction had come upon you. But behold, ye are gone. And the Father, yea, the Eternal Father of heaven, knoweth your state. And he doeth with you according to his justice and mercy. [18]

And now, behold, I would speak somewhat unto the remnant of this people who are spared, if it so be that God may give unto them my words, that they may know of the things of their fathers. Yea, I speak unto you, ye remnant of the house of Israel. And these are the words which I speak:

Know ye that ye are of the house of Israel. [19]

Know ye that ye must come to the knowledge of your fathers, and repent of all your sins and iniquities, and believe in Jesus Christ, that he is the Son of God, and that he was slain by the Jews, and by the power of the Father he hath risen again, whereby he hath gained the victory over the grave. And also in him is the sting of death swallowed up. And he bringeth to pass the resurrection of

---

[18] Mormon 6: 1-22
[19] Mormon 7: 1-2

the dead, whereby man must be raised to stand before his judgment seat. [20]

Therefore, repent, and be baptized in the name of Jesus, and lay hold upon the gospel of Christ, which shall be set before you, not only in this record, but also in the record which shall come unto the Gentiles from the Jews, which record shall come from the Gentiles unto you.

For behold, this is written for the intent that ye may believe that. And if ye may believe that, ye will believe this also. And if ye believe this, ye will know concerning your fathers, and also the marvelous works which were wrought by the power of God among them. And ye will also know that ye are a remnant of the seed of Jacob. Therefore, ye are numbered among the people of the first covenant.

And if it so be that ye believe in Christ and are baptized, first with water then with fire and with the Holy Ghost, following the example of our Savior, according to that which he hath commanded us, it shall be well with you in the day of judgment. Amen. [21]

About 400 A.D.

Behold, I, Moroni, do finish the record of my father Mormon. Behold, I have but few things to write, which things I have been commanded by my father.

And now, it came to pass that after the great and tremendous battle at Cumorah, behold, the Nephites who had escaped into the country southward were hunted by the Lamanites until they were all destroyed. And my father also was killed by them. And I even remain alone to write the sad tale of the destruction of my people. But behold, they are gone, and I fulfill the commandment of my father. And whether they will slay me, I know not. Therefore, I will write and hide up the records in the earth. And whither I go it mattereth not.

Behold, my father hath made this record, and he hath written the intent thereof. And behold, I would write it also if I had room

---

[20] Mormon 7: 5-6
[21] Mormon 7: 8-10

upon the plates, but I have not; and ore I have none, for I am alone. My father hath been slain in battle and all my kinsfolks; and I have not friends nor whither to go. And how long the Lord will suffer that I may live, I know not.

Behold, four hundred years have passed since the coming of our Lord and Savior. And behold, the Lamanites have hunted my people the Nephites down, from city to city and from place to place, even until they are no more. And great has been their fall. Yea, great and marvelous is the destruction of my people, the Nephites. And behold, it is the hand of the Lord which hath done it.

And behold, also, the Lamanites are at war one with another. And the whole face of this land is one continual round of murder and bloodshed, and no one knoweth the end of the war. And now, behold, I say no more concerning them, for there are none save it be the Lamanites and robbers, that do exist upon the face of the land. [22] Behold, I make an end of speaking concerning this people.

I am the son of Mormon, and my father was a descendant of Nephi. And I am the same who hideth up this record unto the Lord. The plates thereof are of no worth because of the commandment of the Lord, for he truly saith that no one shall have them to get gain. But the record thereof is of great worth, and whoso shall bring it to light, him will the Lord bless. For no one can have power to bring it to light, save it be given him of God; for God will that it shall be done with an eye single to his glory, or the welfare of the ancient and long dispersed covenant people of the Lord.

And blessed be him that shall bring this thing to light. For it shall be brought out of darkness unto light according to the word of God. Yea, it shall be brought out of the earth, and it shall shine forth out of darkness, and come unto the knowledge of the people. And it shall be done by the power of God, [23] for the eternal purposes of the Lord shall roll on until all his promises shall be fulfilled.

Search the prophecies of Isaiah. Behold, I cannot write them. Yea, behold, I say unto you that those saints who have gone before me, who have possessed this land, shall cry; yea, even from the

---

[22] Mormon 8: 1-9
[23] Mormon 8: 13-16

dust will they cry unto the Lord. And as the Lord liveth, he will remember the covenant which he hath made with them. And he knoweth their prayers, that they were in behalf of their brethren. [24] And behold, their prayers were also in behalf of him that the Lord should suffer to bring these things forth.

And no one need say, they shall not come, for they surely shall, for the Lord hath spoken it. For out of the earth shall they come by the hand of the Lord, and none can stay it. And it shall come in a day when it shall be said that miracles are done away. And it shall come even as if one should speak from the dead.

And it shall come in a day when the blood of the saints shall cry unto the Lord because of secret combinations and the works of darkness. Yea, it shall come in a day when the power of God shall be denied, and churches become defiled, and shall be lifted up in the pride of their hearts; yea, even in a day when leaders of churches and teachers shall rise up in the pride of their hearts, even to the envying of them who belong to their churches.

Yea, it shall come in a day when there shall be heard of fires, and tempests, and vapors of smoke in foreign lands. And there shall also be heard of wars, and rumors of wars, and earthquakes in divers places. Yea, it shall come in a day when there shall be great pollutions upon the face of the earth. There shall be murders and robbing, and lying, and deceivings, and whoredoms, and all manner of abominations; when there shall be many who will say, do this or do that, and it mattereth not, for the Lord will uphold such at the last day. [25] Yea, it shall come in a day when there shall be churches built up that shall say, Come unto me, and for your money you shall be forgiven of your sins.

O ye wicked, and perverse, and stiff-necked people, why have ye built up churches unto yourselves to get gain? Why have ye transfigured the holy word of God, that ye might bring damnation upon your souls? Behold, look ye unto the revelations of God. For behold, the time cometh at that day when all these things must be fulfilled. [26]

---

[24] Mormon 8: 22-24*
[25] Mormon 8: 25-31*
[26] Mormon 8: 32-33

And now, I speak also concerning those who do not believe in Christ. Behold, will ye believe in the day of your visitation, behold, when the Lord shall come; yea, even that great day when the earth shall be rolled together as a scroll and the elements shall melt with fervent heat? Yea, in that great day, when ye shall be brought to stand before the Lamb of God, then will ye say that there is no God? For behold, when ye shall be brought to see your nakedness before God, and also the glory of God, and the holiness of Jesus Christ, it will kindle a flame of unquenchable fire upon you. [27]

And again, I speak unto you who deny the revelations of God, and say that they are done away, that there are no revelations, nor prophecies, nor gifts, nor healing, nor speaking with tongues, and the interpretation of tongues. Behold, I say unto you, He that denieth these things knoweth not the gospel of Christ. Yea, he has not read the scriptures; if so, he does not understand them. For do we not read that God is the same yesterday, today, and forever? And in him there is no variableness, neither shadow of changing.

But behold, I will show unto you a God of miracles, even the God of Abraham, and the God of Isaac, and the God of Jacob. And it is that same God who created the heavens, and the earth, and all things that in them are. [28] Behold, are not the things that God hath wrought marvelous in our eyes?

Who shall say that it was not a miracle, that by his word the heaven and the earth should be? And by the power of his word man was created of the dust of the earth. [29] Behold, he created Adam; and by Adam came the fall of man. And because of the fall of man came Jesus Christ, even the Father and the Son. And because of Jesus Christ came the redemption of man. Yea, this is wherein all men are redeemed— because the death of Christ bringeth to pass the resurrection, which bringeth to pass a redemption from an endless sleep, from which sleep all men shall be awakened by the power of God when the trump shall sound.

And they shall come forth, both small and great, and all shall stand before his bar, being redeemed and loosed from this eternal

[27] Mormon 9: 1-2, 5
[28] Mormon 9: 7-9, 11
[29] Mormon 9: 16*-17*

band of death, which death is a temporal death. And then cometh the judgment of the Holy One upon them. And then cometh the time that he that is filthy shall be filthy still; and he that is righteous shall be righteous still. He that is happy shall be happy still; and he that is unhappy shall be unhappy still.

And now, O all ye that have imagined up unto yourselves a god who can do no miracles, I would ask of you, have all these things passed of which I have spoken? Has the end come yet? Behold, I say unto you, Nay! And God has not ceased to be a God of miracles. [30]

And who shall say that Jesus Christ did not do many mighty miracles? And there were many mighty miracles wrought by the hands of the apostles. And the reason why he ceaseth to do miracles among the children of men is because that they dwindle in unbelief and depart from the right way, and know not the God in whom they should trust. [31]

Doubt not! But be believing, and begin as in times of old, and come unto the Lord with all your heart, and work out your own salvation with fear and trembling before him. Be wise in the days of your probation. Strip yourselves of all uncleanness. Ask not that ye may consume it on your lusts; but ask with a firmness unshaken, that ye will yield to no temptation, but that ye will serve the true and living God.

Behold, I speak unto you as though I spake from the dead, for I know that ye shall have my words. [32] The Lord hath shown unto me great and marvelous things concerning that which must shortly come at that day when these things shall come forth among you. I speak unto you as if ye were present, and yet ye are not. But behold, Jesus Christ hath shown you unto me, and I know your doing. [33]

Behold, I would exhort you that when ye shall read these things, if it be wisdom in God that ye should read them, that ye would remember how merciful the Lord hath been unto the

---

[30] Mormon 9: 12, 13*-15
[31] Mormon 9: 18, 20
[32] Mormon 9: 27*-28, 30
[33] Mormon 8: 34*-35*

SIGNS

children of men, from the creation of Adam even down until the time that ye shall receive these things, and ponder it in your hearts.

And when ye shall receive these things, I would exhort you that ye would ask God, the Eternal Father, in the name of Christ, if these things are not true. And if ye shall ask with a sincere heart, with real intent, having faith in Christ, He will manifest the truth of it unto you by the power of the Holy Ghost. And by the power of the Holy Ghost, ye may know the truth of all things. [34] And whoso receiveth this record, and shall not condemn it because of the imperfections which are in it, the same shall know of greater things than these.

Behold, I am Moroni; and were it possible, I would make all things known unto you. [35] But behold, that which is of God, inviteth and enticeth to do good continually. Wherefore, every thing which inviteth and enticeth to do good, and to love God, and to serve him, is inspired of God. [36] And whatsoever thing is good is just and true. Wherefore, nothing that is good denieth the Christ, but acknowledgeth that He is. And ye may know that He is, by the power of the Holy Ghost. Wherefore, I would exhort you that ye deny not the power of God; for He worketh by power according to the faith of the children of men—the same today, and tomorrow, and forever. [37]

And now, I Moroni, would speak somewhat concerning these things. I would show unto the world that faith is things which are hoped for and not seen; wherefore, dispute not because ye see not, for ye receive no witness until after the trial of your faith. Wherefore, ye may also have hope and be partakers of the gift, if ye will but have faith.

Behold, it was by faith that they of old were called after the holy order of God. Wherefore, by faith was the law of Moses given. But, in the gift of his Son hath God prepared a more excellent way. And it is by faith that it hath been fulfilled. [38]

---

[34] Moroni 10: 3-5
[35] Mormon 8: 12
[36] Moroni 7: 13
[37] Moroni 10: 6-7
[38] Ether 12: 6, 9 -11

And it is by faith that my fathers have obtained the promise that these things should come unto their brethren through the Gentiles. Therefore, the Lord hath commanded me, yea, even Jesus Christ.

And I said unto him, Lord, the Gentiles will mock at these things because of our weakness in writing; for, Lord, thou hast made us mighty in word by faith, but thou hast not made us mighty in writing. For thou hast made all this people that they could speak much because of the Holy Ghost, which thou hast given them. And thou hast made us that we could write but little because of the awkwardness of our hands. [39] Thou hast also made our words powerful and great, even that we cannot write them. Wherefore, when we write, we behold our weakness, and stumble because of the placing of our words. And I fear, lest the Gentiles shall mock at our words.

And when I had said this, the Lord spake unto me, saying, Fools mock, but they shall mourn. And my grace is sufficient for the meek, that they shall take no advantage of your weakness. And if men come unto me, I will show unto them their weakness. I give unto men weakness, that they may be humble. And my grace is sufficient for all men that humble themselves before me. For if they humble themselves before me and have faith in me, then will I make weak things become strong unto them. Behold, I will show unto the Gentiles their weakness. And I will show unto them that faith, hope, and charity, bringeth unto me the fountain of all righteousness.

And I, Moroni, having heard these words, was comforted and said, O Lord, thy righteous will be done, for I know that thou workest unto the children of men according to their faith. [40] And again, I remember that thou hast said that thou hast loved the world, even unto the laying down of thy life for the world, that thou mightest take it again, to prepare a place for the children of men. And now, I know that this love which thou hast had for the children of men is charity. Wherefore, except men shall have

---

[39] Ether 12: 22-24*
[40] Ether 12: 25-29

charity, they cannot inherit that place which thou hast prepared in the mansions of thy Father. [41]

And it came to pass that I prayed unto the Lord that he would give unto the Gentiles grace, that they might have charity. And it came to pass that the Lord said unto me, If they have not charity, it mattereth not unto thee. Thou hast been faithful. Wherefore, thy garments shall be made clean. And because thou hast seen thy weakness, thou shalt be made strong, even unto the sitting down in the place which I have prepared in the mansions of my Father.

And now, I, Moroni, bid farewell unto the Gentiles, yea, and also unto my brethren whom I love, until we shall meet before the judgment seat of Christ. [42] And then shall ye know that I have seen Jesus, and that he hath talked with me face to face, and that he told me in plain humility, even as a man telleth another, in mine own language, concerning these things. And only a few have I written because of my weakness in writing.

And now, I would commend you to seek this Jesus, of whom the prophets and apostles have written, that the grace of God the Father, and also the Lord Jesus Christ, and the Holy Ghost, which beareth record of them, may be and abide in you forever. [43]

I declare these things unto the fulfilling of the prophecies. And behold, they shall proceed forth out of the mouth of the everlasting God. And His word shall hiss forth from generation to generation. And God shall show unto you that that which I have written is true. [44]

Wherefore, I, Moroni, am commanded to write these things, that evil may be done away, and that the time may come that Satan may have no power upon the hearts of the children of men; but that they may be persuaded to do good continually, that they may come unto the fountain of all righteousness and be saved. [45]

And now, behold, we have written this record according to our knowledge in the characters, which are called among us the

---

[41] Ether 12: 33-34
[42] Ether 12: 36-38*
[43] Ether 12: 39-41*
[44] Moroni 10: 28-29
[45] Ether 8: 26

reformed Egyptian, being handed down and altered by us according to our manner of speech. And if our plates had been sufficiently large, we should have written in the Hebrew; but the Hebrew hath been altered by us also. And if we could have written in the Hebrew, behold, ye would have had no imperfection in our record. But the Lord knoweth the things which we have written, and also that none other people knoweth our language. And because that none other people knoweth our language, therefore, he hath prepared means for the interpretation thereof.

And these things are written that we may rid our garments of the blood of our brethren who have dwindled in unbelief. And behold, these things which we have desired concerning our brethren, yea, even their restoration to the knowledge of Christ, is according to the prayers of all the saints, who have dwelt in the land. And may the Lord Jesus Christ grant that their prayers may be answered according to their faith; and may God the Father remember the covenant which he hath made with the house of Israel. [46]

Awake, and arise from the dust, O Jerusalem! Yea, and put on thy beautiful garments, O daughter of Zion, and strengthen thy stakes, and enlarge thy borders forever, that thou mayest no more be confounded, that the covenants of the Eternal Father which he hath made unto thee, O house of Israel, may be fulfilled. [47]

Yea, come unto Christ and be perfected in him, and deny yourselves of all ungodliness. And if ye shall deny yourselves of all ungodliness, and love God with all your might, mind and strength, then is his grace sufficient for you, through the shedding of the blood of Christ, which is the covenant of the Father unto the remission of your sins, that ye become holy, without spot.

And now, I bid unto all farewell. I soon go to rest in the paradise of God until my spirit and body shall again reunite, and I am brought forth triumphant through the air to meet you before the pleasing bar of the great Jehova, the eternal Judge of both quick and dead. Amen. [48]

---

[46] Mormon 9: 32-37*
[47] Moroni 10: 31 (Compare Isaiah 53: 1-2)
[48] Moroni 10: 32*-33*, 34

Made in the USA
Las Vegas, NV
28 January 2022

42519127R00203